Loving Yourself Whole

Loving Yourself Whole

A Field Guide to Health and Happiness
Through Connection of Spirit, Mind and Body

Patricia Thompson, MSN, RN, CHt

Copyright © 2021 by Patricia Thompson

The author discusses health, how physical and mental dis-ease originate and become disease, and how the progression of this process can be altered. The intention here is to offer valuable information and help others achieve and maintain health and happiness through a natural state of balance. Nothing in this book suggests a diagnosis or medical advice, nor does it imply, recommend or prescribe treatment of any condition or disease. If you are ill or suspect you might be, consult with a medical provider best suited to your needs. Never stop or alter prescribed treatment without consulting a healthcare provider first.

Front cover design by Brad Jackson
Graphic art and layout design by Cindy Segrest
Electronic book layout design by Christy Sparks

All Scriptural quotes are from The New Oxford Annotated Bible with the Apocrypha. New Revised Standard Version. (1977). Oxford University Press.

All rights reserved. This book contains material protected under International and Federal Copyright Laws and Treaties. No part of this book may be reproduced by any mechanical, photographic or electronic purpose, or in the form of phonographic or recording. It may not be stored in a retrieval system, transmitted or otherwise copied for public or private use, other than for fair use as brief quotations in articles and reviews or by an author to quote brief passages with full credit given, without the written permission of the author.

Library of Congress Cataloging-in-Publication Data has been applied for

Thompson, Patricia.
Loving yourself whole: a field guide to health and happiness through connection of spirit, mind and body / Patricia Thompson – 1st edition.
Identifiers: ISBN Paperback: 978-1-7363123-0-8   ISBN Ebook: 978-1-7363123-1-5
1. Mind and Body 2. Spirituality

First Edition

*To my children, my grandchildren and
all the children living on this precious Earth.
May your innocence, love and wisdom
lift humanity up the spiral of evolution
to our true home in Heaven.*

*I want to express my deepest gratitude to my dear friend, Marilyn Stemp.
Thank you for your support, encouragement and, as the editor,
for making Loving Yourself Whole so much more readable
than it would have been. You taught me about reading and writing,
and most importantly, you showed me what it means to be a friend.*

TABLE OF CONTENTS

Important note about this field guide ix

Preface xi

Introduction xvii

Part One: Fundamentals for Understanding 1

    Chapter 1: You Are Much Greater Than You Know 3
    Chapter 2: Does Believing In An Ever-present God Really Matter? 11
    Chapter 3: Reclaiming Your Personal Power 23
    Chapter 4: Understanding the Key Concepts 31
        Energy 32
        Beliefs 40
        Learning 41
        The Mind/Body Connection 54
    Chapter 5: The Guide For Your Future Self — Your Wounded Child 77

Part Two: The Body of Understanding and Wisdom 83

    Chapter 6: The Root Cause of Illness 85
    Chapter 7: It's All About Stress 101
        Reduce Your Stress — What does that mean? 102
        Chronic Stress Becomes Chronic Disease 110
    Chapter 8: Why We Get The Diseases We Do 119
    Chapter 9: Healing Is A Life Changing Experience 147

Part Three: Love Is In Everything 161

    Chapter 10: Love Is The Elixir of Life 163

Chapter 11: Loving Yourself Whole..169
    Connecting With Your Spiritual Nature 170
    Connecting With Your Mental Nature...181
    Connecting With Your Emotional Nature...192
    Connecting with Your Physical Nature 210
Chapter 12: Love And Light—The Essence of All That Is.....................225

Part Four: Love Your Neighbor As Yourself..231

Chapter 13: We Are Social Beings 233
Chapter 14: Distress Is The Call For Change..239
Chapter 15: What Holds Such Desperation in Place?.........................249
    The Myth of Powerlessness..250
    The Myth of Scarcity..256
Chapter 16: The Road Home—The Gifts of Love Wisdom and Power...259

Part Five: Being Love's Expression 271

Chapter 17: The Art Of Mental Transmutation 273
Chapter 18: You Are The Expression Of God's Love 289

Acknowledgements 297

Endnotes..299

About the Author...307

Important note about this field guide:

Dear reader and friend,

Please feel my virtual hug and warm welcome as we begin this journey together. As a fellow traveler and seeker, I'm grateful to be able to share what I've come to understand as a sure and well-lit path to health and happiness. One of my greatest understandings is that we inherently know exactly what to do to feel loved, joyful and peace-filled if only we trust the wisdom of our hearts. It's my fervent desire to help you reclaim your power and in so doing, achieve lifelong happiness…as you define it.

No matter where you start, reaching this goal will take effort and a change of mindset. To accomplish this requires a different perspective, more information and the belief that you *can* make your dreams come true. To that end, this book starts at the beginning—with pivotal concepts and misconceptions, human physiology, the origins of disease from both a scientific and metaphysical perspective, our place in evolution and society and the importance of a relationship with God or a Higher Consciousness. After laying a solid foundation, we'll discuss practices that support our efforts to find the love and meaning we seek. As you read, you may ask: Does all this information really matter? Please hang in there because it does. It's important to know how we got where we are and what's causing our problems so we can avoid the same pitfalls keeping us stuck in this place of restlessness and dis-ease. This foundation then offers a clear understanding that the practices presented later will, in fact, be effective in getting us to our happy place. If you feel the information presented in Parts One and Two is too much, feel free to jump ahead to Chapter Nine and beyond, knowing you can return when the question, "Can it really be this simple?" presents itself.

Throughout the book, I compare Ancient Wisdom teachings with today's scientific understanding to demonstrate how each is describing the same phenomenon and how we can use Ancient Teachings to support our innate wisdom. Empowered with a greater understanding, you will feel confident in cultivating and trusting your inner wisdom when conventional ideologies leave you uncomfortable with more questions than answers.

As with other field guides, *Loving Yourself Whole* offers detailed information to help you identify natural phenomenon in whatever environment you seek to know better. In this case, it's your life, with its hopes and fears and the innate desire to be loved, joy-filled and at peace. Welcome to the conscious journey of loving yourself back to peace on Earth.

Walking with you in Love and Light,
Patricia

PREFACE

Do you feel restless or even a little disappointed with the quality of your life? Are you frustrated with the results you get when you search for answers and implement a course of action proclaimed to be the remedy for your discontent, pain or disease? Whether an issue of health, happiness, goal achievement or a simple sense of satisfaction with life, I believe we all struggle to find a state of peace where we can simply relax for a little while, knowing we're okay and will be okay down the road. The mystery of life seems hinged on the reality that while we are constantly involved in efforts to achieve peace, happiness and fulfillment, we just can't seem to get there. And if we do realize such a state, it's often short lived; after a period of confusion and disappointment we begin the quest again. In my personal and professional experience, this cyclical and often frustrating pursuit of happiness is the result of not asking the right questions. The right questions would lead us to the core of our dis-ease and ultimately direct us to more productive efforts in achieving what we want for ourselves. The right question is the fundamental question of why, "Why am I not happy, healthy or satisfied with my life?"

I have spent a good deal of my own life cycling through ill-informed attempts to make myself happy. So much so that as I was pondering yet another career change, my high school aged daughter shared her inspired observation with me, "Mom, you'll never find a job that makes you happy because you're not a happy person." In that moment, I realized the wisdom in her remark and this allowed me to make significant changes… about a decade later. During that decade of delay, I did make many major life changes. I changed jobs several times, earned a graduate degree, dabbled in a few relationships, moved to several states, visited several countries and helped my aging parents with their health concerns. I learned a lot of things along my journey, but I did not find happiness, peace or fulfillment. In retrospect, all these attempts to find happiness revealed a common thread, one that I believe to be the crux of the problem. My efforts, great and small, were attempts to find answers and happiness outside myself. As my daughter had prophesized a decade earlier, these efforts did not make me a happy person. I was asking myself the wrong questions and pursuing misdirected answers.

It took two rather jaw-dropping work experiences coming within three months of each other to open my eyes and my mind. For the better part of four decades, I had been employed by several different healthcare organizations. As an employee, my performance evaluations were always in the top ten percent…I was a star performer, a model employee. I received great reviews even when I despised my job, a frequent predicament in recent years. In 2016, I was working as a nurse practitioner, alternating between two very different primary care settings and becoming increasingly disillusioned (and outright verbal) about my inability to be effective within the constraints of my work environment. After one particularly frustrating day, I was shocked when I was invited to submit my resignation and not return to work the next day… and this happened twice in three months.

As I drove away from the second place to cut me loose, I was pretty angry. In asking myself why I was so angry, I realized I had been angry for a long time. My anger had overwhelmed my sensibilities. I couldn't keep my mouth shut about things I felt needed to be changed and just do the job I was paid to do…without commentary, and the reason cited for my dismissal. As I pondered how this had happened, I heard myself naming all the people (co-workers and supervisors) who were not effective in their jobs and therefore made it difficult for me to do mine. As I went around the imaginary circle, saying their names in my mind, I came all the way around to my name. And there I realized…I had not been doing my job either. I was working at a job and in a field that was no longer my calling or purpose. It hadn't been my calling for decades, decades in which I'd ignored all the warning signs telling me I was walking down the wrong path. It wasn't that the institutions I had worked for in the past fifteen years couldn't have done a better job, as indeed, they could have. The pivotal point was acknowledging whom I was blaming for my anger. I was blaming other people for my daily distress…until I asked myself the why question. The answer was illuminating and liberating. My distress was caused by trying to be someone I was not, trying to live according to standards and codes of conduct not my own, and knowing deep down inside I no longer belonged in that version of reality. With this understanding, I was able to take responsibility for my life in new ways and make choices that would bring me ever closer to the state of ease, balance and happiness I knew was possible for myself. I would like to tell you this was a light switch revelation, magically transforming me into a happy and satisfied person. It was not, but the revelation did illuminate a more direct path for my transformation toward that place.

I would also like to tell you that this story of job terminations was the only time I required motivation of such major significance to shake me up and get me moving in the right direction. That wouldn't be accurate either. My life has been a journey with peaks, valleys and plateaus. Times when I felt on top of the world, times when I felt dejected or even desperate, and times when my life seemed to level out and I could glide in a more temperate frame of mind. Being discharged from two jobs in three months gave me an opportunity to reflect on my life and ponder…why, after four decades of adulthood and a wide variety of attempts to find my place in the world, was I still wondering what I was going to be when I grew up? Why was happiness so elusive?

As I contemplated these questions and reflected back on the landscape of my life journey, what I discovered helped me find my way to higher and more sustainable levels of peace, happiness and satisfaction. Life is not simply a day-by-day journey between the two points of birth and death. It's an experiential learning opportunity, a field trip in the earth school of our perceptual reality. It's an opportunity to learn, and through that learning, evolve to greater possibilities than could have been imagined with earlier and more limited thinking. Everything that happened to me had a part in shaping who I have become. Tough times and challenges caused me to look deeper and make changes so I could be happy and more content. They let me see patterns of sabotage where I got in my own way, and patterns of synchronicity where momentary disappointment resulted in a much better outcome in the long run. My reflections let me see that the times in my life when I was the happiest happened when I was following my internal guidance system and pursuing my passions. On the other hand, my biggest moments of frustration and distress appeared when I was involved in things that had little in common with my passions and interests. I believe what I found to be true of my life is true for others.

Over the course of my adult life, I have worked as a Registered Nurse, Adult Nurse Practitioner, nurse manager, nurse educator, community educator, massage therapist, life coach, esoteric healer and clinical hypnotherapist…and served as a parent, child and friend. Through my experiences, I have witnessed incredible acts of love, mercy and despair. I have observed people live beyond anything a medical textbook would deem possible in order to complete their unfinished business. I have seen people live for days, sometimes weeks without food or water, often in great pain, because they had a promise to keep, a promise that leaving, even in death, would break. I have worked with seasoned professionals doing all they could to save a life only to watch it disappear, the only plausible explanation for death being that person's absolute refusal to "live that way." I have seen people respond to an unknowable internal clock whereby they were compelled to put their personal affairs in order, if only because it felt like the right time, completing the effort shortly before an unexpected terminal diagnosis or event.

My formal education and my personal and professional learning opportunities have informed my perception of the human condition. I believe it comes down to a few seldom recognized and less appreciated factors. This is what I know:

~ We all have the power to direct and to change our lives, whether or not we are consciously aware of it. The power to live, to let go or to change resides within our focused intention to do just that. We've come to explain life's successes and disappointments as the rewards of tenacity, a stroke of luck—good or bad, or somehow coincidental and unrelated. It only appears this way because, at our level of understanding, we neither understand our own power nor do we grasp the causal link between our intentions and the events resulting from them.

~ We are wise beyond our understanding. We have our life stories, which often contain at least a hint of "What I need to do is…" At some point, we indeed do know what we need to do to make a

better life for ourselves…if only we were listening with our hearts to what we were hearing in our thoughts and saying with our words.
~ We all are inherently drawn to seek love, peace and joy as our deepest desires and ultimate attainments. We won't be deterred; unhappiness and dissatisfaction compel us to keep striving toward that goal. The cycle of searching and disappointment is the result of not understanding our true nature and therefore we wander a path trying to find a poorly defined destination.
~ We are imbued with the gifts of willpower, wisdom and love. We are driven to find happiness and peace because we are part of something much bigger than the physical body and the physical experience that has become the focus of our earthly existence.

The world is filled with great information to help us find answers to our questions. The key to finding the right information is asking the right questions and then as we know and love ourselves more completely, choosing the answers that are right for our individual journey. Pursuing answers and solutions inconsistent with our unique personality, experiences and needs, is like running on a treadmill trying to get to a different location. We can spend a lot of time, energy and money on valiant efforts without making a difference in our state of health and happiness. If we keep returning to the same state of discontent, we are revisiting learning opportunities without understanding the purpose of the lesson. At some point, we must ask ourselves, "Have I had enough of these kinds of learning opportunities and am I ready to change my approach in order to reach my goal?"

The purpose of *Loving Yourself Whole* is to provide information and insight into why we struggle with disappointment, unhappiness and disease so we can ask more productive questions and find the answers that fit our uniquely individual experiences. I believe once we understand how truly magnificent and connected we are, the faster the obstacles holding us back will fall away, opening the door to health and happiness as we each define them for ourselves.

INTRODUCTION

We live in a fast paced and often chaotic world. To deal with this, we have developed helpful techniques to survive and even prosper. We multitask, organize, prioritize and streamline. We have instant access to nearly unlimited information and connectivity via the Internet and social media. As we bustle through our lives meeting demands, deadlines and commitments, how often do we stop to consider how we feel about all this effort and activity? Is it taking us where we really want to go? Why do we think this particular destination or goal is the right one? Are we happy as we work to get there? If we were to acknowledge our hidden twinges of restlessness, disappointment or longing for something better, or ponder the increasing social unrest we see in the world today, it would become clear... most of our efforts to be happy are not actually serving our happiness.

Happiness and health are inseparable in many ways. It's difficult to have one without the other. It's tough to be happy when we don't feel well. On the other hand, disease begins well before symptoms are obvious. Directed in part by physiological processes, nearly all diseases sprout from the seeds of unresolved unhappiness and distress. Chronic unhappiness and stress decreases the possibility of living a long and healthy life. Our persistent inability to be truly satisfied in life increases the probability of chronic disease, premature aging and death. Though it's not plainly stated in ways we can apply to our attempts to stay healthy, scientific research is uncovering more of the mechanisms by which disease and premature aging take place. But, because science is still working on the precise details of these processes (and because the more they know, the more questions they have), there is no definitive consensus on the specific origins of disease or more integrated approaches to reclaiming and maintaining health.

One thing we can be sure of at this point. We don't get high blood pressure, irritable bowel syndrome or any other disease from a lack of medication in our diets. And, we don't get cancer from a lack of chemotherapy in the water supply. Such therapeutic treatments are necessary medical protocols once disease has taken hold in the body, but as treatments...they not a cure because, most of the time, they don't make the condition go away. The need for ongoing monitoring and therapy for chronic diseases suggest that these treatments are managing disease symptoms rather than ridding the body of the actual cause and condition. While science continues to grapple with the determination of "cause" and because once the damage is done it's more difficult to undo, we're left to consider the higher road of prevention.

Unarguably, prevention is a better alternative than trying to reclaim health after it's been damaged. This brings us back to the question, "Why?" Is it just the food choices we make, the sedentary lives we live, the cigarettes we smoke, the alcohol and drugs we consume or the guns that cut lives short? Or is it something much deeper that causes us to make the choices we do? Why do we keep making the same choices knowing they are causing us problems? Why can't we stick to our plans as we try to reach our goals of health and happiness? I believe the answer to these questions can be found in our individual and collective misunderstanding of the basic nature and purpose of our lives.

Loving Yourself Whole is the field guide for exploring your experiences, feelings, thoughts, words and actions in order to develop a deeper understanding of who you are and what makes you react the way you do. Your struggles are the result of not recognizing your true potential and the tremendous capacity you have to be amazing, successful, loving and happy. You are a complex, integrated, energetic and spiritual being. Your life is an interactive learning experience individualized for your unique journey of discovery. Just like scientific discovery, each revelation, coming in the forms of thoughts, feelings and experiences, offers insight. More questions are revealed as your understanding expands. Each revelation is filled with hidden clues to guide you along the path. Learning how to interpret those clues unlocks the potential of personal evolution.

Your efforts to become completely happy and satisfied are hampered by faulty beliefs and misunderstandings that perpetuate limited thinking, missteps identified as mistakes, and the disappointments that emerge from them. The view you hold of yourself in terms of worthiness, importance, lovability, safety and adequacy sets the tone and the parameters for what you will be able to achieve. If you don't feel worthy, good or important enough, it will be difficult to change the behavior patterns that sabotage your best efforts to make productive changes and thus keep you trapped in the rut of disappointment. When you define your life as a solitary effort of pushing to get ahead, you miss opportunities to experience yourself as a part of something much greater. Whether or not you realize it, this limited perspective restricts access to your innate gifts of power, wisdom and love. Restrictions are the result of the power of denial. With your limited perspective, you are denying your great potential.

Loving Yourself Whole is separated into five very distinct parts.

Part One sets the foundational understanding required to utilize the information and techniques offered in the rest of the book. It begins with a brief discussion of who we are and our inseparable and sometimes tumultuous relationship with God, by whatever name you prefer to use. Part One defines the concepts of energy, learning, emotions and the nature of the mind-body connection. These concepts may seem common and mundane, but if we truly understood how they functioned to shape our lives and our perception of reality, we would be much further ahead in making changes and achieving our heart's greatest desire.

With a better understanding of the integrated nature of body, mind and spirit, Part Two looks at the emerging science of psychoneuroimmunology—the study of the link between mind and body—to understand how our innate survival systems either support health and happiness or foster disease and despair. This section focuses on stress, its role in maintaining healthy balance and the detrimental effects caused by an intrinsic and primal system stuck in chronic overdrive. It describes the common mechanism for disease onset and progression. It considers the nature versus nurture debate and the emotional context of diseases through the lens of both evidence-based science and the intuitive understanding offered by alternative disciplines. In this section I submit that scientific understanding is limited to those tenets it has the technology to measure in its priority to provide absolute proof. I don't believe we need to be similarly constrained as we consider options for a more holistic understanding of ourselves and our greater possibilities.

As you read Parts One and Two, you may ask, why is all this information in a book on loving yourself? The answer to that question is written into the pages, but here's a hint: We're human and in order to maintain sanity and move through life, our knowledge is essentially cumulative. Regardless of what's available, we only find the information we're looking for, consciously or unconsciously. We will only assimilate and use that new information when we are ready to embrace its merit. Any incoming information that is inconsistent with what we have previously learned will require a concerted, conscious effort in order to override entrenched information and replace it something more helpful. The tools you have to make a difference in your life are of little use if you don't understand who you are and how you work. Parts One and Two provide information on how you got where you are and why it's so difficult to change. Knowledge is power and this information empowers you with the insight you need to reprogram your unconscious stumbling blocks so you can then move to a more happy and healthy place.

While Parts One and Two set the stage of understanding, Part Three shifts gears toward restorative and healthy practices. It focuses on self-awareness, attention to emotional sensations and cultivating practices that will enrich life experiences and reshape perceptions of reality. It adds personal choice to the same dynamics of energy, learning and the interconnectedness of spirit, mind and body to promote life-altering change and the power to stay the course of intentional change. Part Three provides examples for how to use emotional awareness to locate the faulty belief systems hidden from our awareness and release them so they can be replaced with affirming beliefs that will restore balance and empower health and happiness.

With a more empowered and enlightened understanding of who we are and our potential to affect positive change in our own lives, Part Four steps us into our place in the larger collective consciousness. It discusses how our individual and innate survival imperative is grounded in survival of the tribe, noting that our tribe is actually all the inhabitants of the earth. The overall health of the community, as well as our individual perceptions about the world we live in, are important indicators for our individual health and happiness potential. Part Four encourages individual practices of contemplation, prayer and following our heart's call as we participate in making our world a healthy, safe and loving place for our tribe.

Part Five is the finale. It is short, sweet and simple. It offers easy everyday acts of kindness we can do, mindfully, frequently and free of charge. After working through the earlier processes of learning about ourselves, clearing away useless debris and replacing it with love and life affirming daily practices, these simple techniques offer intentional ways to be a beacon of love. Implementing any of them into your daily life and duties will expand your loving energy and radiate warmth, compassion and enlightened understanding into the world. And this is how you love yourself whole.

~~~

Several themes run throughout *Loving Yourself Whole*. The first one recognizes the importance of discomfort in our lives. Any feeling of discomfort is a significant indication that something needs to be addressed and brought to resolution. This opens the door for the second theme. *Loving Yourself Whole* defines wholeness to include our spiritual—or quantum—nature, allowing that spiritual teachings and quantum science are describing the same phenomenon. According to science and all spiritual traditions running through the history of civilization, we are an intimate part of something much greater than our individual selves. How this is so and the relevance it has to health and happiness are foundational...and this brings me to the names of God. The concept of a Higher Consciousness which some call God, has so many names—and attributes that are also used as names—that it would be impossible to list them all. For ease of understanding, all references to God will be capitalized regardless of the name used. Common examples include Source, Universal Intelligence, Mind of God, Field of Possibility, also shortened to Mind/Field and Still Small Voice Within. As will be explained in the first chapter, expect the pronouns for God to be plural—Their or Them—and also capitalized.

Next, in writing this book I decided to toggle back and forth between first person (we) and second person (you) at regular intervals. This is intentional. I think it is important to understand how magnificent, loving, powerful and filled with potential you truly are. With all my heart,

I want you to know that you are truly amazing and unique. Only the pronoun YOU will convey this.

If you read the word "you" when I discuss heavy topics and think to yourself, that's not about me…no problem. I only ask you to momentarily ponder the possibility that a little piece could apply in a small or remote way. The work of becoming happy and whole is to root out the faulty beliefs lurking beneath the surface of awareness. I have included examples of how this works.

I use the pronoun we to describe processes, events and conditions common to a large percentage of people. The word "we" means you are not alone. You are in great company and you have gotten where you are now through natural processes affecting many, many people. These natural processes don't distinguish gender and affect people regardless of gender identification. For ease of reading, I will use s/he when talking about ideas that apply to people in general.

Lastly, the mechanics of health and disease, as well as the restorative and health promoting practices are not new or original. A wealth of amazing and valuable information is available in a wide variety of formats, books, videos, retreats, online, etc. What I believe is missing from much of this accessible information is a holistic approach that recognizes the essential integration of all aspects of our human experience and the amazing power we have to make a difference once we have a better understanding of our vast potential. *Loving Yourself Whole* is an integrated approach to understanding love, health, happiness and the power we have to control our experience, shape our reality and become truly happy and healthy.

PART ONE

Fundamentals For Understanding

"Knowing yourself is the beginning of all wisdom."
– Aristotle (384–322 BC)

CHAPTER 1

You Are Much Greater Than You Know

"Love is, in fact, an intensification of life, a completeness, a fullness, a wholeness of life." – Thomas Merton

You Are Wired for Health and Happiness

Everything we do in life is driven by two basic imperatives. The first is survival, and immediately following survival is the inherent yearning to be happy and whole. We are born with an innate intelligence that governs both imperatives because one is not possible without the other. Survival is a necessary condition for happiness; this is obvious. Not as clear but equally important is that happiness has a direct and irrefutable impact on the overall survival functions that support health and longevity. This life-altering state of happiness is ultimately—and unconsciously—*determined by whether or not we actually feel happy.* Because happiness is critical for optimal health and long-term survival, our innate intelligence compels us to search for it until we are completely satisfied. This compelling force is the root of *all* desire.

Happiness is a multiphasic state of being which includes three elements, being loved, finding meaning and feeling fulfilled. Almost all of what occupies our thoughts and directs our actions can be traced back to our inherent drive to satisfy one of these three aspects and achieve our deepest desire…to be happy. When we talk about happiness in this book—or as a life-long pursuit—we must remember that we are referring to a cohesive balance between these three essential aspects. To be loved is essential for life, but its critical nature is more informative if it's understood as to *be* love. Finding meaning refers to how we define ourselves and how well we serve the purpose we are innately called to. Lastly, feeling fulfilled is a *knowing we feel* when we are following the guidance of our hearts.

Our never-ending attempts to find happiness suggest we are having trouble finding the kind of happiness that will satisfy our compelling desire for it. It seems that no matter what we do to make ourselves happy, it's not long before we are on the hunt again…for something else. Our insatiable and unsatisfied desire to be happy is the result of not understanding what it is we seek to find. And yet, there is something driving us relentlessly until we have found it.

I believe the force compelling us to find happiness is caused by a distant memory of great happiness and joy. Without some memory or knowledge of the possibility, we simply would not be moved to search for it. Consider for a moment: you've never tasted, seen or heard of ice cream…ever. Would you drive to get some or search the grocery store until you found it? You would have no knowledge of it and therefore no desire for it. The same is true for the kind of happiness we are trying to find.

If we seek love, meaning and fulfillment as the defining elements of happiness, it's because at some point we have experienced them as real possibilities worthy of our efforts now. The exact details of our memories are lost to time, but the sublime feelings attached to them create a desire so profound we cannot be deterred from our quest to experience such happiness again. From birth to death, life is an uncharted expedition to find the holy grail of happiness that somewhere deep inside, we know is possible.

Reclaiming this memory and the happiness that will satisfy our innate longing requires a more complete understanding of who we are and why we are here. The purpose of life and the reason we are here in this three-dimensional experience called life is to rediscover the truth of our essential nature—who we truly are. Our innate intelligence is guiding our efforts to answer these eternal questions. It promotes survival and sustains life so we have time to experiment with our gifts. It also dangles the carrot of happiness in front of us so we never quit searching for the answers that will bring us back to the happiness permanently etched in our deepest memories. Reaching this goal will require understanding beyond what we have come to know through traditional channels of learning.

You Are A Spark In The Mind Of God

To be whole and to love yourself whole requires a deep appreciation that you are much more than you believe yourself to be; you are part of something much greater. You are an eternal Spark within the Infinite Mind of God. You live and move and have your being in this holy space where God Is, and where you are searching for the things you feel you have lost. Being an intimate part of something greater than yourself has important corollaries. First, being part of means being one with. You are one with Source…an intimate part of All That Is. Next, because you are one with All That Is, you are one with everything, including all the inhabitants of Earth. This also makes you one with the earth, the skies and beyond. This is the wisdom handed down through ancient traditions and Indigenous People. Living in the bliss of oneness is the sublime memory that drives you to find happiness. It's also the secret of happiness and the purpose of life. Discovering how to realistically achieve such happiness is the purpose of *Loving Yourself Whole*. If you missed the Introduction, all the capitalized words may be confusing. Capitalized words and plural pronouns identify God by one of Their many, many names.

God is the All-knowing, All-powerful, All-loving and Ever-present Source. As a Spark in the Mind of God, you are imbued with these divine attributes of wisdom, love, power and presence. The more you embrace this truth, the more you understand your magnificent potential and the greater your ability to use these divine attributes to make a difference. Within you lives the Seed of Divinity as your innate intelligence and it contains all you will ever need to be happy, healthy and at peace. This is the Still Small Voice Within speaking to you when you are ready to hear the wisdom and love always present there. It speaks to you through inspirations, intuitions and the wisdom of your heart. This Seed of Divinity is the highest order of your survival mechanism, reminding you that you are a unique expression of God's love and drawing you ever closer to this realization through your inherent desire for happiness.

In God's Image and Likeness, you are eternal. You are an everlasting part of what always was and always will be. You are an essential participant in the expanding consciousness living within the Infinite Mind of God. As you refine your understanding of who you are and the love you have to share, you raise your consciousness to higher and finer vibrations. This brings you closer to the image of God's Will for you, and the happiness you seek. As you do this, you are actively participating in the upward evolution of humanity's collective consciousness. You are a unique expression of God's Love manifesting in this world as you. *Everything you do in this life matters!* This is equally true of each one of your brothers and sisters. We are all being compelled toward the same loving peaceful state of happiness. We are working together to make Heaven on Earth, each participating in our own unique way.

Our disappointments and struggles are caused by the erroneous belief that we are separate from our Source. As a result of this belief, we make choices based on the underlying and deeply hidden belief that we are unworthy...unworthy of love, happiness and abundance in all its forms. *Loving Yourself Whole* is an invitation to think outside the box of convention and preapproved ideologies. It empowers you with information and tools to re-create your life so you can find happiness according to your unique definition of it. As we begin this expedition, let's do a quick review of terrain we will explore. *Loving Yourself Whole* starts by expanding the key concepts of energy, learning, spirit, mind, body and emotions, and the nature of our relationship with the God. I have found that a more in-depth understanding of these particular concepts opens the door to a greater appreciation of who I am and how thoughts, feelings and experiences offer valuable information, and this then allows me to achieve lasting change, balance and peace in my life. Parts One and Two are filled with information basic to the understanding of how we came to be the way we are, experiencing life as we do, and why our struggles and unhappiness lead to chronic health issues. Part Two delves into the stress response, its primary role in disease and premature aging and the emotional context of diseases. The information in these first two parts shine light on the mechanisms by which the healing practices presented in Parts Three and Five actually work to transform health and happiness to a more constant state of being.

Part Three shifts gears into the many practices available to help prevent dis-ease or restore health and happiness. The practices I discuss in Part Three are not new or difficult. The most difficult part of anything new is sticking with the changes we know will take us to a better place. The more we know and love ourselves, the easier it is to choose and maintain new beliefs, attitudes and behaviors. A common thread flowing through *Loving Yourself Whole* is the importance of choice and personal responsibility in achieving the desired states of health and happiness.

In Part Four, I discuss our inherent social nature as it relates to our instinct for survival and the inseparable connections we have with one another because of it. Our perception of the world provides us with valuable information about our individual journeys, even as it calls for our active participation to make it a happier home for all of us.

Part Five is about rewards. The more we love ourselves, the higher our vibration of love and consciousness. The higher our vibration, the lighter and brighter we become, to the point that others notice the difference. Something is different about you! Part Five is about simple acts of kindness you can use in daily life. Not only are these acts a blessing you offer to others, they are also a blessing you feel returning to you as you become even lighter, brighter and more filled with love.

As we move through the five sections, I discuss how science, Ancient Wisdom and intuitive understanding are often describing the same processes as each provides their understanding of the origins and the repetitive nature of unhappiness and disease. While science and technology have added much to our understanding of wellness and disease and in many ways improved the quality of the human condition, science falls short in explaining all of the phenomena obvious to our observations and experiences. This is not a criticism, rather an acknowledgement that science is confined to explanations that can be proven. This is often limited by the ability to measure and control what is being studied. Human behavior doesn't always allow for these rigid testing parameters.

Recent advances in technology have expanded what can be studied, measured and controlled, adding valuable information about the functioning and the mysteries of the body and mind. What researchers are discovering suggests that the understandings of the Ancient Wisdom Teachers and intuitive healers past and present may be accurate and as useful as it was once claimed to be. I believe there is much truth and relevance to earlier and alternative traditions and so I also discuss disease, health and healing from these esoteric and mystical points of view. Observations, experiences, more complete information and an intuitive understanding of our holistic nature may be the most important evidence we need to become happy and whole.

Unhappiness is rooted in the erroneous belief we are separate from God and therefore unworthy of happiness.

Life is an Interactive Learning Experience

Life is a journey, an interactive learning experience. As far back as we can go in recorded history, our ancestors have posed the questions, "Why am I here?" and "What is the purpose of life?" The reason we are here and the purpose of life is to find our way back to that sublime experience of happiness and love we hold in our memory and are intrinsically compelled to find.

How you *feel* about your life is the indicator of how you are doing along that journey. If your experience is anything less than what you want for yourself, then you must participate differently than you currently are. You must change your direction and your experiences in ways that will make a difference...so you can be happy to your core. The struggles and obstacles you encounter along the way are signals indicating you haven't fully embraced your own magnificence and are not loving yourself as God loves you. They're actually gifts of insight reminding you there are better ways to be; to be joyful, peaceful, loving and whole. Learning to interpret the messages encoded in your struggles will guide you along an easier path.

Though it may seem counter-intuitive, becoming happy is an individual effort. Life is the solo journey of discovering who you truly are…the deeper and more expanded version of yourself. You are the driver in control of which roads you travel. Your journey is taking you many places and you have undoubtedly experienced detours and wrong turns along the way. There are maps and interpreters available to assist you, and the village of humanity is providing insights along the way. In addition to these guides, you are equipped with your innate intelligence, your Seed of Divinity, as your internal navigation system. You have access to everything you need to realize your most important reason for being…to be happy and to love yourself whole.

CHAPTER 2

Does Believing In An Ever-present God Really Matter?

"'Within the Mother-Father Mind, mortal children are at home.'
– The Kybalion"

Of course, the answer to this question is yes. Whether you agree or disagree, to move on with a simple yes or no answer is to miss one of the most important opportunities to think outside the box of convention, open yourself to a new pathway and re-imagine your greater possibilities. I encourage you to ponder the concept of God and who you are in relationship to your God. In so doing, you may find more expansive and promising possibilities that were not so apparent without this connection.

Whether you believe you have a solid relationship with God; whether you don't really think about it, or consider yourself to be science-oriented and only think in terms of quantum possibility and larger consciousness; or any other spiritual belief you may hold, everything you read in this book will still work in your efforts to be happy and healthy. I encourage you take these few pages to consider a different understanding about Universal Intelligence, your spiritual—or non-material—nature and how magnificent you really and truly are…because you are part of something you may not have fully understood.

I have had my own challenges relating to the idea of a relationship with God. I have cycled up and down more than once in this concept. I attribute much of my struggle to the image of God I learned as a child and then amplified by my reactionary issues with authority in general. In my youth, a bearded and judgmental white male was presented as the ultimate authority figure. Part of my personal growth has required me to address my unrelenting disdain for authority generally and white male authority figures in particular. It turns out that my issues with the name and the concept of God were based on my learned beliefs about God, rather than the truth of who God is and the potential God represents in my life. It took me decades to sift through what I had learned and replace it with more accurate information. I believe this is true for many of us. Our mistaken understanding about our Source is part of the problems we're having as we try to get out of our own way. But, we have come by these problems honestly.

A long, long time ago, before humankind had science, technology, written language and the Internet, our ancestors had to rely on themselves and on each other. They observed nature and its influences on them. They listened to the only information channel they had—insights, intuitions and instincts—and used their developing cognitive abilities to analyze and reason how all things worked together to create the reality they were living. In time they came to understand how interdependent they were on the visible and invisible forces of nature. Based on their understanding, our ancestors adopted descriptive names for the invisible forces animating their world. A few of those names include Principle, Source, Spirit, Substance of Reality, the Absolute, All That Is, The All within the all, Universal Intelligence and Infinite Living Mind of God. These descriptive names were an acknowledgement of their connection to and their place within the expansive unknowable space many of us came to call God. They couldn't prove the mechanics governing their reality, but they understood *they were an inseparable part of it.*

As time went on and written language, centers of knowledge and recognized authority figures became more common, our ancestors were inculcated by expert opinions and reasoned explanations for how things worked and what constituted the truth about God and our existence. Some cultures were able to retain their concept of an Ever-present Source, whom they could personally access through devotion, contemplation and searching within. In other cultures, the original understandings were re-interpreted, sometimes for easier comprehension and sometimes for consensus and control. The effect of these alterations changed what God looked like and who God was to us. For hundreds of years, the made over image of God has continued to morph as many of us were taught to view God as a white-bearded, father figure who exists in a far away place called heaven—a place we go if we measure up to the standard. This God was assigned other attributes including loving, benevolent, judgmental, angry and even vengeful. We also learned we needed an intercessory to access God—another authority figure—to petition on our behalf and interpret divine truth to us. Handicapped by revised "teachings," we came to believe we were separate and detached from the omnipotent grace of God, and that we were unworthy by most accounts.

My search for meaning and happiness has taken me to many places and exposed me to different people, world-views and spiritual understandings. What became apparent to me was that no matter how different the outward appearance of devotional practices, philosophical beliefs and sacred traditions, the underlying premise was the same. We are each part of all that is, seen and unseen, known and unknown, and above all, *love is the essence of all there is*. Regardless of how divergent religious teachings may have become, a few bits of enduring wisdom have snuck through the cracks of dogma. If we return to the origins of spiritual understanding and dust off the ancient wisdom, we would have a more enlightened understanding of both God and of ourselves.

Occult Mystery Schools and the wisdom teachings they offered pre-date written language and were found primarily in ancient Egypt and Greece. People traveled to these centers in search of answers to the eternal questions about the nature of the universe and the reason for existence. The knowledge taught in these centers was disseminated to remote regions as seekers returned to their homelands. In this way, the wisdom of the ancients and their understandings became the foundation for world religions, including Hinduism, Judaism, Christianity, Buddhism and Islam. Hermetic Philosophy, thought to date back at least 4000 years, was part of the knowledge offered by these schools.

This Philosophy didn't teach through stories, parables and absolute codes of conduct—that would come later. Instead, it maintained that wisdom and true understanding were only possible through a devoted effort to know and understand the Essence of Absolute Truth—and yes, all three are descriptive names for God. What Hermetic Philosophy offered the seeker and the religious traditions emerging from its teachings were seven principles by which the nature of All That Is could be known. These principles were considered the Universal Laws by which the whole of existence operated and understanding them revealed the key to the mysteries of life, but understanding them required dedication, contemplation and discipline.

The similarities between scientific discoveries and ancient wisdom are both uncanny and useful.

Understanding the secrets contained within these principles remains elusive, even today. Fortunately for us, wisdom teachings were encrypted with serial levels of understanding such that even a rudimentary understanding would allow great insight and awareness. At this time in our evolution, we also have the ability to consider these principles alongside recent scientific discovery such that we can recognize parallels and even coherence between Hermetic Principles and quantum science. Though scientific endeavors resist discussing their discoveries in terms of ancient understanding, the appearance of sameness is as uncanny as it is useful. To establish a more informed understanding of ourselves and our potential—and see where we may have been led astray—we are going to visit a few of these principles and the early religious teachings they inspired.

Because ancient wisdom is the foundation for most of the world religions as well as the understanding that flows through many Indigenous cultures, some of the stories and lessons found in their sacred teachings are very similar. This is true of the creation story. I'd like to acknowledge that I was raised in the Judeo-Christian tradition and my familiarity with that tradition will be obvious. If you are more familiar with a different philosophy or religion, please contemplate this section in terms of your own tradition to find the truth for you. And so:

Let's start with the fallacy of our male god image and the resulting choice of male pronouns when referring to God. If we look more closely at the creation story, the first book of *The Bible* implies that God is neither male nor female. Even in a patriarchal society with a pronoun-challenged vocabulary, and the potential corruption of oral tradition and language translation, *The Bible* retains the ancient wisdom passed down through its writing. Genesis 1:26 tells us, "Then God **said,** 'Let **us** make humankind in **our image,** according to **our likeness**...'" This verse is filled with important information; information we haven't yet fully grasped. (Bolding is my emphasis.)

First, according to this specific verbiage, God is using plural pronouns to refer to Them selves. Not he, not she, but both. The Hermetic Principle of Gender advises us, "Gender is in everything; everything has its Masculine and Feminine Principles; Gender manifests on all planes" [of existence]. The Principle of Gender offers a more holistic view of God as the Source of creation. According to this Philosophy, creation is the product of both the masculine and the feminine *attributes* of God operating in union and balance. (In maintaining the understandings recorded in The Kybalion and ancient teachings, the many capitalized words are intentional as proper names referring to God.)

Next, "Let us make humankind in our **image**, according to our **likeness**..." Genesis 1:26 reveals the essence of our own divine nature. This creation story was intended to explain our essential nature in language that could be more easily understood by the masses. Genesis 1:1 starts with "In the beginning, when God created..." and goes on with a story of creation. There is no description of what God looks like, only a description of creation. In this story, the various parts of the universe as we know it, take shape because *"God said..."* and then, *"it was so."* At intervals in the story, *"God saw that it was good."* These three elements are essential to our understanding of who God is and gives us valuable clues about our own potential. What we know from this creation story is that God is creative, powerful and observant, and it implies God is loving, knowing and ever-present. This story informs us that They created by commanding something to take shape, then it happened as it was commanded and then They saw that Their creation was good.

The specific elements of the story convey a simplistic explanation of the Hermetic Principle of Cause and Effect, and provide insight into one of the Hermetic names for God...Infinite Living Mind. The Principle of Cause and Effect is understood as: everything that happens (effect) must originate from somewhere (cause). The inverse is also true: every cause necessarily has an effect—whether or not we can identify the association. In the creation story and in every day life, the idea of cause is not immediately clear, but it's the linchpin for our greater understanding and potential. If we understand God as Infinite Mind, a Presence creating with intention—and the desire to love—through the spoken word, then *cause* is intention moving through the spoken word emanating from the Mind of God. And *effect* is the creation birthed through intention and word. "Seeing [observing] that it is good" is also an essential part of creating reality. Observing is both a cause and an effect. This will make more practical sense when we explore the critical importance of observation in the upcoming discussions on energy, emotions and reality.

There is no way to overstate the possibilities revealed to us by the creation story and what it was meant to convey to someone looking for a more informed understanding. This think-say-manifest-observe sequence revealed how things work in every day life. This sequence is the precise mechanism humanity has always used to create our life experiences. It's also the fundamental understanding necessary for solving all of our problems. What does this tell us about who we are? In God's image and likeness, we are powerful creators of our reality. Our thoughts are the primary cause of our observed reality and experiences, the effect. The creation story offers no descriptions for physical features for either God or humankind because the significance inherent in this story was the encrypted revelation of humanity's magnificent potential and the tools at our disposal if only we understood how to use them. A principle that remains valid even now. If this seems like a leap, just take a deep breath because it will be more tangible in coming discussions. For the moment, know that the image and likeness of God has nothing to do with gender, color or physical features. Instead, contemplate that you are powerful, wise and loving beyond your imagination.

The Principle of Cause and Effect speaks to the mechanics of reality and how we got to where we are. The Hermetic Principle of Correspondence offers understanding into the oneness of All That Is through cohesion and correspondence between the "Three Great Planes"—the Spiritual, Mental and Physical. Everything that exists, known and unknown, operates within and also contains these three planes, resulting in many levels…and beyond the scope of this book. The cohesion and correspondence between all levels is possible through the interconnectedness of the levels, which can be understood more as the spectrum of colors rather than individual steps on a staircase. The information or vibration at one level flows through to the planes above and below it in a consistent—corresponding—manner governed by all seven Universal Laws. It's the glue that holds us together in oneness and the way we can know what is unknowable.

Correspondence is the Principle behind the Hindu understanding that we are a microcosm of the macrocosm. These Planes are disguised in religious and esoteric teachings with concepts such as the hierarchies of divine messengers, levels of energetic vibration or dimensions beyond our physical reality. It's the Law granting access to higher realms when we pray and meditate, as well as the Principle that delivers inspirations to us in moments of quiet or need. Regardless of the words used to discuss the different levels of existence, they refer to the planes of correspondence flowing through one another to offer us a more complete understanding of ourselves and all other things. The creation story uses the Planes of Correspondence to suggest the truths many of us were taught in our religious indoctrinations, though we missed the larger truths and the most beneficial meanings.

The Law reads, "As above, so below; as below, so above" and governs the flow of knowledge moving through the spiritual, mental and physical planes of energy, above and below. In its absolute simplicity, it tells us:

~ Everything, visible and invisible, exists within God and God exists within every thing. We are one with God because God (above) flows through all lower planes, and we, on the dense physical plane (below), can reach upward through those same planes in our search for meaning and Truth. Through our indoctrinations we may have misunderstood this as a separate God figure up in heaven. In Hermetic wisdom, God is the highest (above) and finest vibration permeating all things that exist at lower vibrations (below).

~ At its most rudimentary understanding, the Law tells us everything is a unified whole of three planes, spiritual, mental and physical. This makes us spiritual, mental and physical beings functioning on this physical plane with access to ever-higher levels of knowledge. The complexity of this Law is beyond simple understanding, but one thing we can be assured of…we are part of something greater and are capable of realizing greater possibilities through the higher planes available to us.

~ Correspondence means what is Truth on higher planes is also true at the lower planes. This is equally true in the opposite direction, what is true on this lower physical plane is also true at the higher planes. Understanding this Principle is pivotal because it gives us a way to know what we can't prove—at least at this point in our evolution. It informs us that the Universal Laws governing reality apply to all planes of existence. This means we cannot escape the Laws of Cause and Effect, Rhythm, Vibration or any of the others because they are universally applicable.

Armed with an understanding of the Planes of Correspondence, let's look again at the creation story and what we were taught about the Ever-present, All-knowing, All-powerful and unconditionally Loving attributes of God. How do we know this is true? Through inference, the story establishes the Infinite, Knowing, Loving and Powerful attributes of God. How else could such a magnificent, complex and organized creation exist? From our lower perspective, creation is obviously the product of something big, powerful and intelligent. We can know God is all these things because we are experiencing the wondrous reality They created. "In the beginning, when God created…" (Genesis 1:1) suggests God was in existence before everything else, making Source Ever-present, Eternal and Infinite. This is the "as below, so above" principle helping us more fully understand the nature of God.

Love is the other attribute of God implied in the creation story and is an easier demonstration of the Planes of Correspondence. How do we know God is All-loving? Consider the love parents have for their children, especially their newborn. Think about how they feel and what they might be thinking. There is nothing they wouldn't do to help their children survive, thrive and grow to their greatest potential. Knowing they have given their children everything they need to go into the world, parents love and trust their children enough to allow them to move into a larger world and make their own free-will choices, even as they know mistakes will be made as part of the learning process. This is the depth of love parents have for their children here "below." Based on our understanding of the love we have for our own children, we can know that the God "above" loves all Their creations this much and more.

The other half of Correspondence tells us about who we are. If God above is All-loving, All-knowing, All-powerful and Eternal, then we here below share those attributes. "As above, so below" is hidden in the words "created in Their image and likeness" and inform us that we are likewise endowed as eternal, knowing, powerful and loving beings. We just don't think about ourselves that way, yet.

We receive from our God-parents as we receive from our earthly parents. Among other things, this means we have the power to create and, as in the creation story, we create our reality with our thoughts, words and observations. The problem is, we don't perceive ourselves this way and so we're handicapped by this lack of awareness. Our limited awareness is due, in part, to where we are in the process and timeline of human evolution. We are still babes in the woods of understanding. With our current level of understanding, it's difficult to access knowledge when we don't trust the messenger within us, and it's difficult to see how powerful we are when we don't recognize the connection between our thoughts and the reality they create. Only a handful of humans have grasped the complete understanding of the Universal Laws which animate all of creation…we call them Masters, Teachers, Anointed and Enlightened.

We return to the original question, does believing in an Ever-present

God really matter? One possible answer is no. In this paradigm, life will go on in just the way it always has; according to the Universal Laws offered by Hermetic Philosophy, slowly validated by ongoing efforts of mathematic and scientific research. Like gravity, the Hermetic Principles (Mentalism, Correspondence, Cause and Effect, Polarity, Rhythm, Vibration and Gender) function to shape our reality whether or not we think about them or understand the mechanisms by which they operate.

The answer we need to seriously consider is yes, because believing in a powerful, loving, knowing Presence brings us into relationship. In this relationship we become more aware of the support and encouragement available to us if only we are open to the possibility. Such an understanding can give us access to more wisdom, power and potential for love and happiness than we have as we struggle to get by on our own power and limited knowing. The name we call this Presence does not matter, whether God, Spirit, Mind or Allah. What does matter is the inseparable connection strengthened by a conscious relationship.

The old saying, "It's not what you know but who you know that counts" applies here. Knowing yourself as a Spark in the Mind of God and developing a relationship with your Source is the "who" that counts—the One you need to know. Whatever you learned about God and whatever you think about God's influence in your life, now is the perfect time to replace the mistaken belief of separation with the whole and empowering truth of your oneness with the Source of All That Is. You may find that changing how you think about yourself and about your relationship with an Infinite Loving Creator begins to ease your discomfort almost immediately. It will certainly decrease the time and effort required to get where you want to be.

If you're still on the fence about the concept of God or the idea that you have a spiritual nature, there are other ways to understand the concepts presented here. Ongoing research in the fields of mathematics, quantum mechanics, consciousness and the physical and psychological sciences offer ever more evidence in support of the Hermetic Principles as explanations for how reality works. Though there is much work to be done before science can explain the mechanisms proving the validity of all that Ancient Wisdom has to offer, there has been some significant progress made in that direction. So much so that the field of possibility described by quantum mechanics is right in step with the Principle of Cause and Effect, Vibration, Rhythm and Polarity offered by Hermetic Philosophy. Science and Hermetic Philosophy are two different paradigms describing the same thing. So for the disbelievers among us, I will use Mind of God/Field of Possibility or Mind/Field as names of God when it suits ease of understanding.

This is the proper time to restate that you are the creator of your reality, and due to its critical importance this won't be the last time. To be happy, healthy and whole requires your acknowledgement of this truth, and the degree to which you embrace it defines the level of power you possess to direct your life toward happiness. And...now that we have established how important you are, the more complete truth is that you are not alone; in actuality, you are a co-creator. The constant factor supporting your inherent power to create *is* the Ever-present Power that moves in, through and around you and all things. Your creative thoughts emanate from you and interact with the Divine Presence holding all of creation in place. God is the Matrix and the Universal Laws you are unwittingly using to sculpt your reality, thus you are co-creating with God. As a Spark in the Mind of God, you are one of many other Sparks who exist within the Divine Matrix. You and all of your brothers and sisters are working together as one to co-create the reality we are experiencing as individuals and as the human race living together on Earth.

CHAPTER 3

Reclaiming Our Personal Power

"A hero: a man or woman who is unsatisfied by his condition, and resolves to do something about it."
– Bangambiki Habyarimana, Pearls of Eternity

What happened to our personal power? Very simple...we gave it away. Not intentionally, or even consciously, but it happened over the course of humanity's quest for enlightenment and discovery. A brief trot through the history of civilization will demonstrate that we relinquished our power over time—like a helium balloon slowly losing altitude—in a process supported by well-intentioned instruction, role modeling and coercion. Through these mechanisms, we abandoned our connection with Source and all the planes of divine intelligence and power available to us through this connection. This departure from God, and therefore from ourselves, is the basis for our disappointments and struggles, and it's why we often feel powerless to fix the problems we encounter. Again, this is not our fault; it's the result of generations of conditioning, socialization and specialization, most notably the separation of religion and science.

We owe our existence to the fact that our earliest ancestors survived and advanced through the discoveries of their times, unaided by microscopes, petri-dishes, telescopes and computers. They spent most of their time doing things to ensure survival. Their knowledge came from trial and error, observation, recurring conditions, repetitive successes and contemplation.

Contemplation allowed them to accept revelations and intuitions as messengers guiding them to a better understanding of how things worked or how they could improve the current situation. (These revelations and messengers were sometimes described to others as angel visitations, burning bushes or dreams.) With experience and insight they came to recognize that the world around them was orchestrated by a power greater than themselves and that they were part of it. They were free to follow their insights and use their discoveries to advance their societies. There was little conflicting information or acclaimed experts telling them they were foolish to use their internal guidance and observation as sources for new ideas and progress. Today we recognize the amazing accuracy with which they tracked the movement of the planets and stars and then used them to determine planting and harvesting seasons and to navigate their expanding world. Interestingly, the trial-error-success-observation-repetition sequencing they used to discover and validate how things worked then are some of the same tools used by researchers in order to prove accuracy and validity today.

The shift from believing in an ever-present guiding force intimately involved in every aspect of life to the illusion of separation and reliance on self was a natural progression of humanity's evolving sophistication. Scientific discoveries and technological advances spawned an "every man for himself" mentality. As part of the collective "we" of humanity, the more we learned about the world and the way it worked, the more independent and capable we believed ourselves to be. The more dominion we were able to exercise over our environment and the expanding world we lived in, the more using our power to control our dominion enticed us. The tremendous expansion in human awareness, complexity and potential allowed us to make choices about what to believe, how to think and how to live. This was true for our ancestors and it is true for us now.

This growing world of knowledge allowed us to feel smarter, more capable and more powerful than ever before. The world was our oyster! This was the fork in the road where we collectively began to see ourselves as the source of wisdom, knowledge and power. We quit looking to the heavens and our inner voice for guidance. As knowledge continued to expand, we started listening to those who appeared to be more intelligent and learned than we believed ourselves to be. With our own agreement, and sometimes through coercion, we accepted and endorsed the answers put forth by designated authorities. In time, we came to readily accept that these experts knew better than us. They became the defining word on what was true and what was right for all of us.

Scientific and technological advances have continued to expand, pushing our knowledge to heights previously belonging only to storytellers and fantasy. The oceans, skies, space and the internal mechanics of body and mind became the new frontiers. Science became the sole purveyor of certainty and accuracy. It established more precise rules for research, experimentation and proof, thus claiming ultimate authority over the designation of "truth." In deciding what criteria would be necessary to distinguish fact from fiction, experts added measurability and control as necessary criteria in determining validity and factual reality. Repetition, observation and efficacy were no longer the adequate proofs they once had been. As a result, knowledge that had been validated through repetitive efficacy, accumulated over time and then shared through wisdom teachings, gifted healers and the science predating man's ability to precisely measure cause and effect was abandoned. To believe in any of it, teach it or use it became heresy, witchcraft, wives' tales, quackery, nonsense, sham, anecdotal and just plain silly depending on where on the timeline of history we look. Ridicule and retribution became the consequences of believing in old science and practicing the ancient healing arts. Being the survival oriented and evolving people our ancestors were, most of them distanced themselves from the Source of knowledge and the practices of their distant past. This distancing was handed down to us over many generations. They learned—often the hard way—and then taught us not to discuss intuition, instincts and other foolishness with educated people.

The advances of science and technology have brought many benefits to the world and in so doing, the world has become appropriately reliant on the good that has come from them. As a natural extension of this reliance, we continue to discount our innate wisdom and internal guidance system—our sixth sense—and sometimes even our common sense, for the steady stream of information originating from outside ourselves. Additionally, the speed and complexity of life has become so fast paced that it's difficult and unlikely we will find the time to contemplate the accuracy of information as it passes through the chaos of our lives. We simply don't have the time or energy to discern truth from hype and consider how the incoming information might impact our lives...or better or for worse.

More importantly, we have been socialized through family, schools, churches, government and social media to trust the experts as the ultimate authority on just about every aspect of life. In a kind of all encompassing "father knows best," *we are giving away our power* to someone or some entity who will interpret information for us. These recognized authorities now determine the accuracy of information, discern its merit and relevance and then convey it to the general population through popular media sources and other designated experts. We latch on to this flow of information, assimilating it into our beliefs, priorities and routines, rarely pondering the accuracy or considering that it might not be the right choice for us as individuals.

This is the long and winding path of sophistication, socialization and evolution we collectively have participated in for hundreds of years. We have used our intelligent minds to logically dismiss the truth of our oneness with God and with each other. We have discounted our connection to everything and our oneness with all things as a myth or fallacy...if we consider it at all. We've rejected our connection to the Earth and nature, as well as our intimate reliance on them. We've forgotten how to listen to our own intuitive wisdom—our Still Small Voice Within—to find the answers that would direct right thoughts, words and actions towards a more balanced and joyful existence. Lastly, we've given our power over to those who have declared themselves experts. Those who claim to have the answers to problems which were initially created by separation and the faulty belief systems seeded by that separation...problems for which they have no answers.

Our individual struggles are the result of faulty beliefs and thought patterns that hold us trapped in our own discontent and misery. Likewise, society's struggles are the result of beliefs and thought patterns each of us hold in common with the rest of humanity. We are active participants co-creating our collective experience of reality. The only way to achieve health, happiness, peace and fulfillment is to change the beliefs and patterns holding us stuck in the same old disruptive patterns. The peace and joy we instinctively are driven to seek are the magnetic forces drawing us back to the love and oneness that is our true essence. Remembering that we are each an intimate part of God and fully embracing the wisdom of divine guidance will support and nurture us along our life journey. We all walk this path together, but the journey to loving yourself whole is an intense and individual adventure.

Reclaiming your power is a matter of strengthening the connection with your Seed of Divinity. Your Seed, like all seeds, contains everything you need to know to grow to your full potential as the healthy, happy and peace-filled person you were meant to be. If you are disappointed with your efforts to be happy and content, it's only because you don't have all the information you need to be successful in finding that happiness. You are operating from outdated, faulty beliefs and information that keep you locked in the same box of confusion and disappointment you've been experiencing. If you want your life to be different than it has been, you only need to commit to a different path and find the right information and tools for you—as the unique individual you are. Then you must actually use them to change the faulty beliefs you unconsciously cling to in the shadows of your mind.

The shift from where you find yourself now and where you want to be is a solo journey—one only you can control. As with any journey to a new destination, you will interact with others who are on their own journeys. There will be important signs to pay attention to and there will be alternate roads if you take a detour or get lost. No matter what, there will always be a path back to the high road when you stop and ask for directions.

Understanding how to interact with others, decoding your internal signals and accepting the help that comes through your innate wisdom are all part of the information that went missing when we collectively relinquished our spiritual connection and the power that came with it. The good news is that this information is all still available to us when we choose to reclaim it. In more good news, the science that enabled the disconnection from our inner resources is now offering a wealth of information on just how connected, powerful and magnificent you actually are. It's up to you to find the right information that will help you reconnect with your true self and then decide how to integrate it into new and uplifting ways to create your happiness.

Family Tree of Humanity

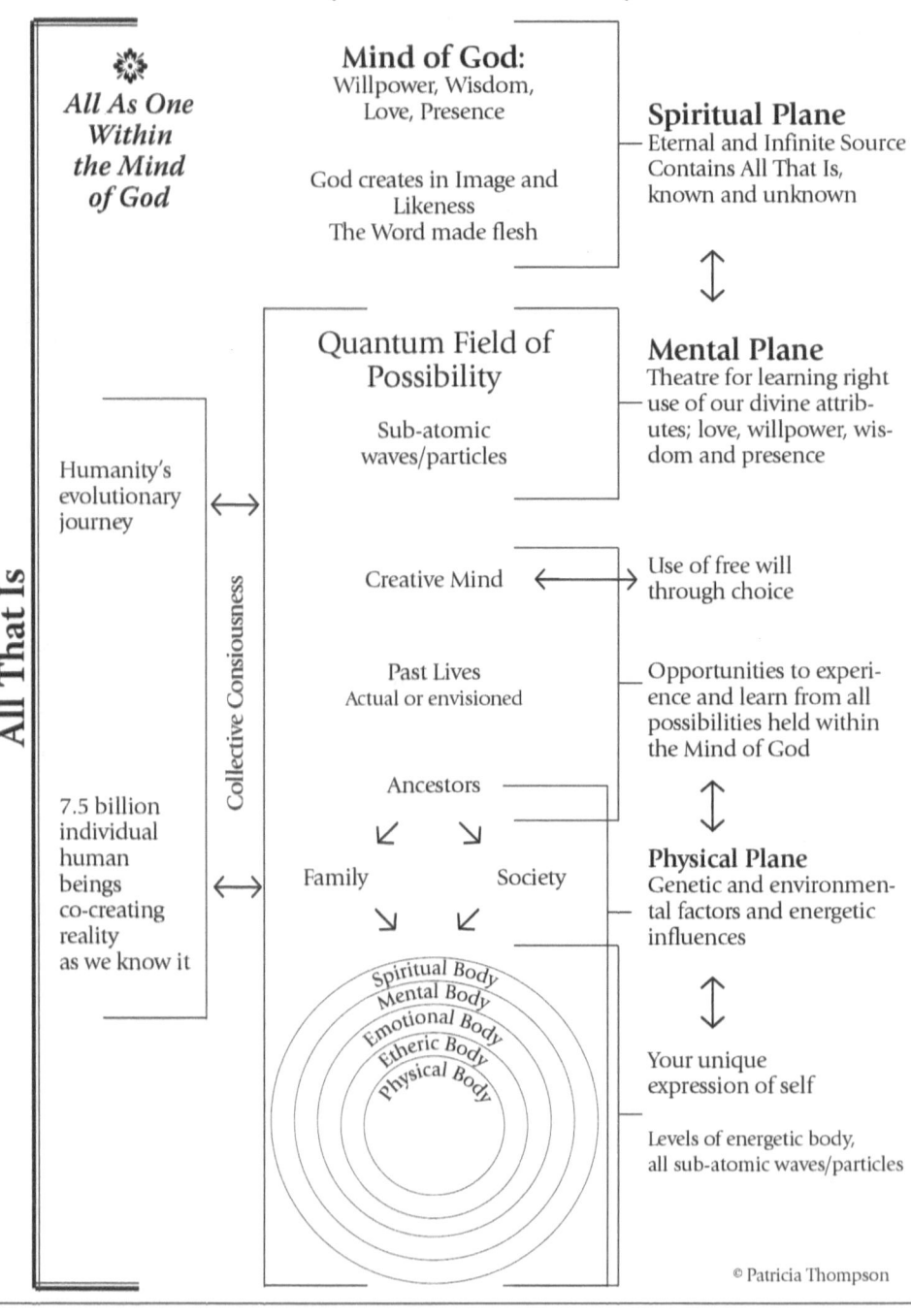

© Patricia Thompson

Family Tree of Humanity

This diagram demonstrates how science and ancient teachings merge together to explain oneness, existence and human potential. It is difficult for a two-dimensional schematic to portray a multi-dimensional reality, so imagine each of the three columns as descriptors that show the interrelatedness of all aspects within the Mind/Field. Imagine the top to bottom hierarchy in each column as an interwoven and multidirectional continuum rather than a stepladder.

Though time is an illusion, the diagram infers a familiar timeline flowing through the history of humanity's evolution, linking the experience of our ancestors to our own. Oneness with our ancestors, our history and the experience of 7.5 billion other earth travelers make up our collective consciousness, which we define as our reality.

Science is not yet able to quantify the size of the quantum field or what came before the Big Bang, leaving us to ponder what has remained unknowable for eons of time. The Infinite Mind of God is at least as big as the quantum field. The large box represents the Mind of God and Their participation in All That Is. This means that human possibilities are not limited to human determination alone. There is energy, movement, interference and coherence and we are all co-creators participating in and dependent upon this infinite field.

The diagram illustrates the Planes of Correspondence on two levels. It implies a hierarchy of spirit above passing through the mental plane to the physical plane below, as seen in the third column. The same planes of correspondence can be seen at the bottom of the second column representing our individual and holistic nature within the physical plane itself. The bidirectional arrows in column three remind us that energy moves between the levels giving us access to higher realms of vibration. This same bidirectional access is implied at all levels listed in the second column. Understanding our origins, connectedness, evolution and potential in this way is a key to finding the happiness we are drawn to seek.

CHAPTER 4

Understanding the Key Concepts

"Those who cannot change their minds cannot change anything."
– George Bernard Shaw

We don't get too far into adulthood before we realize that our goals to achieve health, happiness and contentment require effort and perseverance. The only true path to achieving these goals comes through loving ourselves as the unique, one-of-a-kind individuals we are. We get lost in our efforts because we are walking paths we learned were right for us, in a one-size-fits-most kind of way. To find the specific path that's right for us as an individual, we need to understand the natural processes that brought us to where we are so we can use those same processes to correct our course and get where we want to be. The first step in this process is having accurate definitions and better understandings about the foundation of reality. Our foundations, our experiences and our reality are functions of energy, beliefs, learning and the integrated nature of spirit, mind, emotions and body. Because these functions determine our experiences and perception of reality, we are going to explore them in detail now.

∽∽

Energy

"The energy of the mind is the essence of life."
– Aristotle (384–322 BC)

The concept of energy cannot be overstated. Energy is the glue that holds everything, seen and unseen, together as one big magnificent interwoven field of reality. It's the force that moves and shapes everything there is. In its more obvious and physical application, energy is the air you breathe, the water you drink, the food you eat, the physical body you live in and the gravity keeping you attached to the Earth. At the mental level, your thoughts are the energetic medium radiating out from you to create your reality. Taking to a grander level, your thoughts are the energetic force contributing to the expanding universe we are living in, whether you are conscious of it or not. Your thoughts are not only a creative force in their own energetic manifestations, they also direct how you speak and act, which definitely have an impact on your life and your participation in the world. To better understand how energy is the foundation holding all things together, let's consider what Ancient Wisdom and quantum science tell us about energy.

"'Nothing rests; everything moves; everything vibrates.' – The Kybalian"
This is the Principle of Vibration from Hermetic Philosophy. The Masters of Ancient Wisdom believed that everything lived and moved and had its being in the Universal, Infinite, Living Mind of God. This Principle encouraged wisdom seekers to contemplate the premise that everything was energy, including their own nature. According to the Mystery Schools, understanding this principle fully was to possess "the scepter of power."

$E=mC^2$

Fast forward through thousands of years of mathematical and scientific insights and advances. Albert Einstein's theory of special relativity postulated that matter and energy were essentially the same, differing only by rate—defined as the speed of light. This standing theory not only explained the relationship between energy and matter, it supported the teachings of Hermetic Philosophy with scientific credibility.

It may seem as if ancient teachings and scientific theories have little relevance in our lives. Nothing could be further from the truth. Appreciating how energy and matter are the same and that our bodies are simply energy in the form of matter is the key that opens the gates to change, health and happiness. To fully appreciate our energetic nature, consider what we know to be true of the human body.

Everything in our body functions through action potentials and electrical impulses; from the beating of our hearts to the flexing of our toes; from growing hair to pushing food through our digestive tracts; from healing a broken bone to fighting cancer; from remembering how to tie our shoes to writing a grocery list, college thesis or business proposal. All thoughts, words and actions, conscious or unconscious, are the result of electrical impulses originating at some point in the body, flowing along cellular membranes and jumping across synapses to create an effect in another area of the body.

Beyond this energetic communication animating all bodily functions, we are pure energy at our smallest unit of measure. Our physical bodies are made up of systems organized around one goal, to support life. If we continue to dissect down through the muscles, organs and tissues we'll find our basic unit of function—the human cell. Though we may think of the cell as the basic unit, we give little thought to the potential held within these tiny structures. All cells contain vital components including DNA, genes, and their own power generating stations. All cellular structures are comprised of molecules, which are made of atoms, and atoms are made of sub-atomic waves and particles—protons, neutrons and electrons energetically bound together in space. In fact, all atoms are 99.99% open space. This means we are made up of waves and particles moving in space. We are energy, bound together by energy, vibrating in space. How this energy works is the critical piece informing us of the innate power we are using to create our reality.

Neutrons and protons consist of fine particles called quarks, which operate within their energetic fields. Energy bonds hold quarks, neutrons and protons together in the tight package we know as the atom's nucleus. Electrons are waves and particles orbiting around a proton/neutron pair…but they are not limited to a single orbit around that nucleus. Shifting to another orbit is called a *quantum leap* and appears reliant on interactions within a larger field—beyond the atom itself. Electrons interact with and are affected by the electromagnetic field to create photons—units of light. These photons then affect the behavior of the electrons themselves. This is the constant and dynamic give and take of energy. In all of this, our basic unit of function is pure energy and it's filled with potential…the potential for change and even a quantum leap. Now, it's a matter of who is in charge of the change.

Science also tells us that our photons, electrons and the electromagnetic field they interact within are not limited to our physical bodies. The universe we live in consists of the larger electromagnetic field with quarks, electrons, photons and energy bonds of its own. Our photons and electrons are constantly interacting with the larger field, and together, all those sub-atomic waves and particles are behaving according to quantum theories physicists are still trying to fully understand. Could it be that this larger electromagnetic field is one and the same with Infinite Living Mind of God?

Our interactions within the Mind/Field determine our reality… even when we can't prove how it works.

What quantum science is revealing has important ramifications when it comes to our magnificent potential. At our most elemental form, we are vibration—energy in motion. We are made of units of light, confirming our divine nature as vibrant beings of light. We are part of something greater than ourselves because the electromagnetic field holding us as physical matter in this space and time is part of a much larger field. According to quantum theory, this electromagnetic field contains all possibilities because anything and all things are possible as energy interacts and changes waves into particles, gives shape to matter and becomes the reality we experience. This larger field means we are living in concert with everything else because information in the form of energy is also part of and interacting with the collective field to contribute to humanity's perceptions of reality. This makes us co-creators in the Quantum Field of Possibility as quantum theory offers us a better understanding of the dynamics operating in the Mind of God where we live, move and have our being.

We are energy, bound together by energy, vibrating in space.

The Power of Our Mind

So then, how do we create our reality? How do we explain that weird discomfort we feel when we walk into an unfamiliar room or when a stranger stands too close? How do some people sense when a loved one has been hurt or has passed on? How does a child prodigy play an instrument with such mastery? How do we explain spontaneous healing? How did Copernicus, Edison, Einstein and others come up with the brilliant theories that revolutionized the world? How did the intentional efforts of a group using Transcendental Meditation™ cause the crime rate in Washington, DC to drop by 23.3%? The answer to these questions is energy and the electromagnetic field. We cannot see subatomic particles and waves, but there is no denying their existence as the essence of all things. Hermetic Philosophy and quantum theory again provide the insight and mechanics we need to understand how the power of our thoughts works to create reality.

According to the *Kybalion*, the Hermetic Law of Mentalism taught, *"The Universe is Mental—held in the Mind of THE ALL."* This informs us that everything in the Universe is a mental phenomenon, thus reality has its foundation in thought. The Universe is contained within the Infinite Mind of God, The ALL. In this way, all that happens not only takes place within the Mind of God, it also originates there as an option in all that is possible. Since we exist in this Infinite Mind, our thoughts are also part of the mental power operating within the Universal Mind. This is how we are co-creators of our reality. The Law of Mentalism, where thoughts are creative energy, then joins the Law of Causation to determine what reality looks like for each of us.

The Hermetic Principle of Causation—also known as the Law of Cause and Effect—offers, *"Every Cause has its Effect; every Effect has its Cause; everything happens according to Law; Chance is but a name for Law not recognized…"* As discussed earlier, this law creates our reality, and it's in agreement with the laws of physics. The easiest way to understand the application of this law is to imagine dropping a pebble into a pond of still water. The pebble (cause) must create ripples (effect) in the water. The ripples are energy waves moving out from the cause. No matter how far the ripples travel, even as they become less visible, they continue until they interact with the pond's edge where they turn around and return as ripples to the point of origin. Our thoughts (cause) are like the pebbles prompting ripples (waves) into the electromagnetic field to shape reality. They interact with the larger field (edge of pond) and return to us as an observation (perception) of our reality (effect). This is true even when we don't recognize the direct association between our thoughts and the reality we experience as a result of them.

These Hermetic Laws are also explained at least in part by quantum science. Our thoughts are actually sub-atomic waves interacting with the electromagnetic field to influence the energetic behavior of other sub-atomic waves and particles. The quality (vibrational frequency) of our thoughts (as cause) changes the behavior of other sub-atomic particles in the field to influence the outcome (effect) that is produced (our perception of reality). Without being aware of our power, we are active participants, and co-creators, in the electromagnetic field within the Field of Possibility and the Mind of God.

The Law of Cause and Effect has two important ramifications. First, it helps us understand the Law of Mentalism. Our thoughts are the mental phenomenon creating our reality. On a more simplistic level, our thoughts are the context and impetus for our words and actions, which definitely have consequences. Secondly, the Law of Cause and Effect places responsibility for the conditions of our lives squarely in our own hands. If thought is causation, then what we think is important and how we think about ourselves is what defines us and our possibilities.

The Observer and The Observed

The biblical creation story gave us three elements in the creation process; the spoken word (originating in the Mind); then it happened according to the Word; and then the observer (God) saw that it was good. This third phase, observation, is what holds creation in place... until different thoughts modify the perceptual bias of our observation.

In their best seller, *Spontaneous Evolution: Our Positive Future (and a Way to Get There From Here)*, Bruce Lipton and Steve Bhaerman discuss recent scientific discoveries that help us understand how thoughts become reality. The magnetoencephalograph (MEG), one of the more recent technologies for mapping brain activity, clearly shows that the brain transmits thoughts across open space as their energetic signals are received and measured by this electronic device...which is not touching the body. In the opposite direction, visual and auditory stimulation from the surrounding environment travel through open space to the eyes and ears and are received into the brain as electrical impulses that can be measured and mapped as activity in various regions of the brain. These electrical impulses from our senses pop into our conscious awareness as thoughts that trigger feelings. Research with MEG tells us the brain is not the mind, but rather, a powerful transmitter and receiver. This also implies we have the natural ability and capacity to receive information in the form of insights, intuitions and instincts triggered by sources external to our brains...but not external to our minds, as we will explore in detail.

Our thoughts are heavily influenced by what we have learned and come to believe about ourselves and the world we live in. What we learned, mostly in our earliest years, is the foundation of our personality and personal perceptions. It's our thoughts, tempered by our attitudes and perceptions, which shape our reality. How is this so? The Double Slit experiment helps us understand the process.

The Double Slit experiment was first performed in 1803 by Thomas Young and has been repeated many times since then in attempts to understand the unexpected results. This experiment demonstrated that the smallest elements of light and energy (photons and electrons) can be: 1) in two places at once and 2) both a wave and a particle at the same time. Additionally, *photons and electrons behave differently when they are observed than they do when left unattended* in their own "interference patterns." Repeated experiments proved that the power of observation, or even the intent to observe, changed the behavior of the waves and affected the resulting patterns...the outcome or effect. While the complete explanation for this phenomenon is still being studied, a prominent theory is that observation collapses waves (energy) into particles (matter). In his article, *"What Is The Double Slit Experiment?"* Matt Williams informed readers of Universe Today, "The Double Slit experiment...made scientists aware of the incredible, confounding world of quantum mechanics, where nothing is predictable, everything is relative, and the observer is no longer a passive subject, but an active participant with the power to change the outcome."

Quantum theory suggests that reality is the result of individual and collective perception broadcast out into the field of possibility (observer/cause) and then reflected back to us as "the way it is" (observed/effect). Since we believe that what we perceive is actual reality (now the cause), we reinforce our beliefs and thoughts as true in our own minds (now the effect). Albert Einstein quipped, "Reality is merely an illusion, albeit a very persistent one." If reality is an illusion and only real based on our perception, then we are not bound to the way things are, except through our own choice to continue the status quo by clinging to the same thought patterns. If we don't like what life looks like, then, according to science and Ancient Wisdom, we can change it. Dr. Einstein also said, "Problems cannot be solved with the same mindset that created them."

This is the secret to changing your reality. As the observer of your life, you are projecting your belief-biased perceptions and thoughts into the electromagnetic field as you bear witness to your life and the world you live in. The field instantaneously reflects back to you *what you believe to be your reality*. What you believe to be true about yourself and the world are creating your reality over and over again. To change your reality, you must change your beliefs, perceptions and thoughts.

The most important take away of this section is that you are a powerful energetic being perceiving yourself in material form. Your limitations are rooted in two common beliefs. First you believe you are only a physical body. Second, you believe you are separate from God, the Mind/Field, where you exist. Further, your possibilities are restricted to the beliefs programmed by early learning, before you had enough awareness to reject them as a detriment to your magnificent potential.

Don't be limited by how others define you, whether they are family, friends or experts. You have the power to change those things causing you to be unhappy or unhealthy. You are an energetic being of light shaping your reality through the power of your mind and the beliefs you hold there. As an active participant and co-creator in the greater and expanding consciousness, you have access to information and inspiration available from levels that are as yet unknown to you.

Love Is Energy

Energy is the vibrational force of change that holds things together and pulls them apart. It's the expanding particles and collapsing waves which manifest as all that is visible and invisible. But, does energy have a quality that defines it? Science measures energy as rates of frequency using units called Hertz (Hz); high vibrations/frequencies are faster and finer; lower vibrations/frequencies are slower and more spread out. We can know this is true because hot temperatures move particles faster and cold slows them down, even to the point of making substances thicker or more solid. When we think of emotions, we see a similarity. Love makes us feel light, bright and warm all over. I believe we feel this way because our waves and particles are moving at a higher vibration. Fear and hate have the opposite effect because they are of a lower vibration.

I believe Love is the energy that moves all things. The Planes of Correspondence suggest this. Consider a mother who runs into the street and lifts a car off her child after an accident. How is such strength possible? Only in this one instance is she able to lift such tremendous weight. The bond of motherly love is the energy flowing through her entire being. In that moment, she is driven by something beyond thinking and what she believes is possible. So it is with the energy that supports and sustains our lives. Love is the highest and most powerful level of vibrational force radiating at the Source of Creation. God is Love. Because God is Love and you exist in the Mind of God, you are also Love. You are the Love and Light created in God's Image and Likeness. Love is the energy that gives you life and it's the magnetic energy in the Mind/Field compelling you to find happiness, peace and fulfillment with every breath you take. As you love yourself, you are coming ever closer to vibrating at this higher frequency and living its peace-filled reality.

Beliefs

"Beliefs are choices. First you choose your beliefs. Then your beliefs affect your choices." – Roy T. Bennett

Webster's dictionary tells us that beliefs are "the state of believing, conviction or acceptance that certain things are true or real; [belief] implies complete unquestioning acceptance of something even in the absence of proof and, esp. of something not supported by reason..."

Beliefs is a word that will appear throughout *Loving Yourself Whole* because it's the firmly held beliefs we adopt, mostly before the age of four, that are the key to freeing ourselves from our pain and struggles. Consistent with the definition, they're not necessarily grounded in truth, proof or reason. Our beliefs are spawned from immature thought processes we used to make sense of the experiences and attitudes we encountered in our earliest years. What the significant adults in our lives believed to be true and the way we were treated became the basis for our beliefs—whether or not they were true or reasonable. When our experiences were repeated over and over, our immature minds took this as confirmation that what we were learning about the world was true and affirming it as reality...even if it wasn't. Thus our beliefs were formed and etched into our memories becoming the focal reference point that dictated thoughts, attitudes, coping patterns, feelings, reactions, words and behaviors...pretty much everything in life. They also constitute the basis of understanding we use to interpret everything happening in our lives. As we grew up, our interpretations of similar life events then became our "proof" that those early-formed beliefs were actually true. This was a circular cause and effect sequence taking place over and over again without any conscious awareness it was happening. Even identifying the belief or the process at the root of our trouble remains elusive when we attempt to make changes. To break free of the bonds keeping us trapped in old patterns, we must expose the boogeyman in the closets of our minds.

Learning

"Learning is a treasure that will follow its owner everywhere."
– Chinese Proverb

Your life is an experiential journey mapped out by your perceptions of reality, your experiences and the choices you make along the way. Your learning opportunities are uniquely and collaboratively designed by you and the Mind/Field in order to guide you to higher levels of self-understanding and love. If your experience of reality is less loving, peaceful and fulfilling than you wish it was, then as ancient wisdom and science suggest, the energy of your thoughts, words and actions are causing some degree of turbulence along the way.

The progress you make along your journey is accelerated or hindered by a number of factors. Two of the most important factors in determining the ease of your path are the choices you make and how fast you alter your course based on the learning opportunities—life experiences—you encounter along the way. The ability to choose is grounded in the innate gift of free will. You always have the ability to choose. In every moment, you have the ability to choose your thoughts, the words you use, how you respond to others, how you feel about and react to situations, and the actions you take to make life better for yourself and others. Your ability to choose differently is limited by what you have learned about yourself, your possibilities and the world around you.

Learning is the process of receiving, analyzing, assimilating and applying information in all its forms. What you have learned about yourself through this process informs your beliefs, which then automatically and unconsciously dictate your thoughts, words, feelings and actions. Your beliefs were solidly programmed into your subconscious mind at a very early age, before you had the capacity and maturity to accurately analyze the incoming information and reject it as untrue about you. It was easy to get it wrong and, like most of us, you probably did.

That said, it's important to understand that you came to this place of disempowering beliefs and recurring struggles through innocence, misunderstanding and the long-held belief that you are separate from your own divinity and Universal Intelligence, as we discussed earlier. Separation from God and our divine nature is a commonly held belief and since we tend to cluster with like-minded people, it's natural to feel certain that your way of thinking is spot-on. If you likewise share the perspective that life is a struggle to get ahead, resources are scare and its "every man for himself," then your life is going to reflect the suffering you believe is inevitable. But, in the Mind/Field, suffering is not inevitable. Suffering, unhappiness and disease are the possibilities manifested as a result of faulty beliefs, which are based on learning handed down to you. Once you recognize their origins and the process by which you became burdened with them, you can choose to learn a different way of believing, thinking, speaking and behaving.

The ability to choose is grounded in the innate gift of free will.

Childhood and How We Learn What We Do

Learning is an essential part of the innate imperative for survival. The process for learning is hardwired into our brains and nervous systems in an automatic and definitive way to ensure we are able to quickly identify threats and immediately respond to them. Throughout our lives, learning follows the same wiring program regardless of what is being learned, and most of it happens without our awareness. A baby cries when it's uncomfortable. Whether hungry, wet or cold, a baby quickly learns that crying brings relief. Learning that crying when hungry brings food may seem different than learning to walk, but the process is the same. It requires *repetitive experiences to form neuronal pathways*. Learning to run from a sabertoothed tiger used the same hardwired processes, though this lesson required fewer repetitions to stick in one's memory; the loss of a loved one to a tiger's dinner was quickly stored in memory and handed down to future generations with fear provoking emphasis. No matter the time period we live in, survival means learning to respond appropriately. This means making changes in ourselves or in our environment.

> *"Give me a child until he is 7 and I will show you the man."*
> *– Aristotle, The Philosophy of Aristotle*

Understanding how we learned in our earliest years is important to understanding how we got where we are and how we can tip the scales in favor of unlearning outdated or faulty information and replacing it with new ideas and empowering beliefs. When we were very young, we learned new things incredibly fast. As we get older, it isn't as easy to absorb and assimilate new information, especially if it conflicts with beliefs and thoughts we've held for most of our lives.

Regardless of age, learning happens through two mechanisms, repetition and hypnosis. Repetition is just that, repeating the same thing over and over until it sticks, like learning to roll over, walk, tie shoes or memorize multiplication tables. Hypnosis is a state of mind defined by slower brainwaves (alpha, theta and delta) than the brainwaves of focused attention (beta) or intense concentration (gamma). These slower brainwaves are simply states of mind more open to new information, insights and alternative ideas, and they offer a huge advantage when it comes to learning new things. The brainwaves of infants and younger children are naturally slower and so they live in a state of mental openness which enables rapid learning. The younger they are, the slower the waves. This allows a tremendous amount of new information to be assimilated before the age of two years. They remain incredibly fast and pliable learners until about age six when the rate of their brainwaves begins to more closely resemble those of adults, and the ease of incorporating new information tapers off. Adults and children over the age of 12 spend more time in the faster brainwave state of attention and analysis. That said, we spend more time in the hypnotic states than we realize. Daydreaming, reverie, meditation, introspection, contemplation, prayer and sleep are all slower brainwave states

Brainwaves in Childhood and Beyond

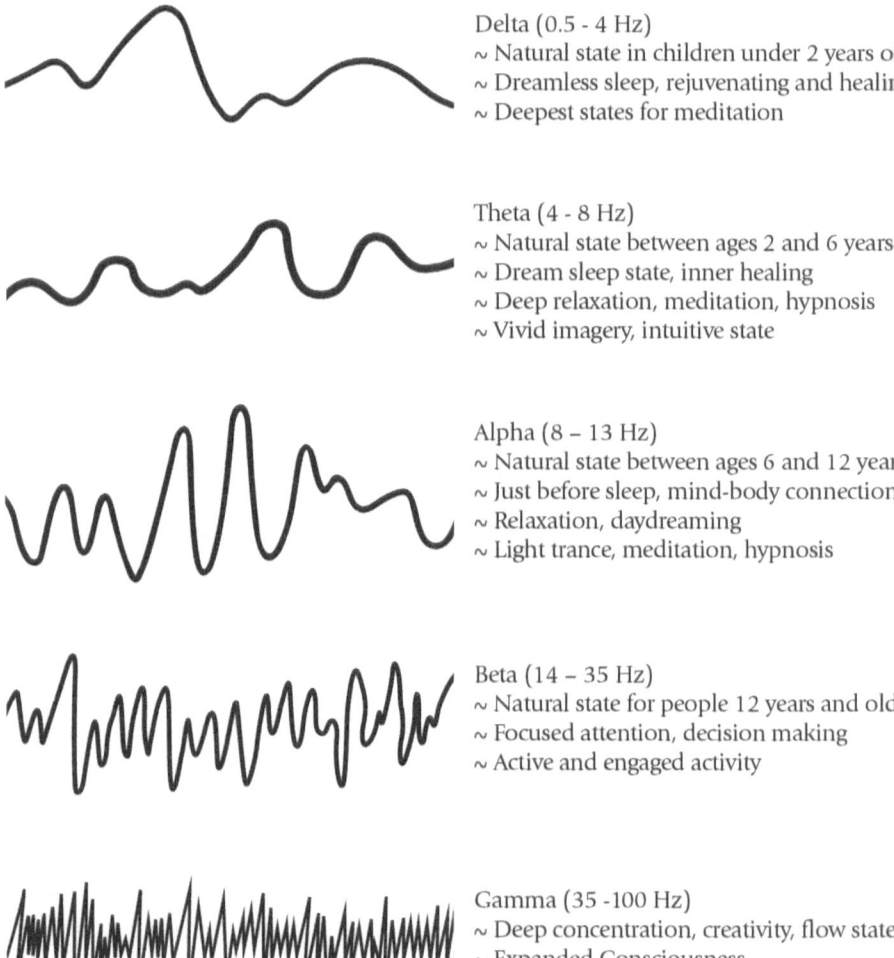

Delta (0.5 - 4 Hz)
~ Natural state in children under 2 years old
~ Dreamless sleep, rejuvenating and healing
~ Deepest states for meditation

Theta (4 - 8 Hz)
~ Natural state between ages 2 and 6 years
~ Dream sleep state, inner healing
~ Deep relaxation, meditation, hypnosis
~ Vivid imagery, intuitive state

Alpha (8 – 13 Hz)
~ Natural state between ages 6 and 12 years
~ Just before sleep, mind-body connection
~ Relaxation, daydreaming
~ Light trance, meditation, hypnosis

Beta (14 – 35 Hz)
~ Natural state for people 12 years and older
~ Focused attention, decision making
~ Active and engaged activity

Gamma (35 -100 Hz)
~ Deep concentration, creativity, flow state
~ Expanded Consciousness

These brain waves are natural states of mind. Babies start with slow brainwaves and increase their range as they age. After age 12, alpha and beta are regular wake states and higher frequencies happen in sleep and unintentionally, but are beneficial for intuition, learning and healing when accessed intentionally through a contemplative mind.

where the mind is more open to new information, even new information that conflicts with what was previously learned.

Learning through hypnosis and repetition can be fast-tracked in several ways. Both are accelerated by the simultaneous use of the other. Using them together generates a synergistic affect requiring fewer repetitions and therefore less time to learn something new. This synergistic approach is useful for adults trying to make changes in beliefs, thought patterns and behaviors. Repeating inspirational affirmations in a slower brainwave state, whether meditation or self-hypnosis, can offer quicker and long lasting changes if practiced with diligence and intent.

Other factors that accelerate learning are driven by our primal survival instinct. Because primal instinct is involved, these factors not only affect the speed of learning, they also affect how we will respond physically, mentally and emotionally to future events. Information accompanied by high emotional charge makes a big impact on memory. The brain's memory function will hold onto moments of joy and happiness, but negative emotions, especially fear, will make a more significant and lasting impression. When incoming information or experiences are accompanied by fear, the subconscious mind prioritizes the learning so fewer repetitions are required for memory and learning. Spanking as a deterrent to undesirable behavior or hiding whenever a violent parent is drinking are examples of accelerated learning. Highly charged positive emotions also move information into memory. The experience of being loved promotes brain growth and development in childhood and helps shape behavior and attitudes as children learn about themselves. Further, we can all appreciate that being in love helps us remember favorite foods, interests, birth dates and happy times in much better detail.

Historically, being part of a tribe was associated with better chances of survival and as a result we are still intrinsically drawn to belong to a group or groups. Belonging to a group requires some compliance with group standards. This makes remembering information coming from authority figures and peers an important factor for inclusion in a group. Perceived importance has a weighted impact on learning and as a result, less repetition is required when information comes from peers and authorities, especially if being part of that group is regarded as desirable. This applies to people of all ages.

Along with their slower brainwaves, infants and children have another impressive advantage. Their brains grow at an astonishing rate. In the first year, the thinking, reasoning and coordinating networks in their brains grow 88%. Researchers at Harvard University report that the brains of very young children form "more than one million new neuronal connections every second." As the brain continues to develop, the neuronal connections that have information passing through regularly—repetition—continue to develop, while those that don't have information passing through are "pruned" away. This growth and pruning process ends in childhood, after which the regeneration of brain cells and their connections slows dramatically. This means adults can still learn new things and change old ways, it just takes longer and requires much more effort. As adults, repetition is still necessary for learning and making new connections. But if we want to make positive changes, it's also necessary to stop repeating the same old thoughts and behaviors and allow those old neuronal connections to die away. Repetition is the process by which we learned the habitual patterns we now have and it is the process we will use to get rid of them.

Researchers tell us that our brains process about 400 billion bits of information per second; we are consciously aware of about one percent of that. Of those 400 billion bits approximately 11 million per second come through our sensory organs and we are only consciously aware of about 50 bits per second. That's a lot of information running through our brain circuitry without any effort on our part. This is important because the information that becomes our accumulated knowledge, memories and belief systems comes mostly from our environments and our experiences. Our senses (sight, hearing, taste, smell, touch) are the open doors through which a lot of information flows. Mechanisms within the brain scan those 11 million bits per second to determine which 50 need to reach our conscious thoughts. To speed processing and learning (and preserve sanity) the bits making it to conscious awareness, and ultimately to memory, are the ones which have relevance and similar patterns based on past experiences, learning and previously stored memories; or they have a real sense of urgency in a dramatic or life-altering way; or we make a conscious choice to pay attention, such as learning a foreign language, school work or business projects. This means any new information not needed for survival, inconsistent with what we already know to be true or not consciously prioritized will be dismissed without any recognition of it ever having been sensed. Along with the faster brainwaves and much slower neuronal growth working in the adult brain, this sorting and discarding process makes learning new things a slower and more conscious effort as we get older. It is interesting to note that while children's brainwave activity and their information processing ability is closer to an adult's by the age of 12, the reasoning and analyzing part of their brains, the frontal lobe, is not fully developed until about 25 years of age.

Children's slow brainwaves and rapidly developing brains allow them to gather information like a giant sponge, indiscriminately absorbing information from everything they touch, taste, see, hear, smell and feel. Information just flows in, unfettered by analysis and discernment while the analytical parts of their brains are just getting started. With their brains still under construction, younger children don't have the ability to analyze and discern the relevance, truth and accuracy of new information the same way adults do. As children experience life and their brains grow so does their ability to analyze and discern truth and relevance more accurately. The younger a child, the more difficulty s/he will have sorting fact from fiction and disregarding faulty information, unhealthy patterns and beliefs. But once planted, that's what grows.

At birth, children have no knowledge of the world, themselves or their environment, so as part of the survival imperative they must figure things out quickly. They gather information, arrange it in some order and make meaning out of it. They take in everything they encounter, sorting it, contextualizing it, making associations and then store it in memory. They make associations and assign meaning (why things happen the way they do) based on the age they are at the time of an experience and in contextual agreement with whatever their immature reasoning ability has decided about themselves and the world to that point. This age-dependent timing and cumulative understandings are the key factors forming the beliefs they will carry into adulthood.

Young children perceive themselves as the center of the world. They cry, smile, coo, throw temper tantrums and behave in ways to attract attention, which helps them get what they need to survive. In their developing brains, all their actions get results; what they do makes things happen. So, when bad things happen to them or important people in their environment, they naturally decide they are the cause of it. Because they can't verbalize this to anyone, there is no way to correct this erroneous thinking as it gets programmed into their memory. Everything happening around them is making a lasting impression. All the while, they lack the capacity to think analytically and discern relevance or factual reality as they figure out, for themselves, how the world operates and how they operate in it.

This is where repetition in the form of consistency is critical in a child's evolution from birth to adulthood...and how we came to the point we are now. Children's rapidly developing neuronal connections are formed through interactions they have with their environment (experience), especially their interactions with parents, family and caregivers. The quality, character and regularity of their interactions are fundamental to the growth patterns being constructed in their brains. Loving, stimulating (not overwhelming) and repetitive interactions with consistent people have life-long positive effects on behavior, health and cognitive ability. Stressful environments, that can include stressed out parents and caregivers, and inappropriate, irregular or ineffective interactions, have life-long detrimental effects on behavior, health and cognitive ability. Parental stress, discord and violence from conception to birth also have life-long consequences. In fact, the pre-birth period of growth is quite possibly the most crucial time as far as brain development and future health potential are concerned.

The brain's development and the learning accumulated through early experiences and interactions become the contextual foundation for how future incoming information will be analyzed and assimilated into beliefs, perceptions and thought patterns. Once this foundation is formed, all the information and experiences we are exposed to later in life are then interpreted through the filter of beliefs and understandings we learned before the age of six. Our beliefs along with our subsequent interpretations of life experiences provide the repetitive sequencing that confirms we are correct in our beliefs about ourselves and our world. This is the cause and effect that keeps us stuck in the same reality.

Here's an illustration of how experience, learning, timing and making meaning can form faulty beliefs and make a life-long impact:

When I was three years old, my family lived in a small towable trailer. I slept in an upper bunk at the rear of it. One evening, after my parents had put my younger brother and I to bed, they stepped out for date night. I cannot tell you all the things that might have gone through my three-year-old mind, however, based on prior attempts at misbehavior, I'm pretty sure I wouldn't have gotten out of bed if my parents had been home. Knowing they weren't, I got out of my bunk and walked into the larger living space to tell my babysitter I wasn't tired and I wasn't going to bed yet. In an instant, she picked up her sweater from the back of a kitchen chair and twirled it over her shoulders as she said, "Oh, I can see you're a big girl and you don't need a babysitter, so I'll just go home." Without another word, I ran back to my bed.

To this day, I can still feel the tension I felt in my body as she announced her plan to leave. I can still see her towering over me as she spoke. And to this day, my parents can't believe I can describe the layout of that trailer. Why do I have such a palpable memory of something so seemingly insignificant from so many, many years ago? Timing is everything. This was a significant learning event for me. This brief and innocuous-appearing event took place at a critical moment in my psychological development and it hit my survival instinct dead on. Disobedience and having an expressed difference of opinion was not safe; it resulted in abandonment, or at least the threat of it. Did I think all this through in my three-year-old mind? Of course not, but the meaning I gave to it at the time helped form the belief that I was not safe on my own and to be safe I was going to have to comply with rules and authority. The belief that I was not safe would come to be the foundation for my relationship with money, significant others and authority in general. It was pervasive, and even when I had nothing to worry about it was running in the background of my mind affecting choices and decisions in many areas of my life.

Children pay attention to everything going on around them as part of their rapid learning process. They are also very sensitive to and affected by the vibe—energy—in their environment because they have not yet learned to disregard it as "just their imagination." What made that one situation life defining for me was not that it happened. It was that it happened at just the right moment in my life and it was consistent with other events suggesting the same thing. At the time, my parents were struggling with finances, job stress and three children in three years. My father also struggled with addiction problems. At age three, the world already appeared somewhat unsafe in my developing brain and personality.

This example demonstrates how even the tiniest and most insignificant-appearing events can have a major impact on our lives, especially when they are consistent with other repetitive information (experiences) and our inability to analyze situations accurately at the time.

The belief that we are not safe can originate in other ways. In my professional life, I've worked with many people who had problems with decision making, changing unhealthy behaviors or reaching goals. As we worked to uncover the underlying reasons for these issues, a few of my clients told me they'd had rather idyllic childhoods…nothing there to be concerned about. But as they talked a little more about their younger years, they described a childhood rather lean on parental interaction. They were left to make their own decisions, push poorly defined and poorly enforced boundaries, and make mistakes with little parental guidance or supervision—and often without consequences. Ultimately they did not feel worthy of their parents' attention. They did not feel protected or safe. And most importantly, they did not feel loved. Nothing terrible happened. It was just the consistent pattern of emotional distancing from parents who, most likely, had learned to be that way from their own parents.

Most of us grow up in homes with loving parents who did the best they could. We were not abused, neglected, unloved or ignored. And yet, all of us are limited to some extent by faulty beliefs that we learned in our earliest years. Our parents had their own patterned ways of thinking, speaking, behaving, coping and reacting to their world. They learned to be that way from their upbringing and their life experiences. By virtue of the survival imperative, constant contact, emotional tone, repetition and brain development, we learned to be very much like our parents, though many of us would deny this. If they were anxious, depressed, angry, selfish, hopeless, kind, good-natured, hopeful, helpful, forgiving or generous, chances were very good we would exhibit these attributes as well.

Each one of us experienced a childhood, one with events that would play a major role in our spiritual, mental, emotional and physical development. Between events as benign as a babysitter threatening to leave to those as serious as sexual abuse, there are endless possibilities including, but not limited to, natural disasters, unsafe neighborhoods, wars, divorce, domestic violence, new siblings, separations through military assignment or incarcerations, major moves, parental illness or death. Even a strong parental reaction to innocent but dangerous behavior such as running into the street, sticking a knife in an electric socket or sitting on the new baby can have a life-long impact. Whether the events happening in our lives were big and obvious or so small as to seem insignificant, timing and the behavior and attitudes of the significant adults in our lives influenced how we interpreted life and ourselves in the wake of these events. Ultimately, we determined our worthiness, lovability, importance, safety and hopefulness based on our earliest experiences.

Early Learning Sets the Stage for Greater Understanding

Consider how would we be and where would we be if, from the moment of our conception and with every heartbeat, we heard only loving messages of how powerful, capable, loving and intelligent we were. What if we were encouraged—with loving adult guidance—to daydream, honor our intuitions and follow where our hearts led us? What if our childhood experiences supported these messages, and the beliefs we adopted for ourselves affirmed that we were worthy, loving, powerful and intelligent? What would our thoughts be now? How would we speak and act? What would the Mind/Field reflect back to us as our reality?

It's safe to say that none of us were born to fully enlightened parents in a fully enlightened society. Nor were our parents or their parents before them. Handicapped by their own upbringing and learning, our parents did the best they could. Unfortunately, ancestral trauma, drama and faulty messages have been passed on through them to us. We have come by our perceived shortcoming naturally and innocently. This is true for each one of us.

What is difficult to comprehend but may be easier to recognize from the events we're observing in the world today, is that each one of us is individually contributing to the struggles, the achievements and the evolution of humanity. Our personal distress is mirrored in the collective problems of society. We are all on this timeline of human history together, so while our experiences and perceptions are not exactly the same, we are all observing our reality with the same faulty beliefs holding our collective reality in place. Regardless of our stories, what we learned in our early years resulted in a few basic beliefs that shape not only our life experiences, but contribute to the collective experience in like manner. As stated in the beginning, the root cause of unhappiness is the belief that we are unworthy. Collectively and individually indoctrinated with this root cause, our earliest experiences morphed separation and unworthiness into our personal beliefs of not loved/lovable, not important, not safe and not (strong, smart, pretty, rich, etc.) enough, or some variation of these few. And now, steeped in our individual stories and beliefs, we project our bias-based perceptions into the Mind/Field to create the world we live in. The state of our world rests with our ability to love and heal ourselves.

When we believe we are not worthy, we just can't seem to follow through on the positive changes we want to make. Even though we have no conscious recognition of these foundational errors, they are influencing our every thought, word, feeling and action. This in turn has profound affect on our health and happiness. It's only through loving ourselves, getting to know ourselves and striving to relieve our pain at the core level that we will turn onto the path of greater ease, higher vibration and happiness.

How we learn and how we were potentially affected by our early experiences is important. With this understanding we can appreciate how we arrived at the mistaken beliefs that are having a dramatic impact on our lives. The blessings of forgiveness are more forthcoming with this awareness. Knowing that learning as adults takes a more concentrated effort in order to assimilate and utilize new information helps us appreciate that change is not a light switch we simply flip on and everything becomes sunsets and rainbows. As we attempt to figure out why we feel the way we do about ourselves and why we struggle to make positive choices in our lives, it's not necessary to know the exact circumstance that caused us to believe and think the way we do. But it *is* important to realize that somewhere deep inside we have erroneous beliefs about ourselves. With this realization, we are able to expose, release and replace them.

We are experiencing this three-dimensional life in order to learn to love unconditionally—as we were created. We are compelled to search for happiness so in time we will discover this highest form of love. By our soul agreement with God as Universal Intelligence, we are participating in healing the soul of humanity by healing ourselves. This only happens as we address our pain, find the error patterns and heal them. Because we are intimately connected with every human being as part of All That Is, all healing we accomplish for ourselves makes us an active participant in the evolution of humanity. By increasing our vibration, we are increasing the vibration within the collective conscious and the Mind/Field where we all live.

What we don't realize as we move through our lives is that the status and station we were born into and the subsequent learning opportunities shaping our beliefs actually set the stage for our participation in the universal healing and evolution of us all. The faulty beliefs we unwittingly adopted are programmed into our brains in order to trigger and support the experiences of struggle and triumph throughout our lives. As Gary Zukav explained in *The Seat of the Soul*, the purpose behind the circumstance of our birth, family of origin and the society we were born into was to set the stage for the lessons we agreed to learn on behalf of ourselves and the human collective. Understanding how to use learning opportunities to find the hidden wounds, erroneous beliefs and the guidance encrypted within them is the purpose of our experiences. Knowing how we learn helps us understand how we got where we are. It also gives us the tools we need to move to a better place.

Whether we come from idyllic childhoods or from abusive ones, and everything in between, each of us was affected by events in our earliest years that paved the way for struggles, learning and healing. This might seem like a leap, especially for those who have suffered great trauma and injustice. On the other hand, seeing life as a learning opportunity changes how we can move forward. Blaming our parents or any one else has no functional purpose in the long term. Even if we believe they could have and should have done better, this is where we find ourselves now. Placing blame on someone else robs us of the opportunity to make things right for ourselves going forward. Recognition, forgiveness and healing our broken beliefs, and then replacing them with the truth of our magnificence is the only way we are going to be happy and at peace. This is a process. It is the life journey we are on. Learning to use life experiences to change what we believe and create a happier reality happens through repetition, which involves dedication and discipline. It's accelerated through the practices of meditation, contemplation, introspection and self-hypnosis—slower brainwaves—just like all learning.

The Mind-Body Connection - Spirit, Mind, Body

*"We are not human beings having a spiritual experience.
We are spiritual beings having a human experience."
– Pierre Teilhard de Chardin (1881-1955)*

The holistic integration of mind and body is the basis for health and happiness. Our inability to feel whole is the foundation of unhappiness and disease, even when we think we are doing everything "right." The mind and body are so connected that even in our attempt to separate them for discussion and better understanding here, we won't be able to talk about one without referring to the other. Many of us have some understanding of the mind-body connection and may have used some of the healing modalities that embrace the concept. What is obviously missing in the more common understanding of our integrated nature is the other aspect of this paradigm…the spirit.

From our discussion on the relevance of God and our energetic composition, it's clear that our physical, mental and spiritual bodies are indisputably connected. We might also ponder that without the benevolent and loving energy of Mind/Field holding all things together as reality, we would cease to exist. Our bodies, minds and spirits are inseparable from our Source, and our limited recognition of our oneness and spiritual nature is short-changing our ability to be happy and whole.

Spirit
"For in [Them] we live and move and have our being." – Acts 17:28

There is no place where you begin and Spirit ends. You and Spirit are One. As you open to the amazing potential inherent in this truth, you are able to live in the State of Grace where you have better command of your innate gifts of love, wisdom and power. This understanding alone allows you to become happier, healthier and more at peace.

Our spiritual body, which we now know as a spiritual plane of correspondence at our physical level, is the part of our survival system compelling us to greater understanding, love and happiness. To my knowledge, science has not found the physical focal point that initiates an impulse to search for happiness, yet the impulse is undeniable. If physical survival was the only component of the survival imperative, we would still be sitting in caves around a fire, grunting our communication to one another; yet we seek more. Unfortunately, in our quest for meaning and happiness, we have become misdirected. The intrinsic yearning pulling us towards happiness can only be found through the love of self and knowing beyond doubt, we are one with All That Is.

Our spirit, which we can also call our Spark of Divinity and Seed of Knowing, is at the core of who we are. Our individual spirits are our intimate connection with the Mind/Field and the loving energy that sustains us. This is the connection guiding us back to Heaven by any name, whether Kingdom of God, Garden, Enlightenment or Nirvana. Our Seed of Knowing is just like the acorn of a mighty oak tree. The acorn possesses all the knowledge needed to become the image and likeness of its parent tree. The earth, sun, rain and wind are the environmental support team nurturing its evolution to become like its parents. So it is with us and our relationships, interactions and experiences as they form the elements of our support team.

Our spirit, eternally dwelling within the Infinite Mind of God, is the Seed of Knowing that has access to all we will ever need to achieve peace, happiness and fulfillment. We access this knowledge through faith and through our minds.

Mind
"This mind is the matrix of all matter." – Max Planck

If Spirit is synonymous with Mind as taught by Hermetic Philosophy, and the Mind of God is the Infinite Field where all possibilities exist, then our own spiritual and mental bodies, as levels of correspondence, are also one. Our minds are the space where we are aware of our experiences, whether they come in the form of insights and intuitions or as acknowledgments of pain, pleasure, disappointment or happiness. Mind is the space where we know we exist, and where we are both the observer and the observed, creating our reality within the Infinite Mind of God/Field of Possibility.

For ease of understanding, mind can be thought of as the connection between spirit and body and the space where we can experience and understand that connection more fully. The mind is not the brain and it isn't inside the head. The physical brain is the processing facility where memories can be accessed and the thoughts and insights of the mind can come to our attention. While the mind is working all the time, we are aware of about 5% of what is going on there. The other 95% is essentially automatic and programmed to run without active engagement in our thoughts. To better understand how this applies to achieving a happier and healthier life we will first look more closely at what the 95% subconscious mind is doing for us. Then we will explore what the 5% conscious mind is doing and could be doing—if we understood its role better.

Subconscious Mind

It would literally blow our minds if we had to consciously think through everything our subconscious mind manages automatically. This part of the mind is the form, foundation and glue holding our internal and external reality together. It's the primary influence for our physical, mental and emotional characteristics and nuances. The subconscious mind has a powerful effect on the operations of the physical brain. How we think about ourselves, the world we live in and the experiences we are having affect our emotional tone. Our emotional tone and attitude toward life, as well as the ups and downs of joy and heartbreak, have a direct impact on our chemistry, biology and health. Our emotional tone and attitudes are a direct result of early learning and are held in the subconscious mind, along with our memories.

One of the reasons the subconscious mind gets credit for 95% of the processing capacity is that the body's functions and most of our movements take place without any conscious thinking on our part. Growing and repairing bones, digesting food, producing offspring, fighting infections, beating hearts and breathing are just a few of the obvious life-sustaining functions managed independent of conscious thinking. Even what appears to be conscious, such as tying our shoes, riding a bike, driving a car and many of the tasks we perform repetitively are mostly functions of the subconscious mind. Once we go through the conscious efforts and neuronal connections required to learn how to do these things, the mechanics of doing them become automatic—mostly subconscious efforts—habitual processes.

The subconscious mind is also the access point for inspiration, intuition and instinct. Though we largely have dismissed these forms of communication, the necessary hardware for receiving them still exists as it always has. We continue to receive these seemingly external sources of information through this channel, although we minimize their frequency and benefits when we don't acknowledge the possibility or the fact that we are actually receiving them. Aha moments, bright ideas, premonitions, gut feelings and heart calls are tangible experiences we all have from time to time. These are forms of information flowing through the subconscious, into our nervous systems, registering in our bodies and then being acknowledged by our conscious mind. They represent information from sources outside the brain even though we don't think about it in that way. Consider how great you feel when you come up with a fresh, new idea to solve a persistent problem. The source of your novel approach came from some place other than your brain...that idea wasn't from your memory; it existed as a possibility in the Field, the Mind of God. *It came to you as you allowed it in and acknowledged its presence.*

The blessings of love, appreciation, gratitude, forgiveness, compassion, humility, equanimity and others come to us through the subconscious. These virtuous feelings originate at a higher spiritual plane, flow through the levels of our subconscious mind to be felt by the physical body and recognized by the conscious mind. They are inspirational messages telling us that we're in alignment and coherence with our divine essence.

Lastly, the subconscious mind holds our deepest secrets and our greatest pain, whether or not we have any awareness of them. It knows every darkness we hold in our hearts, every terrible mistake we have ever made and it knows just how unworthy, unimportant, unsafe and inadequate *we believe ourselves to be*. In concert with the Law of Cause and Effect and free will, the subconscious mind uses all the nonsense we came to believe before we were six years old to create learning opportunities so we can discover how we sabotage our best efforts to be happy and more loving. It uses our faulty beliefs and now entrenched attitudes and reflexive responses to dictate the thoughts we have, the words we use, the feelings we experience and the manner in which we behave.

It might appear that our word choices don't make much difference, but they do. Our words indicate how we think about ourselves and the world in a "glass half empty or half full" kind of way. Consider what you say as you acknowledge a mistake to another person. Do you say, "I'm sorry?" Or, do you say, "I apologize?" The latter says you are acknowledging you made a mistake. The former is a rather harsh statement. It acknowledges you made a mistake, but "I am" implies that the reason you made the mistake was because you are a sorry state, or in a sorry state. When you speak the words, "I am…" you are making a powerful statement, declaring you are whatever words follow I am and then projecting that thought into the Mind/Field. Repetitive negative word choices such as "I'm sorry" and "my bad" arise from a belief that I'm not good enough. If life sucks or the world is in dire straits or I can't get out of my own way are regular thoughts and vocalizations, they are revealing the beliefs and attitudes entrenched in your subconscious mind.

How we interact with and react to others is largely influenced by the subconscious mind. The context and tone of interactions in our small world as children was repeated over and over again, and that consistent repetition provided the template for our own adult interactions. Consider how different people might respond to a similar situation. If we were to receive a critical performance review, some of us might be grateful for an opportunity to grow and for being appreciated enough to have our work and potential noticed; some of us might feel bad about ourselves because this confirms our belief that we aren't good enough; and some of us might be angry with the ignorant reviewer who has no appreciation for all we do. Each of these reactions is normal. Our reactions are consistent with our beliefs about ourselves. Our prejudices come from this same preprogramming. Considering whether a man or a woman is more suited for a position, when their qualifications are equal except for gender, is based on early learning; as is how we react when a person of one gender is hired over the other. Likewise, the discomfort or outright fear we feel when we come into close proximity with a person we perceive as different reveals what is hidden beneath the surface. Our reactions, word choices and behaviors emerge, or even erupt, from our subconscious mind. We know this to be true when we just can't hold our tongue or stop a behavior we know, even as we are doing it, will cause a problem.

Those same childhood patterns continue chattering in the background of our mind, reminding us of our place in the world, our worth, our safety and our love-ability. We learned early on how to act and react to get what we needed and maybe even what we wanted. We also learned how to react to environmental cues in order to avoid painful situations. These unfiltered learning and immature understandings now shape the way we view the world and our place in it. How we think about ourselves also *dictates what we think others are thinking about us.* This is known as projection. We think we know what they are thinking, not by verifying what they're actually thinking, but by projecting our beliefs onto the interaction and then interpreting their verbal and non-verbal communication as proof we are correct. We move through our world using the responses of others as confirmation that we are exactly who we believe ourselves to be. Sometimes, we act in ways that will cause others to treat us the way we expect to be treated. This is called self-fulfilling prophecy. Our projection and self-fulfilling behaviors are choreographed at such a deep subconscious level we have absolutely no suspicion that we are the cause of our own disappointment and suffering. We blame others for our hurt, not sure how we got ourselves into this situation…again.

Our subconscious mind holds our perceived reality firmly in place. It sets expectations, interprets events, dictates reaction and normalizes our day-to-day existence so we can live a seemingly stable life. Our subconscious mind directs the character and quality of our thoughts and emotions and how we express them in words and actions. In doing all this, it determines the quality of our lives, mentally, emotionally and physically. Held deep within the subconscious mind, our perceived quality of life is the bias-based observation that collapses waves into particles to shape what reality is for us…individually and collectively.

Conscious Mind

With all that is going on in the subconscious mind we have to wonder, what exactly does the conscious mind do? The conscious mind is credited with executive functioning, things like analysis, logical and inductive reasoning, setting intentions and goals and implementing the strategies for accomplishing them. It interacts with our external environment through incoming sensory information and through outgoing thoughts, which often become spoken and written words, coordinated movement and a wide range of behavior. And, all of this is heavily influenced by the subconscious mind. Our conscious mind interacts with our internal environment, readily accessing stored memories, feelings, perceptions and information available from the subconscious mind. It's the part that "thinks" about our emotional experiences. The conscious mind analyzes and rationalizes our feelings to determine what the emotion is about and then decides what, if anything, to do about that feeling. The conscious mind is also where we can lose a lot of valuable time and energy worrying about the past and ruminating about the future, as opposed to living and being present in the moment.

Our conscious mind is the space where new information and ideas received through our senses can be taken in and accepted as worthy of memory space and learning efforts. This is how we learn calculus, economics, cooking, driving and all the other useful information we need in order to do what we do. It's also the place where previously unknown information, in the forms of new ideas, intuitions and instincts make an impression on our conscious awareness as "aha moments" or the answer to our prayers. These thoughts that seem to come from out-of-the-blue are external only because they don't come from memory and previous learning. Intuitions, insights and inspirations are ideas from the Mind/Field flowing through our subconscious minds to be acknowledged by our conscious minds in moments of openness and surrender—slower or gamma brain waves.

Life presents us with many moments to receive these revelations and intuitions. They come when our guard is down. Moments of joy, grief, appreciation, despair, meditation, daydreaming, surrender and prayer are a few such occasions. When we become consciously aware of these new and captivating thoughts, we have a choice to truly experience and integrate them into our beliefs, attitudes and plans, or not. Integration of new information is not an instantaneous result of the revelation or intuition. Whether from the classroom, life experience or divine inspiration, all new information that is not consistent with our now entrenched beliefs and attitudes will take repetition, time and effort to integrate and assimilate. This is true no matter how beneficial the conscious mind might determine such information to be.

While the subconscious mind is the primary operating system creating our reality, the conscious mind is the place of power—willpower. It's the place where we take our power back because we must consciously choose to think, speak and act differently than our beliefs dictate and approach life from a higher perspective if we want our reality to be different than what it's been. The conscious mind is where we reflect on our lives, decide on goals and develop strategies for accomplishing them. As we set goals and develop strategies, we are honoring our desire, setting our intention and expressing our will. This is the power of the mind and the point of creation. Our intentions, formulated in words are fueled by our desire (energy) to create the change we want, as in the creation story. Intention is the power of our will, conveyed through our thoughts. As we express our intention, it interacts with the loving and benevolent energy in the Mind/Field. To the extent we feel worthy, loving, important, powerful and adequate as our underlying beliefs, we are in coherence with the Mind/Field, which reflects back a changing reality consistent with our desire. The degree to which we feel unworthy, unloved, disempowered, unsafe, unimportant or inadequate shifts our energy in a way that is discordant with the loving, benevolent energy ever-present in the Mind/Field. Free will and the Law of Cause and Effect dictate that the Mind/Field must reflect our belief-biased perspectives back to us. And so, we are minimizing, or even rejecting, the support and assistance we might benefit from if only our energy was more in synch with God's Will for us. The secret of our magnificent power lives in our ability to accurately define and balance intention (will) and love to achieve greater happiness, and then be persistent in pursuing a different reality than we are currently experiencing.

Part of this power comes from acknowledging our oneness with Source and accepting the significant assistance that comes from being open to our Source. The other part of this power comes from consciously choosing, in each moment, to think, feel, speak and act in a way that is more in alignment with our true essence than what we have come to believe is true about ourselves. As we consistently and consciously choose different thoughts, we are building new neuronal connections in our brain, we are learning. Before long, these new life and happiness affirming thoughts become imbedded in our subconscious and replace the old beliefs. If we avoid our old and habitual patterns and keep our focused attention on empowering new beliefs and thought patterns, our progress towards happiness multiplies logarithmically. In so doing, we are upgrading the subconscious operating system creating our reality 95% of the time. This is how our life journey becomes so much easier and our future learning opportunities become reflections of how wise, powerful, loving and happy we are becoming. This is also how we access the tremendous help available to us during troubled times.

Emotions
"Pity those who don't feel anything at all."
– Sarah J. Maas, A Court of Thorns and Roses

Emotions are the fuel that propels our intentions and thoughts into Mind/Field. When we feel loving and powerful, we are in coherence with the loving energy in the Mind/Field and this synergy amplifies our ability to manifest health and happiness. The opposite is true of fearful and disempowering feelings based on negative self-beliefs. When we are fearful, we project fear and it disrupts our synergy with the loving energy in the Mind/Field. What is reflected back to us are the belief-biased negative thoughts and perceptions we hold in our minds. It's a blessing of mercy and love that we don't get back all the negativity our minds project into the Field. We are spared from the extremes of suffering because as individuals, or even as the collective consciousness, we cannot overpower the higher vibrations of love and benevolence supporting all life within the Mind/Field. The All-powerful and Loving Presence tempers our negative energies so we experience dis-ease rather than destruction. At the same time, do not doubt for a moment that we have the power to destroy ourselves. Too many of us are doing this one poor choice at a time. Remember, we are in this three-dimensional learning experience to discover the proper use of the power of our minds.

Love and fear operate along a continuum, a frequency scale. The more intensely and frequently we love ourselves the higher our vibration and the greater its impact on our lives and in the collective consciousness. This is so because our vibration is in alignment with and being amplified by the unconditional Love in the Mind/Field; we are in coherence with the Love of God. Even if we love ourselves just a little bit once and a while, we still benefit from a more cohesive connection with the Mind/Field, though our connection isn't as strong and we're vibrating at a lower level than we would if we learned to love ourselves more completely. The same is true at the opposite end of the spectrum. Absolute fear is the absence of love. At its extreme, it's a very low vibration and a violent disruption broadcast into the coherent energy of the Mind/Field to be reflected back to us as terrible suffering. If our fear is less intense, then our vibration isn't as low and it creates less of a negative impact on our energetic field of possibilities. Though the Love of God is always present and beckoning our return to love, we are simply receiving back what we are transmitting.

We know this is true from our own experiences. If we truly love what we're doing, we have more interest and stamina to do the work. We have trouble pulling ourselves away from our passion-driven efforts. When our hearts aren't into what we're doing or we don't love our work, it's hard to stay engaged and diligent. The same is true when we don't love ourselves. We don't have the emotional and mental stamina to make the changes necessary to be happy and healthy. And so it is with fear; the greater the fear, the lower its vibration and the more it pulls our energy to lower levels on the continuum. A little fear can cause anxiety and make life uncomfortable as we are out of synch with the benevolence in the Mind/Field. More fear can provoke anger and depression as we resist the benevolent energy drawing us back into alignment with our true essence. Extreme fear creates chaos in our field as we, in affect, reject our oneness and the support available through this awareness. As a result, we become more hopeless or hateful, depending on our experiences.

Emotions are also messengers connecting our mental body with our physical body. *Love and fear are the emotional triggers activating our innate survival mechanism* as we will explore in Part Two. As we discuss love and fear, please understand this includes any other emotions you might experience. All emotions are variations of either love or fear in their effect on the body; positive feelings like gratitude, compassion, joy are, in effect, love; and resentment, envy, hate are about fear, which is linked to our sense of separation and unworthiness. Our emotions are influenced by our memories, beliefs and coping patterns. They are felt in our bodies and transmitted to the conscious mind where we interpret them and decide how to react to them…or justify our reaction when it was reflexive. The key to getting the most from these messages is to understand what they are telling us.

To accurately interpret the message and its guidance, you must first *be aware of how you feel*. Think for a moment: how do you feel when you recognize love or joy? You might feel lighter and brighter and no matter what else is going on in your life, your shoulders relax a little and a smile spreads across your face. Positive emotions are high-level vibrations you may sense as flutters, warmth or peace, to name a few possibilities. You literally *feel* them rush through your body in those special moments. They are powerful messages springing up inside and calling out, "Wow, you got this!" Love and all other positive emotions are offering support and affirmations that you are on the right path. They let you know that in this moment, all is well in your world. This is you experiencing your true essence.

Fear and all other negative emotions are low frequency vibrations offering guidance as they sound the alarm that change is necessary if we are to be happy and healthy. They are a warning signal, like the foghorn's blast heard by a ship's captain when clear vision is obscured by darkness and fog. They are warning you of the danger lurking beneath the surface and advising you to alter course. Because of your innate wisdom and programmed patterns, the low vibrations of negative emotions stick with you until you alter course. Or more compelling, they become stuck in the background of your mind as you shove them beneath the surface of your awareness. Out of sight, out of conscious mind, but you are not out of harm's way as they set the tone for your life and your health on the subconscious level.

Emotions are messages we feel in our body. How we react to them is determined by beliefs and patterns of coping we learned very early. If we were taught that showing our anger was inappropriate or harshly disapproved of, we learned to suppress our feelings. If we learned that anger is caused by an outside event, we may have learned to lash out or to suppress it depending on the beliefs and patterns we adopted. But fear and love operate in a balance. If we spend too much time in the low vibrational energies of fear, we drastically reduce our ability to let love alter the perception we have of ourselves. Feeling loved and valued is less of a possibility in this negative state. If we suppress our feelings of fear, we also suppress our ability to feel love and peace. This is life on mute. Not acknowledging our feelings doesn't make them go away, we're just ignoring what's going on inside. When we don't heed the warnings and make the necessary changes, our experiences will become more intense and the messages more compelling.

No matter which emotions we experience, they are always blessings. They're part of the inspirations, intuitions and instincts coming to us from Spirit, entering through our bodies and minds to guide us ever closer to the peace and love we truly desire. High vibration emotions are the loving energy that nurtures, guides and supports us along our journey of evolution. Lower vibration emotions are not lacking in love, sustenance and guidance, it's just that we haven't chosen the easier road and so we're being guided by something we will pay a little more attention to…pain.

Along the ups and downs of my life, I have often contemplated: If I know happiness comes from meditation, loving myself and making choices that promote health and happiness, why do I keep making lesser choices? Even knowing the dynamics of unhappiness and disease and understanding that there is an easier path to get where I want to go, I still choose poorly on occasion. The answer always comes back to one central belief…I'm not worthy of such a state of peace and harmony. And, with that, around the spiral of poor choices and poor outcomes I go again, each time learning a little more about myself and doing a little better the next time. Life is a process.

Why Emotions Are Critical to Survival and Healing

Emotions are critical factors in our survival system. Fear triggers the innate survival mechanism, also known as the fight-or-flight response, and this immediately shifts physical and mental resources so we have what we need to make appropriate changes. When we are no longer in a state of fear, this innate response system returns to a health-sustaining balance. Love is the emotional trigger that maintains optimal balance in our mental, emotional and physical functioning.

Emotions are an innate part of our subconscious mind and a major pathway integrating the mind and body as a functioning whole. As part of the innate survival imperative, the subconscious mind is designed to interpret incoming information and evaluate it first for indications of a threat. If a threat is perceived, we feel fearful and our bodies mobilize physical resources to respond in life-protective ways. This happens whether the threat is real, like a person aiming a gun at us, or programmed by learning, such as being afraid to venture out in public because we grew up in a violent neighborhood. When we experience situations that trigger emotionally charged childhood memories, we can re-experience the same uncomfortable emotional sensations and this then activates our survival response...even when there is nothing to fear in the present. Distressing emotions are simply signals telling us change is needed to bring us back into balance and avoid bigger problems later. Ignoring or burying emotions result in a lack of appropriate and necessary change. Whether or not we're consciously aware of these emotions, they become an ongoing and debilitating problem affecting our health and the quality of our lives. Learning to recognize painful and negative emotions, locate their origin, forgive and release the pain is the key to returning to love, health and oneness. This is the vital element to healing our problems and it's the focus of Part Three.

Emotions are important messages alerting you to pay attention to what is going on in and around you. They are an integrated, life-sustaining communication system necessary for survival, and divinely crafted to protect and nurture you throughout your life. Therefore, emotions cannot be labeled good or bad; they are simply energetic messengers with the purpose of guiding you. It may not appear so, but you always have a choice in how you deal with your emotions. One choice is to act them out. Acting out with negative behavior can have problematic consequences, but these consequences will provide you another opportunity to re-examine what's really going on inside. When it's safe to do so, an alternative choice is to take time to contemplate the why. Why am I feeling this way? As you search honestly for this answer, you will receive information and guidance to help you make the changes necessary to move away from situations and the long-held faulty beliefs that result in the pain and negativity you are experiencing.

Another common choice is to push negative emotions from your awareness; bury them so you don't feel your distress. This is the most debilitating and destructive choice. When we turn down the volume on our negative emotions, its like putting our cellphone on vibrate. We are indicating to our spiritual, mental and physical bodies that we are not taking calls. On vibrate we can't hear our wake up calls and we barely feel our emotions. Whether a positive or negative emotion, all we hear is a distant hum of the vibration. We have cut ourselves off and muted the alert for both fear and love. Limiting the sensation of pain also limits our ability to experience happiness. This can become so severe as to feel numb all the time. Because negative and positive emotions are intimately linked to our physical health, ignoring and burying our negative emotions have life-long and detrimental effects on our body's ability to repair, rejuvenate and maintain health. Disruptive emotional states are the root cause of illness, premature aging and death, which we will explore in depth in Part Two.

Body
"But if one observes, one will see that the body has its own intelligence; it requires a great deal of intelligence to observe the intelligence of the body."
– Jiddu Krishnamurti, The Flight of the Eagle

There is no way to appreciate the complexity, beauty and majesty of the human body. Amid all we know and all that science is discovering, there are ever more questions as to the diverse, integrated and entangled operations allowing us to experience life in the way we do.

After a brief description of the systems of the body we are all basically familiar with, I will share a few interesting discoveries that have been the focus of various fields of science. It's important to note that there is so much more going on in the body than we have appreciated until very recently. The most essential understanding arising from these latest discoveries is that our health—and potentially our existence—relies on factors science doesn't fully understand...yet. In considering the greater possibilities brought forth in these new revelations, keep in mind that every system, structure and process is the product of sub-atomic waves and particles interacting within your electromagnetic field, which is part of and interacting with the larger electromagnetic field...in the Mind of God.

~~~

A quick overview of the systems of the body:

Nervous System — Consists of the brain, spinal column and the nerves that communicate back and forth from all other parts of the body, from hair follicles to toenails and everything in between. The brain is one part of a central nervous system; the complete nervous system also includes a peripheral nervous system with its own branches. No need to figure this out as I will discuss specific parts as we progress through their importance to health and wellbeing.

Circulatory System — Consists of the heart, arteries, veins and smaller blood vessels. It functions as the pump and conduit serving the entire body by transporting oxygen, nutrients and various forms of information to every one of the 50 trillion plus cells.

Respiratory System — Includes the nose, sinuses, trachea, larynx, bronchial tubes and lungs. It's an energy exchange system that adds oxygen to and removes carbon dioxide from each and every cell, in cooperation with the circulatory, nervous and renal systems.

Digestive System — Mouth, esophagus, stomach, small intestines, large intestines, rectum, anus, liver and gall bladder. From mouth to anus, this system is one long tube that processes anything entering through the mouth. It's responsible for breaking down and extracting nutrients from food and passing them as usable energy to the circulating blood for distribution to the cells. It's also responsible for keeping toxins and harmful microbes out of the rest of the body.

Renal/Urinary System — Maintains fluid, electrolyte and the delicate pH balance for optimal cellular functioning. It filters the blood and eliminates excess fluids, electrolytes and some toxic substances.

Skeletal System — This system works with other systems for mineral balance, movement and protection of the internal environment.

Muscular System — There are different types of muscles but as a system it's about movement and mobility. It also helps maintain proper body temperature.

Endocrine System — This is a system of glands throughout the body that responds to stimuli from the pituitary and hypothalamus glands deep in the brain. It's responsible for regulating and maintaining the many hormone levels that keep the body in healthy balance.

Reproductive System — Includes organs that allow for procreation and the continuation of the species. Ovaries and testes are part of the hormonal balance supporting other body functions beyond reproduction.

Immune and Lymph Systems — This is a complex system of circulating chemicals, antibodies, blood cells, lymph tissues, spleen, thymus, bone marrow and more. This system protects us from foreign invaders and cancer cells. It's responsible for the inflammatory processes that heal damaged tissue regardless of the cause. When disrupted or out of balance, it's the system that causes many other diseases.

Integumentary and Exocrine Systems — Includes skin, nails, hair and sweat glands. The skin is our largest organ and it forms a protective barrier that keeps our internal environment separate from the external one. It releases some waste and toxins and helps regulate body temperature. It's the sensory organ of touch.

~~~

To fully comprehend the messages our bodies are sending, why we feel poorly when any one organ or system is ailing and why medications have side effects, we must appreciate how interrelated these systems really are. Not one of them performs only one function, and nothing a particular system ostensibly controls happens without the coordinated effort of other systems. Consider the kidneys: They have delicate pressure and chemical receptors which evaluate the flow and constitution of blood as it passes through. Approximately 120 quarts per day flow through them to produce about two quarts of urine per day. Urine is not just excess water being expelled. The kidneys also filter out certain drugs, toxins and by-products of metabolism. The kidneys produce hormones which maintain blood pressure, initiate red blood cell production and participate in maintaining healthy bones. They regulate the critical fluid and electrolyte balance and maintain a fairly rigid pH balance, both necessary for everything else the body does. To accomplish each of these functions, the kidneys must communicate and coordinate with other systems. For pH balance the kidneys must work, via the circulatory system, with the nervous system and the lungs. For production of red blood cells, the kidneys work in cooperation with the liver, gut, thyroid, bone marrow and nervous system. To maintain blood pressure, they work in unison with the heart, blood vessels and nervous system. There is more to this, but the intention here is to demonstrate how complex and integrated our bodies are. Each system operates in the same multi-function and coordinated manner, and all without a single conscious thought on our part.

The heart and gut each have their own independent brain and nervous system.

The independent brains of the heart and gut are proven facts so let's consider how that information can be used to improve both health and happiness. The independent nervous systems of both the heart and gut are smaller than, but similar to, the nervous system involving the brain in our head. According to the science, the heart has an intelligence that operates autonomously from the intelligence and system-wide control credited to the "head brain." This "heart brain" actually sends more information to the head brain than it receives from it. All of this is true of the independent intelligence discovered in the gut as well...the "gut brain." For our discussion, I will use the terms heart brain and gut brain to refer to these independent intelligences and the nervous systems that communicate information to and from other parts of the body, including the head brain and its associated nervous systems.

The heart brain and gut brain both receive information from internal and external sources and they have the ability to learn new things. They both hold memories independent of each other and separate from the head brain. These capabilities allow them to process incoming information and then communicate with the head brain thereby contributing to mental and emotional interpretations, habitual thought patterns and reactionary behaviors, as we discussed in earlier sections. They make chemicals, known as neurotransmitters, which affect physical processes and communicate with the head brain to trigger hormonal, physical and mental changes.

We will be exploring the Autonomic Nervous System (ANS) as an integral part of the fight-or-flight response in more detail in Part Two. At this point it's important to note that researchers are adding the gut brain as the third branch to what was formerly thought to be a two-branch system; they have properly named the gut brain the Enteric Branch of the ANS. The gut brain is responsible, at least in part, for identifying fear and relaying the message to the head brain. Much of the communication between the gut and the head brain is via the vagus nerve, and contrary to previous thinking, only 20% of the vagus nerve fibers send information in the other direction. This means an astounding 80% of its fibers are transmitting information up to the head brain. The neurotransmitters made in the gut—dopamine, serotonin and ghrelin—are linked to the physical stress response, survival and our states of happiness, satisfaction, anxiety and depression.

The heart brain operates in a similar manner. It communicates with the head brain via the vagus nerve, and like the gut, more of its fibers are dedicated to conveying information to the head brain than receiving instruction from it. In addition to producing the pleasure, reward and happiness hormones of dopamine and serotonin, the heart makes oxytocin in amounts nearly equivalent to the head brain. This hormone is related to trust and bonding with others.

These discoveries provide credibility to inherent wisdom and the "language of the body" we use regularly in conversation. "What a rush!" "I have a broken heart." "My gut reaction is telling me not to go there." "I feel lighter than air." "I just have a feeling that…" Statements such as these are examples of the heart's intuitions and the gut's instincts being received by our conscious mind for recognition, verbalization and appropriate action.

Science is uncovering much more about the heart and gut brains and their miraculous capacity to receive information, process it, commit it to their own memory and then influence thoughts, feelings, words and behaviors. Because researchers are still working on the dynamics that make this possible, there isn't much information available with regards to how these organs communicate with our external world. However, if we consider their atomic nature, we can be assured that they are indeed transmitting as they are receiving. We can know this is true when we feel love radiating from our beloved or feel our own love beaming outward toward our child. The same is true of our gut reaction when we encounter a stranger and get an unsettling feeling warning us to move away. It's all energy transmitted from and received by our heart, gut and head brains.

Our human cells are far outnumbered by bacteria, viruses and other organisms living in our bodies.

Another fairly recent discovery is the incredible number of foreigners living with us. In the last 15 years, the Human Microbiome Project discovered that microbes, including bacteria, fungi, protozoa, and viruses, outnumber human cells by about 10 to 1. If a 100-pound person has 65 trillion cells (1 trillion per kilogram), 10 times that is a lot of microbes traveling around the body. Researchers also found that the genetic information from these microbes plays a critical role in our physical functioning and survival. The majority of them live in our gut, though significant numbers populate the surface of our skin and various cavities and openings. Their genetic profiles contribute more to our health and survival than our own human genes.

The microbes living in our gut provide necessary enzymes required to digest food—enzymes our body doesn't make on its own. They manufacture vitamins and certain anti-inflammatory compounds we need and would not have without them. And through as yet unknown mechanisms, a rather specific combination of assorted microbes rushes into the birth canal to greet emerging new life. As full-term babies pass through the vagina, they pick up some of these microbes to support their immune system as they enter their new environment. No matter where these microbes are found, one of their most important functions is to protect us from the harmful microbes that cause disease. Science does not yet understand the mechanisms by which these beneficial inhabitants can turn destructive and start causing problems in places where they had previously lived in balance and supported health.

In addition to the estimated 650 trillion microbes living in our body, there are extracellular vesicles that also outnumber human cells by about 4 to 1. These vesicles are very tiny little bubbles of information manufactured by individual cells and released into the general circulation. They are found in almost all bodily fluids, including urine, synovial fluid, bile, breast milk, amniotic fluid, semen and tears. All cells are capable of producing these little bubbles of information and once released, they are directed to other cells according to some instruction or force still not understood.

Though researchers are still working to uncover all the purposes and mechanisms of the vesicles' action, they have discovered some very remarkable things. Exosomes and Microvesicles, two of the three known subtypes of extracellular vesicles, were once thought to be the cells' port-a-potties. Now they're understood to be a communication system connecting cells to each other. They promote health through efforts such as repairing tissues and supporting the immune system. Conversely, they can be instrumental in disease and disease progression. At this time, researchers believe the information carried by these little bubbles are responsible for transferring mutated genetic information from a cancerous cell to healthy cells in other parts of the body where they become a cancer found later. They also contribute to the growth of a tumor once it takes hold.

While we ponder the abundance of life and communication going on inside the body, there is one other bit of information I want to offer. It has been said that we have an entirely new body about every seven years. While this is not entirely accurate, it has some merit. Most of our cells have a limited life span and replace themselves before they die. This happens at different rates for different types of cells. White blood cells, responsible for fighting infections, have the shortest life and last only a few days; colon cells only 4-5 days; liver cells about 160 days; bone cells about 10 years. It was once thought that brain cells lasted a lifetime with no new cells being produced after the brain's rapid expansion in childhood. Researchers now know some parts of the brain have the ability to make new cells, especially in the deepest parts of the primal brain, related to memory, emotions and the health-altering stress response.

I think most of us live with a fairly simplistic view of our bodies. The brain thinks and controls the rest of the body, the heart pumps blood, the kidneys make urine, the gut digest food and so on. Oversimplified understandings grossly underestimate the complexity, integration and elegance of our physical form. Our limited understanding makes it less likely we will take advantage of the fact that we have the ability to improve our health and wellbeing if we choose to think and act differently.

We have three independent yet integrated brains operating with their own nervous systems. Each of them affecting our hormone levels and chemistry and providing us with a wealth of information and guidance. We are teeming with biodiversity as hundreds of trillions of microorganisms and their genetic information support and enhance our own genetic inheritance. Hundreds of trillions of tiny information-carrying vesicles connect cells and systems together to produce the integrated and coordinated activities that support health and life itself. The turnover of our cells implies we are refreshed and made new over and over. Our biodiversity, communication and cellular rejuvenation all promote health…until they don't. What causes them to shift from health promotion to disease progression is still not completely understood, but….

There are increasing bodies of evidence which indicate it is our choices that trigger the shift. How we think, how we feel and how we treat our bodies are important factors impacting our overall health and wellbeing. Our ability to be happy and healthy is not limited by the circumstances of birth or family. We can choose to stay locked in a box of limited understanding and therefore limited possibilities or we can choose to make our way to a new state of mind with many more uplifting possibilities. In concert with our minds, our bodies receive all of the information we need to achieve happiness. Our emotions tell us how we are progressing along in this effort. Our conscious minds interpret the information we accept into our awareness and from there we develop plans to use what we know to help us get what we want. Hopefully, the plans and changes we make bring us closer to the peace and fulfillment we desire.

*** Ultimately, it's your choice that produces the shift. ***

Becoming the balanced, healthy and peace-filled person you wish to be happens much the same way you got where you are now. Pay attention to your environment and experiences, identify what's working for you and commit it to your memory for future use. Stop repeating what doesn't serve your happiness so the repetitive pathways can be pruned from your brain. The difference between your childhood and now is that you are the person in charge. In truth, you are the only one in charge. You are the adult choosing the lessons and making the decisions that form your life experiences. Ultimately, you are the master of your reality by the energy you put forth into the Mind/Field as an expression of who you are and who you want to be. You have all you need to re-create your life using the guidance of your body, the wisdom of your mind and the power of your loving energy to reclaim your birthright as it was breathed into you at creation.

You are in the process of an awe-inspiring evolution. You are also an essential part of humanity's evolution. It's no accident or coincidence that you are here now, participating in this magnificent mess we call life. It's not a mistake that you are exactly where you are in life right now. A mistake is simply an opportunity for learning and growth and nothing more. We are at a point in our collective evolution that requires your unique personality with your gifts, understandings and skill set to assist in healing the collective conscious…one person at a time. You, learning to love yourself, are the perfect remedy for this struggling world.

CHAPTER 5

The Guide For Your Future Self – Your Wounded Child

"The Wounded Inner Child is the primary gateway to healing and integration."
– Markus William Kasunich

We live in an imperfect world with a struggling society. Even perfect appearing families have some degree of dysfunction and so we are all products of dysfunctional families. This is simply where we are on the spiral of human evolution. Each one of us is trying to figure out how to get the happiness, love and peace we inherently know is possible. But our efforts are often misguided by a hidden force we don't understand…our inner child. No matter how idyllic our childhood, at some point early on, there was an event or events that impacted our young minds to shape what we believed about ourselves and the world. This is part of the web of life that connects us all and it's how our personal stage was set for the growth opportunities we would encounter throughout our lives.

Some of us might say our childhoods were fine and it was a major event that happened later in life causing our distress now. This is a misunderstanding based on the fact that we can remember later and possibly larger experiences in adulthood while belief-altering events in childhood have long since been forgotten. The truth is, we are energetically drawing such experiences to us so we have the opportunity to go back and heal our wounded child. If our inner child had grown into adulthood with everything s/he needed to cope more effectively, we would be able to deal with major events and release the emotional baggage we still carry around as a result of them.

It's not uncommon for us to partially blame our parents for our state of unhappiness. Some of us have done enough soul searching to move past the point of blaming our parents for our problems. We've come to an adult understanding of why they did the things they did, right or wrong. We forgave them and moved on. Yet, after all the soul searching and forgiving feels complete, we still find ourselves struggling with the same thoughts and behaviors that get in the way of happiness and peace. This is because we haven't healed the part of ourselves that was hurt initially. Whether or not we've forgiven our parents or others, we still live in the shadow of our wounded child. Somewhere deep inside is the child who still believes s/he is unloved, unworthy, unimportant or not good enough. These underlying beliefs are stronger than our willpower and repeatedly sabotage our best efforts to change for the better. When change is too difficult, we develop strategies or habits to quiet the discomfort we incessantly feel. But no matter how much we drink, smoke, buy, cry, exercise, eat or lose control, the nagging dis-ease we feel is our wounded child still believing s/he is not worthy, important, safe, loved or enough. Even without addictive tendencies, our unhealthy choices are the result of trying to appease an unhappy child we are not communicating with effectively.

We have become masters at ignoring our wounded child, burying our emotions and overriding the psychic pain in any way we can. Our individual pattern of dealing with our discomfort is much like sweeping dirt under the rug. After several decades of hiding it, there is a pile that can no longer be ignored. In real life, this pile takes the form of increased susceptibility to illness and chronic diseases. Problems like insomnia and poor concentration can cause other seemingly unrelated problems like accidents and work difficulties. Most health problems are rooted in the emotional pain caused by something unseen and unknown to us. Healing our wounded child requires much more than simply understanding the child's fears from our adult perspective. The key to finding peace and happiness is building a loving and trusting relationship with our inner child.

> **Listen to the wisdom of your inner child.**

Healing your wounded child is not a mystery. It happens with the same approach you would use with any troubled child. Kindness, compassion, understanding, consistency and love are the answers. Like any frightened child, your wounded child is hiding deep in your subconscious mind because s/he feels unsafe, neglected or abandoned. Ignoring this child only makes her/his complaints more compelling and uncontrollable. Each unhealthy or unwise choice you make confirms to the child that you can't be trusted to make good decisions on her/his behalf. Like any frightened child, it will take patience to coax your child out of hiding and get him/her to tell you exactly what s/he needs in order to feel better. It will take commitment to follow through on promises you make to give your inner child the love and support s/he needs to grow up healthy and happy. This means not caving into the cravings of immediate gratification and addictive behaviors. It will take consistency in repeating loving and supportive thoughts, words and behaviors so s/he can trust that you will always be there to love and keep him/her safe. No matter what happens in your life, your wounded child must believe that s/he won't be abandoned again. This is what is required to grow up happy and whole, no matter when you start.

As the voice of your inner child, your discomfort is the message calling out for the recognition and resolution of your unfulfilled needs for true love, peace and a sense of safety that can only be accomplished through self-love. You do this through introspection, self-awareness, forgiveness, compassion, following the guidance of your heart, and by correctly interpreting the messages of your emotions and physical conditions. Start where you find yourself now and follow the path of your emotions to uncover the faulty beliefs getting in your way. Make choices and changes that keep the promise of "I love you and I will always be there for you." As you love, nurture and protect your inner child with happy, healthy thoughts, words and actions, you will find you are doing a much better job of caring for yourself. As you heal your wounded child, s/he becomes your joy-filled, curious, wide-eyed guide who embraces life's experience with trust, openness, excitement and love.

Approaching Change—Be As the Little Children

Change, no matter how beneficial and desirable, pulls you out of the comfort zone of the familiar into the off-balance state of the strange and unknown. As an adult, you may have adopted a "Let's hurry up and get this done" or "I'm not really sure this is for me" kind of attitude toward change. This is a natural part of an innate mechanism that keeps you safe from perceived instability and danger. It's also the mechanism that keeps you trapped in the rut of life. As you explore some of the alternative perspectives and possibilities for change presented here, consider approaching the journey with the wide-eyed curiosity of a child. This too will be a learning experience. A child-like approach to mastering new ways of being is worth your time and energy because it will accelerate your efforts to reprogram your mind with beneficial beliefs about yourself and change your life for the better.

Infants and very young children start with few preconceived notions about how things work. Their play is the work of discovery. On an innate level, they understand the survival imperative to know themselves and their world. They are compelled to learn; they want to learn. Every moment is filled with curiosity about their connection with things and how to interact with them. Their willingness and tenacity to figure out how to hold a toy, roll over, crawl, walk and get attention are all just a matter of course in their day. They are surprised and delighted when their efforts are successful. Before long they have memorized the process that makes something happen exactly as they wanted. Their brains are making lasting connections. Once a skill is mastered, they are off to the next effort, satisfied, happy and curious.

Indeed, as adults, our lives could be our play. Much like children, everything we do is to figure out how to connect, navigate and control the elements in our lives. Whether or not we are aware, we keep repeating the same process over and over again until we figure it out or get it right. The play of adults may be more complex and the time allowed for trial and error may seem more compressed, but the bigger difference is that adults approach their learning and growing with preconceived ideas about "how things are in the real world." Armed with this once learned and now unconsciously embedded knowing of how things are, we adults act out our knowing by repeating the same unproductive, self-sabotaging behaviors that create the rut-like reality we have trouble waking up to each morning.

It will take some time and effort to unpack the learned response patterns and faulty beliefs that are now invisible but still hold you in place. Have compassion for yourself as you would a child who fell down while learning to walk. Admire your effort and tenacity. Giggle with glee at every little success and aha moment you experience. Reclaim the innocent, playful curiosity of your Inner Child and embrace your unique journey to the mastery of your life.

PART TWO

The Body of Understanding and Wisdom

"He who knows others is wise; he who knows himself is enlightened."
– Lao Tzu

CHAPTER 6

The Root Cause of Illness

"All disease is the result of inhibited soul life, and that is true in all forms in all kingdoms. The art of the healer consists in releasing the soul, so that its life can flow through the aggregate..." – Alice A. Bailey (1935)

Now that we know *what* we are: spiritual beings; love and light vibrating and interacting in electromagnetic fields of possibility with the purpose of knowing ourselves and finding our way back to the higher vibrations of Love and Harmony from which we originated.

We know *who* we are: each one, a Spark of Divinity expressing the Love of God as a unique one-of-a-kind individual; a unified presence of spirit, mind and body enabling a deeper understanding within an expanding consciousness.

And we know *how* we got to where we are now: We are participants in the journey of human evolution, guided by Divine Wisdom, Love and Power, and misdirected by poorly informed free-will choices of lower vibrations, which have been perpetuated through ancestral, societal and familial heritage, misinterpretation, faulty understanding, learning and beliefs.

So now it's time to look at how and why we become unhappy, diseased and die prematurely. A better understanding of the holistic nature of disease also unveils the essence of disease prevention and healing. Such an understanding coupled with strategic changes in beliefs, thoughts and actions shifts our trajectory toward health, happiness and an increased quality and length of life.

Alice Bailey's quote speaks to the role of the healer. It's not generally understood, but we are *all* healers; we are here to heal our own misunderstandings. Her instruction is an interpretation of the Hermetic Principle of Cause and Effect. It's also refers to the guidance of Matthew 6:33, "But strive first for the kingdom of God and [Their] righteousness, and all these things will be given to you as well." These teachings remind us we are spiritual beings and we need to embrace that truth if we are to move back into balance and alignment with our true nature.

Distress, unhappiness and disease come to us in a very logical and orderly way. It's just that we don't fully understand the logic or the process. Humanity's original sin, the place where we collectively missed the target and went off course, was the point at which we started to perceive ourselves as separate from God. At least according to early Judeo-Christian teachings, this all happened early on…in the beginning. Genesis 1 is a metaphor informing us of our magnificent origins and great potential. Genesis 2 tells us of a powerful, wise and loving God who created a garden to give us a purpose and the opportunity to learn and grow. Our perspective of duality came as God split Their creation into masculine and feminine entities so we wouldn't feel alone and could learn to love others as we were loved…unconditionally. Genesis 3 and 4 clarify what went wrong and how we got to where we are now. The problem is that we have misinterpreted those teachings to believe we were disobedient, judged unworthy of Paradise—another metaphor for the love and peace we seek—and punished with expulsion and separation from the Kingdom…and this separation and expulsion are now a permanent state of being.

If we read these few chapters with a different perspective, we could have a more beneficial and informative understanding of how we got here and what we can do about getting back to Paradise. A more discerning read of Genesis 3 reveals a God who is looking for us with the questions: Where are you? Why are you hiding? How do you know you are naked—or separate and unworthy? In answering for all of us, Adam responds from his newfound knowledge of good and evil, which includes a now *altered and faulty understanding based on inexperienced reasoning*. Though his condition hasn't changed, his perception of his condition has and Adam answers that he and Eve were naked, ashamed and afraid (important to note, God didn't tell them they were naked or that they should be ashamed and afraid). Without judgment, God lovingly and respectfully accepts Adam and Eve's choice to follow a less informed and inspired path and the perceptions resulting from it. Their choice to eat the forbidden fruit and how that perceived evil (cause) banished them from Paradise (effect) is a metaphor for what happens when we ignore or disregard divine guidance and go our separate way. Because of their choice, they must deal with the consequences of the knowledge of good and evil. They decided they were bad, much like we decided we weren't good enough in our childhood, and now they must walk the road of toil and suffering, just as we decide we are stuck with the suffering in our lives. Adam blaming Eve and Eve blaming the serpent was instructive for how we perpetuate our own misery by not accepting responsibility for ourselves.

In the story, God tells Adam and Eve what life will look like from this point on. Considering this biblical accounting was told in retrospect, all of humanity's suffering was already well underway; it's like a child's story tale with simplistic explanation of why life looks like it does. God was not sentencing humanity to misery, They were offering a forecast based on cause, effect and trajectory. It's no different than what happens today. If we go out with friends and party too hard, we go to bed knowing what tomorrow is going to feel like. And if we do that repeatedly, we can forecast what the future will feel like as well. It's a projection based on thoughts, behaviors and trajectory, it's cause and effect, not God's punishment.

Even in the middle of all the mayhem and mistakes, the remedy is offered to us. In Genesis 4:7-8, "The Lord said to Cain, 'Why are you angry and why has your countenance fallen? If you do well, will you not be accepted? And if you do not do well, sin is lurking at the door; its desire is for you, but you must master it.'" The story is another instructive metaphor. This passage is an invitation to understand that we choose our feelings and we allow them to disturb our wellbeing. It's an opportunity to appreciate that if we perceive we've done well, we can expect to attain that loving state we're trying to achieve, and if we're not doing well, it's because sin (misperception about what will bring us happiness) is lurking close by. The things that tempt and distract us won't bring true happiness, but they are constantly and seductively present. It's up to us, individually, to master them.

What Ancient Wisdom, Scriptural Teaching, Masters, philosophers and esoteric healers are all telling us is that we are spiritual beings and our one big mistake, our original sin, is in interpreting ourselves as separate from God. With this understanding and perception of separation, we have come to believe we are unworthy…unworthy of love, peace, abundance and our magnificent birthright as the holy children of God that we are.

The belief that we are separate from God is the original sin and the root cause of all disease.

The experience we are living is the product of Universal Laws, whether we call them quantum or Hermetic, and the mental ideologies humanity has developed over eons. With the help of ancestors, religious dogma, science, society and family we have long ago dismissed our spiritual nature. And even though this is where our distress and disease begins, we no longer have a frame of reference allowing us to think and heal at the spiritual level. So we must step down to the next level to find our answers. This is the realm of our mental bodies, and even as we feel our Divine Spark urging us toward peace and love, we are now *thinking* for ourselves. At this level and with the help of the same ancestors, society, family and friends, we have come to believe happiness and love are to be found outside ourselves. The spiritual dilemma of separation is now a mental dilemma where we are using subconsciously programmed beliefs and thoughts to guide our choices. We use our conscious minds to rationalize our choices as reasonable and worthy of our efforts to achieve happiness, connection and love. Some of our choices are well founded and do bring us love, joy and health. But if they are grounded on faulty self-beliefs and misguided actions, they become sin's "desire for you" and cause discomfort and distress. If we had the awareness, discipline and discernment to look deep at the source of our *mental* distress, we would find our *spiritual* distress. Unfortunately, most of us did not learn to look within to find the origin of our discomfort and so we can't recognize the true source of our struggles. Many of us will miss the root cause of our distress even at the mental level.

We have become quite masterful at pushing troubling thoughts out of our minds. We justify the continual mental strain and anguish as part of the price we pay to live the life we believe we deserve. We have convinced ourselves that having more, bigger and better is worth all the headaches it creates as we seek happiness from external sources. Because we are ignoring our mental pain and struggles, or at least justifying them with our reasoning abilities, we again miss the opportunity to uncover our faulty beliefs as the source of our distress. This means our innate wisdom and messaging system is going to have to step down another level to get our attention.

The next level of communication and distress signaling is our emotional body. The messages we feel in our bodies appear as a form of discomfort letting us know something is out of rhythm and balance. Fear and all the other negative emotions become compelling messengers trying to get our attention. They are alerting us that we need find the source of our distress, change what is causing it, and head back toward balance, peace and harmony.

If we are honest, many of us have become quite masterful at dismissing or repressing our emotions. For some, the emotional pain associated with life has become so great that we have banished all emotions to a place where there is no access or memory. The degree to which we have repressed our emotions and painful memories doesn't matter. Our negative emotions, whether hidden or on full display, stay with us and continuously drag us down. They are intimately entangled with the healing opportunities we missed at the mental and spiritual levels and they are directly associated with the problems we will have physically. Missing the opportunity to recognize our emotional distress and heal our pain, we step down to the next level…the physical body.

In this way, what started a very long time ago as a spiritual dilemma became a mental, emotional and then physical problem through our well-established thought and behavioral patterns. This pattern of dealing with distress through deferred awareness is not new to us. We have been practicing, reinforcing and refining it for millennia. It has been handed down parents to child for eons. These patterns are also woven into our inherited genetic information. The conventional approach to dealing with mental and physical disease is not working. It's time to live and heal in a new paradigm.

Your physical body is a magical, mystical, holographic, time traveling machine supporting your journey. No matter your size, color, gender, gender identity or perceived handicap, your body is the perfect vehicle to explore, learn, grow and evolve as you progress through life. Each descriptor, whether white, brown, black, him, her, their, big, small, deaf, mute, blind, wheelchair-bound or otherwise normal in someone's opinion, presents unique opportunities to know and accept yourself, and to learn to love yourself on deeper and deeper levels. In addition, your physical descriptors give you a point of reference when you interact with others. This provides additional opportunities to grow in acceptance, compassion and love for yourself and for others.

Beyond being the perfect vehicle for your journey, your body is the ultimate communication device, providing you with all the information you need to be healthy and happy. It receives information from internal and external sources. It transmits this information to you in various ways, such as insights, intuition, instincts, feelings or memories, depending on how you best receive information and learn from it. It warns you when you are being pulled into situations and choices that will knock you off balance, cause you distress or put you in danger. It automatically monitors and adjusts internal resources to assure survival, stability and growth. Everything about your physical body was divinely created to be everything you need to survive, succeed and be happy.

How Disease Gets Started

Disease starts with the belief of unworthiness and the frequently unrecognized feelings of fear. From this point, it works its way through the brain and into the body where it slowly disrupts healthy cells and erodes the processes supporting balance and health. The older parts of our brain take care of all the primal and necessary survival functions like balancing hormones, digesting, reproducing, breathing, circulation, memory and infection control. While there are many structures in the brain that support life, I'm going to focus only on those that regulate function in order to meet the demands of our constantly changing environment. The small organs and glands of the limbic system, part of the primal brain, shift energy resources so the body can deal with stress and ensure survival, even in the most severe environments.

Our primal brain has been functioning in the same way pretty much from the beginning. It caused us to reflexively run from unexpected noise in the bushes (saber-toothed tiger) and puff up to confront a threatening stranger. It even caused the body to store fat and quit reproducing in times of prolonged famine. As we survived and evolved, we learned to grow our own food rather than travel for it, interact with mates and fellow humans on deeper levels and live in larger communities. As life became more complex, so did our brains. As we developed language, writing and reasoning skills our brains kept making new connections. We learned new things through trial and error, contemplation and repetition, just like we always had. It took a long time, but we were evolving the complex brains we have today. Unfortunately, our advanced thinking and reasoning skills took us to a place where we began dismissing things we could not readily explain through logic and science. Because we don't fully understand the complex, integrated functioning of our minds, brains and bodies, we have become more estranged from the intuitive knowledge and innate wisdom that were once vital information sources for our ancestors. We forgot how to listen to our own messaging systems until we muted them entirely.

We have used our rational, analytical minds to discount and disconnect from the once readily available intuitive messages. Even as science recognizes the vast network of neuronal connections linking our newer, more evolved brain to our older primal brain, we have failed to recognize that *this new brain does not replace or supersede the control functions of the older, innate brain.* It's there, still functioning as it did thousands of years ago, ensuring survival, balance, growth and evolution for each of us. We cannot override the functions of the primal brain by simply "thinking it through." Unfortunately, we *can* think ourselves into predicaments that will push our primal brain beyond the point of balance and health. As we continue to distance ourselves from our inner knowing and messaging systems, we slide further down this path of imbalance and dis-ease.

As I was writing *Loving Yourself Whole*, I struggled with how much detail to include. How much would be too much? This was especially true as I considered how much information was enough to fully appreciate the brain, the stress response and their preordained contribution to disease and despair. I believe knowledge is power and being able to see a clear connection between childhood brain development, life experience, stress and disease is both illuminating and empowering. Realizing the physical brain was divinely crafted to allow us to change the erroneous beliefs and habitual patterns we have adopted can liberate us from the distress we are experiencing. This is the information missing from health classes, clinical office visits and Internet searches. Understanding how esoteric knowledge and science all fit together shines light on greater possibilities and empowers us with information we can use to heal our most troubling problems.

There is no way to appreciate the vast network of nerve cells and their innumerable connections to other cells, tissues and organs. We just need to understand that information from a single organ or gland travels to multiple places simultaneously, and all parts of our brains and branches of the nervous system are designed to both send and receive information. No part of the brain acts alone. Since the brain is the interface between the mind and the body and connects with all the structures ultimately dictating our health and wellbeing, we will start with a brief walk around the parts of the limbic brain in control of the

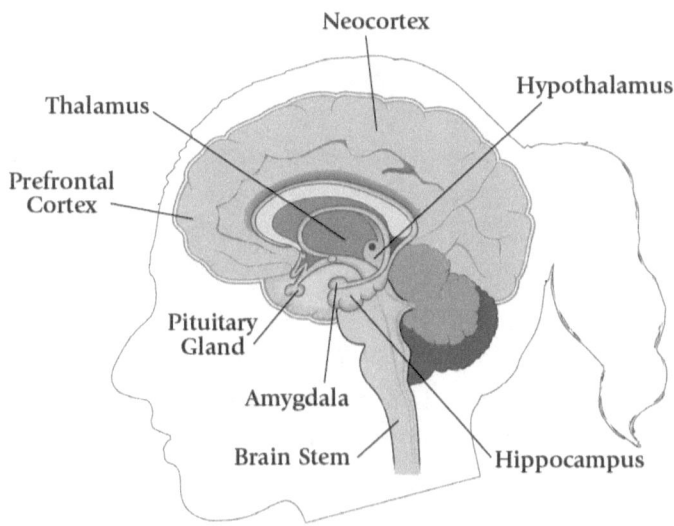

95% automatic functioning we discussed earlier.

The CORTEX is the outer layer of the brain and surrounds the more primal structures. It's a huge processing plant that works with structures in the primal brain to interpret incoming sensory information, coordinate movement and construct how we interact with the world...some of this without a conscious thought. The prefrontal cortex sits behind the forehead and is largely responsible for our personality, reasoning, logical thinking, learning, impulse control and conscious thought processes. It's one of the rapidly developing areas during early childhood learning and it houses the bulk of those entrenched patterns of thinking, coping and reacting to the world. Emerging research suggests that severe childhood traumas and toxic environments, whether mental, emotional or physical, can shrink connections in this part of the brain. This shrinkage in turn keeps the brain focused on fear-based emotions and survival behaviors, and limits learning and more effective reasoning and coping patterns. While much of what happens in this prefrontal cortex still falls within the 95% subconscious thought processing, this is where a significant portion of the 5% conscious thinking happens. It connects with many other places in the brain to move us through our lives. For our purposes, it connects with the amygdala and hippocampus, and together these parts of the brain influence our unique perception of our experiences, memory, learning and emotional interpretation and reactivity. The prefrontal cortex is also the place where we can plan and initiate the changes we want for ourselves.

The AMYGDALA gathers information from our five senses, visceral organs (gut), thalamus, hippocampus, cortex and more. It's important for arousal, emotional learning and motivation. It's part of the system that senses and responds to fear and pleasure, making it the trigger for the fight-or-flight stress response. Recent discoveries suggest that fear-provoking events, especially in early childhood, increase neuronal connections in the amygdala. This sensitizes a person to further fear-provoking events, which may intensify reactions to perceived threats in the future.

The HIPPOCAMPUS is responsible for learning, short-term memory, retrieval of long-term memories, emotional context, spatial associations and control of cortisol production. It connects with the amygdala, the hypothalamus and other parts of the brain including the prefrontal cortex. Along with the prefrontal cortex, it functions as a gateway through which information must pass to get to memory and learning. This is especially true when new information conflicts with older and longer held memory and learning. The hippocampus' influence on cortisol levels makes it a critical factor in the health-promoting chemical balance and the fight-or-flight survival system.

Just as the amygdala and prefrontal cortex are affected by traumatic childhood or prolonged adult stressors, the hippocampus is also affected. Toxic events shrink the number of neuronal connections, affecting memory and learning. This *heightens the stress response and reduces learning, mental flexibility and the ability of the brain to stay healthy* through cellular regeneration.

Recent studies have shown that the hippocampus has the ability to generate new cells, change in size through the number of neuronal connections, and potentially alter how we respond to stress. In an otherwise healthy state, stimulated with enrichment, emotionalized learning and exercise, the hippocampus can produce stem cells, which migrate to other areas of the brain to become new cells and new connections.

This means we have *the potential to change* our minds about what we have learned and how we react to our experiences. This potential for structural and functional change is a relatively new concept, and one to keep in mind as we move forward.

The HYPOTHALAMUS is wired to send and receive information from both the amygdala and the hippocampus. It also receives input from the prefrontal cortex. It regulates the balance of hormones responsible for health and wellbeing. The hypothalamus is the first gland in the balance-maintaining complex known as the Hypothalamus-Pituitary-Adrenal (HPA) axis. In response to our internal and external environment, it makes minute adjustments to control such processes as body temperature, blood pressure, heart rate, breathing and caloric expenditure based on the needs of the moment. It maintains the balance of hormones like thyroid, estrogen, testosterone and cortisol to keep us functioning at our best. When it senses an insufficient quantity of any of these important hormones, it sends a signal to the pituitary gland to increase production and maintain optimal balance. This includes sending a message to the adrenal glands, which rest on the kidneys, to maintain adrenaline and cortisol levels according to changing demand.

In addition to directing the pituitary gland to increase production of certain hormones, the hypothalamus makes and releases a few of its own; oxytocin, better known for its effect on laboring mothers, is being recognized as the "cuddle hormone" for its part in compassion and bonding behavior in general; and vasopressin, which in addition to managing blood pressure and urine output, appears to have an influence on social interaction and sexual behavior.

The PITUITARY gland is considered the "master gland" because it's responsible for signaling glands downstream to adjust their hormone production in order to maintain a healthy balance. For our purpose and simplicity, the pituitary gland affects the production of cortisol (the stress hormone), thyroid hormone, growth hormone (its not just for kids) and two other hormones affecting testosterone (also active in women) and estrogen (also active in men). The later two hormones affect sexual interest, function and the ability to procreate. The pituitary gland is the second gland in the HPA axis and all the hormones it influences have a major affect on how we feel and how our bodies function. Chronic stress is known to have a negative impact on the hormones affecting bone growth, thyroid function, libido and reproductive functioning. And, through the effects of cortisol, stress has an *impact on the functioning of all cells*. There is no way to overestimate the effects a distress signal has on the whole body as it passes through this HPA axis.

The THALAMUS is a network of cells that communicates with and influences other areas of the brain. It governs sleep, wakefulness and arousal. Its connection to the hippocampus affects memory and learning, and it plays a part in emotions, mood and motivation. It serves as a relay to interpret incoming sensory information including pain, temperature and gross motor movement.

One last bit of important information on the structures of the brain: Studies are now telling us that the pro-inflammatory response caused by prolonged stress and cortisol dysfunction can damage the blood-brain barrier. This is a circulatory loop in the center of the brain, which filters the blood supply as it enters the brain. Damage to this barrier allows harmful and toxic agents into the very delicate structures of the brain that in turn regulate every little thing about us. The list of potential diseases in which this may be a factor is of growing interest to research efforts.

Now that we know a little about the distinct areas the limbic brain, we can turn our attention to the downstream effects. Health and survival are dependent on the 24/7 monitoring and controlling functions of the limbic brain, which manages hormonal balance through two separate but interconnected systems, the Hypothalamus-Pituitary-Adrenal (HPA) axis and the Autonomic Nervous System (ANS). The ANS has three divisions; the parasympathetic and sympathetic branches and the enteral branch, which we mentioned earlier as the gut brain. These three divisions, along with the heart brain, send action-provoking communication to the amygdala, as well as receiving activity-oriented messages from it.

When we are calm, happy and content, the amygdala holds chemical, hormonal and biological functions in a balanced state. It signals the parasympathetic branch to maintain an optimal flow of neurotransmitters to the heart, lungs, gut and other vital organs via the vagus nerve. Messaging from the amygdala allows the hypothalamus to maintain a balanced production of the hormones regulating all the functions of the body. This combined effort is nicknamed the rest/digest/reproduce system. When it's in charge, the flow of hormones and chemical transmitters are balanced so we can relax, sleep well, digest food properly and have the right hormonal mix for interest in sex, conceiving children, supporting immune function, building healthy bones and repairing and rejuvenating tissue all over the body. When all is well, all body systems are getting the resources they need to function properly. This is our happy place.

Physical survival is essential for evolution and so the brain is designed to prioritize survival above all else. Always on alert for a threat, this same system initiates the innate stress response programmed into the subconscious brain. Regardless of the severity or source, when the gut brain, thalamus or hippocampus perceive a physical or psychological threat, the amygdala is instantly alerted and immediately triggers the HPA axis and sympathetic branch of the nervous system to shift gears. This is the fight-or-flight system that redirects resources so we have the energy we need to *make changes and deal with the threat*. The sympathetic branch releases larger amounts of norepinephrine and adrenaline causing blood pressure, heart rate and breathing to increase. Blood vessels constrict and blood sugar starts to rise. As the hypothalamus is triggered, it expands the stress response by changing the hormonal balance and increasing the supply of cortisol. Blood is shifted away from the digestive, reproductive and immune systems because they have very little to do with immediate survival. The constricted blood vessels preferentially send blood, with the oxygen and nutrients it transports, to the systems most needed for survival. These are the heart, lungs, muscles and the parts of the brain necessary to stay focused on the immediate problem and survival…rarely the thinking brain. When the threat has been effectively dealt with, either through overcoming it or by confirming it wasn't really a problem to begin with, this same integrated messaging system signals the hippocampus, amygdala, hypothalamus and the parasympathetic and enteric branches of the nervous system to return to rest/digest/reproduce mode.

Over a period of hours to days, hormonal and chemical balance is restored and shifts the body's resources back to a state of equilibrium and optimal function.

The primal brain also has a provision for threats lasting longer than it takes to fight with or run from potential danger. In times of prolonged struggles such as war, famine or the long hard travels that our ancestors experienced, the primal brain caused the adrenal glands to maintain higher cortisol levels. Cortisol stimulates the liver to make more glucose (sugar) fueling the increased workload of muscles, heart and lungs. If this extra supply of sugar is not used immediately, it's warehoused around the midsection in readily available fat stores. The prolonged and higher levels of cortisol work with the other systems of the body to channel resources toward the systems focused on fight-or-flight rather than rest, digest and reproduce. In this way, the primal brain—with no thinking required—is the master control directing all systems of the body to cooperate in survival efforts during hard times...all hard times.

Pausing here for just a moment, I want to emphasize what I regard as a critical and yet unappreciated relationship. The amygdala, hippocampus, thalamus and prefrontal cortex are instrumental in memory, learning and emotions, which are fundamentally established in early childhood. The neuronal structure and functions of these organs were also shaped by early childhood experiences. What you came to believe and all the thoughts, perceptions, coping and reaction patterns you adopted then, are now the deciding factors dictating how your brain functions...right here at this point. This is exactly where what you learned, what you came to believe about yourself and the world, and the emotional countenance you assumed as a result, determines your health and happiness. It's also where your feelings and life experiences continue to jive with and reinforce what you learned then. From here, it's fear that triggers the amygdala to start a chain reaction down the ANS and HPA axis, and love that brings the system back into balance. Where do fear and love come from? This is the point where mind, emotions and body are woven together as inseparable.

Whether someone points a gun at you, your child runs into a busy street or you are struggling with some negative emotion such as anger, resentment or guilt, you are experiencing a threat to the integrity of your being. This is also true if you are struggling with a physical ailment. On some level, you are afraid because your world is out of order and you don't feel safe. Your response is innate and preprogrammed. The amygdala signals everything downstream to shift to a different operating mode. Through the influence of adrenaline and cortisol, every function in the body is affected. There is nothing you can think, rationalize, ignore or bury that will alter this innate process. *The fight-or-flight response is automatically triggered by fear, whether the threat is an actual danger or a perceived threat based on learning and past experiences.* Only your state of mind and how you truly feel can shift from the fight-or-flight system to the one that promotes rest, digest and reproduce. There is no reasoning with the way it rules over the body.

CHAPTER 7

It's All About Stress

"Its not stress that kills us, it is our reaction to it."
– Hans Selye

Science has known about our fight-or-flight response since the 1930's when Hans Selye, MD first identified the survival mechanism he called the General Adaptation Syndrome (GAS), so named because it described the process the body went through in order to adapt to changes or noxious stimuli in its environment. Eventually, this adaptation syndrome became known by the more common names of stress response and fight-or-flight response. Over time, researchers have added more information to how this stress response worked and what triggered it. In our more sophisticated times, saber-toothed tigers and warriors with spears have been replaced by other types of stressors.

All major life events trigger the stress response, even when fighting and running aren't effective methods for dealing with change. Whether change is recognized as beneficial or threatening, it triggers the stress response to liberate the resources needed to *adapt* to our changing environment. Thus life-impacting events like:

Losing a job	Getting a new job or position
Getting married	Getting divorced

Buying a house	Moving to a new location
Having a child	Death of a loved one
Accidents/Trauma	Chronic illnesses
Surgery	Natural Disasters

And many others were viewed as activating events that shifted our biological functioning into the stress response mode. Eventually, we will come to terms with these life events, and once we effectively deal with the changes, we automatically shift back into a "normal" where the HPA axis and parasympathetic can restore balance.

Researchers continue to explore stress, the stress response and an expanding awareness of its effects on the whole body, and as they do, new information is challenging what was once accepted as sure science. According to Dr. Bruce Lipton, the discovery of DNA and later, mapping the human genome led to the premature and inaccurate determination that our inherited genetic structures caused most of our chronic diseases and cancers. As recently as the 1980's, conventional ideologies didn't recognize stress as a significant factor in disease formation. There was an ongoing debate of "nature versus nurture" regarding the true origins of disease. In this debate, nature represented genetic predetermination and nurture represented environmental influences. Neither side was able to definitively prove they were correct or the other side was wrong. Today, medical science and practitioners generally agree that at least 90% of healthcare concerns are stress related, tipping the scale more toward environmental influences and the stress response. Unfortunately, disease treatments are focused on managing the end results of stress and not the stress itself. In a sign of the growing awareness of stress and its substantial role in disease, today's practitioners often add the caveat, "reduce your stress."

Reduce Your Stress—What does that mean?

Being totally healthy means developing a greater understanding of what stress is and how its long-term effects hijack resources and damage our physical, mental and emotional wellbeing. Most of us don't realize that even in the absence of war, drought and famine, we're drowning in a state of constant stress. Unaware of the true source of our discontent, we're unable to make the appropriate changes that would move us back to a calm state where the primal brain can maintain a better balance for long-term health and happiness.

A stress or stressor is anything, physical or psychological, actual or perceived, that moves us out of our comfort zone and renders our usual ways of thinking and coping ineffective. Stressors can represent a change, a need for a change, an unmet expectation, a challenge or a threat to our safety on some level. In this way, stressors and our built-in response to them can be beneficial and even life enhancing. They allow us to greet change with the resources we need to adapt, grow and progress in productive and purposeful ways. Through awareness, well-intentioned strategies and effort, we can overcome the stressors we encounter and in so doing, we may learn new skills for coping with life.

Some stressors can cause serious harm or pain and yet, even these life-altering events are opportunities to grow to higher levels of self-awareness. Dealing effectively with stress allows us to overcome adversity and reach new levels of understanding, especially when we connect with our innate wisdom, which reminds us we *do actually have the power to make a difference* in our lives. The most damning part of stress is not the stressor itself but our lack of appropriate response. Stress is the call to change—to change something internally or externally so we can move back into balance. As we have become more distant from our intuitions, instincts and inner knowing, we often fail to recognize that our feelings of restlessness, dis-ease or pain are signals calling for change, as well as the stress triggering our destruction. Our lack of recognition and meaningful change holds our stress response in a sustained "on" position as if we were in the midst of a war or famine, and in some ways this is quite true.

The fight-or-flight response is the innate survival system created to keep us safe and sustain our evolutionary progress by maintaining the integrity and optimal functioning of our bodies and minds. While stress is both a response initiating system and a call to action, too many of us have unwittingly chosen a different kind of response when faced with threats we don't recognize as detrimental or modifiable. We freeze; a kind of dear-in-the-headlight response where no effective change takes place. We don't stand up and fight for our right to be safe, loved and treated with respect, nor do we run away from situations that don't serve our highest good. We march on day after day as if our restlessness, distress and disease are either of no consequence or simply unavoidable. This distancing from our own power and knowing and the resulting freeze response is the natural consequence of years of careful conditioning and repetitive practice. Regardless of our awareness, this default freeze response is the mechanism by which we are destroying our health and happiness. The prolonged stress response with its sustained shift in hormonal and chemical balance is tearing down the very tissues and organs it was intended to protect.

We have come to this default mode through the early learning that taught us how to perceive, cope, respond and survive in the world. Predictably, what we learned became reinforced and compounded through many repetitions as we interpreted events according to our beliefs and responded to them the same way we always have. Some of us learned it wasn't okay to cry or express anger or disappointment, or even disagree with authority. Some of us were raised with the belief that we were powerless and had no options to make life better. There are many variations to the erroneous programming we learned and are repeating daily. As a direct consequence, we have learned to bury our feelings in a place where we feel little or we feel nothing at all.

The complexities and technology of today's culture have increased the degree to which we have become even more estranged from ourselves. We have more devices to connect us, access to more information than we can hope to sort through, experts to help us navigate life's complexities and personal lives allowing little time for self-reflection and awareness. In all of this, we are more separate from our true self and increasingly unaware of the struggles taking place inside. For many of us, struggles have become life as we know it, and we just deal with it. The problem is this: the way we are choosing to deal with our demanding, challenging and ever-changing lives is also the mechanism of disease.

When we no longer feel our emotional signals or are conscious of the negative thoughts accompanying them, it becomes very difficult to hear our inner guidance system sound the alarm. Being unaware of the stress affecting our mind and body doesn't mean the brain is failing to send an alarm. It just means we are not responding appropriately to our problems as they threaten our integrity and healthy balance. To stop the physical and mental wear and tear caused by unresolved and prolonged stress, we need to start with a more comprehensive understanding of stressors.

A stressor can be physical, emotional, mental or spiritual in nature and your amygdala doesn't differentiate or respond differently based on its origin. Stressors can be acute, arising suddenly and lasting for a relatively short time. They can be long-term or chronic, lasting weeks, months and years. They can even become a way of life. Remember, your primal brain can be relied upon to respond in the same way each time it perceives change or a threat to the balance of life. Your stress response system can be in the "on" position continually if your amygdala and hippocampus determine this is what is needed to deal with an ongoing threat.

It's important to know that stress is an individual experience; what stresses you doesn't necessarily stress others; how you respond to a stressful event will be different than the response of someone experiencing that same event. Consider these examples as a starting place for your own exploration.

Physical Stressors
~ Some physical and emotional conditions can be both a stressor and the result of prolonged stress. All chronic conditions, such as diabetes, heart disease, cancer, anxiety and depression, put a strain on our whole mental, emotional and physical being. They are part of a vicious cycle and they can keep us in a chronic stress response.

~ Physical illnesses like flu and colds and injuries such as broken bones and twisted ankles naturally stress the body because the stress response is part of the innate mechanism of repair and rejuvenation. As we work through recovery, many aspects of our lives will be impacted including our emotional demeanor. How

we feel about our physical problems can cause additional stress.
~ Pain is a warning sign advising us something is wrong. It could be a broken bone, a headache, a twisted bowel or muscles knotted up by the way we hold tension in the body…unconsciously of course. Pain can come from many different places but it's always a warning.
~ Food, beverages and many things you put in your mouth can stress the body. Processed foods including junk, fast and snack foods and most beverages we consume have lots of calories but lack the nutrients the body needs for optimal functioning. Chemicals in the form of pesticides, herbicides, preservatives, artificial sweeteners, alcohol, food additives and even your prescribed medications, though necessary as prescribed by your healthcare provider, are foreign and not-natural occurring molecular substances. While deemed safe by authorities, they still need to be detoxified by your body, primarily the gut, liver and kidneys. Depending on the amounts of high calorie, low nutrition and chemical-laden food you are taking in, you could be shorting yourself on solid nutrition while asking your body to do a lot of extra work to detoxify. There is growing evidence that high-calorie, low-nutrient, processed foods and chemicals are contributing to leaky gut syndrome, a precursor to inflammation, food sensitivities and autoimmune diseases. Poor nutrition is also linked to chronic fatigue, which may be due to its negative impact on mitochondria, the energy-generating component in each and every cell. Proper nutrition with whole and preferably organic food cannot be emphasized too much.
~ Additional sources of physical stressors include:
  – Acute illnesses like colds, pneumonia and heart attacks.
  – Chronic illnesses like obesity, diabetes, arthritis and cancer.
  – Inadequate or disrupted sleep patterns.
  – Foreign substances like cigarettes, drugs, alcohol, and pollution.
  – Major injuries like car accidents, sexual assault and any form of physical violence.

Emotional Stressors

Negative emotions are messages that indicate the need for change in order to restore balance. They become long-term stressors when we don't fix the underlying causes of them. We may choose to ignore or bury our negative feelings, but they remain a continual threat to the integrity of our wellbeing. At a very intimate level we are tearing ourselves down. When we don't make changes to resolve our problems, we are literally a threat to ourselves. Emotional stress triggers can include:

~ Any negative emotion, such as fear, hate, resentment and unworthiness.
~ Feeling out of synch with ourselves and at odds with others.
~ Feelings of isolation and hopelessness.
~ Emotional and verbal abuses are often unrecognized forms of domestic abuse.
~ Unresolved mental health concerns such as chronic anxiety and depression.
~ Depression is part of a disease-begets-disease cyclical pattern where one problem stresses the body so much that other diseases begin to appear.
~ Even when we can't feel our emotional distress, we will behave in a manner that expresses it. Behaviors such as gossip, bullying and emotional or physical abuse are the result of feeling inadequate, unworthy or unlovable. To deal with these faulty beliefs and feelings, we somehow justify our behavior to degrade and belittle others—a learned response. Victims of these types of activity necessarily feel threatened. How they choose to deal with such assaults will determine how fast they return to balance. For some people, being on the receiving end is more than a one-time event. It's a miserable, damaging way of life, also held in place by feelings of being unlovable, unworthy or not good enough. The same is true of manipulative relationships where we feel pressured to behave according to someone else's expectations.
~ Long-term caregiving is a prolonged life event that can take a huge toll on physical, mental and emotional resources, even in the most generous and loving of circumstances.

Mental Stressors

Mental stressors are things we ruminate or catastrophize about repetitively, including:

~ Financial troubles.

~ Community, societal or political unrest.

~ Job stress: Unreasonable schedules or workload, lack of appreciation, bullying.

~ Time management issues: Too many obligations, whether voluntary or otherwise.

~ Life events: exams, presentations and major decisions about cars, homes or jobs.

Some of our mental stressors are short lived. We get past the exams and presentations. We settle into new towns, homes, jobs and relationships. Our financial situations change for the better. Unfortunately, more and more of us are feeling trapped by our commitments and overwhelmed with lives that offer little real satisfaction and we have resigned ourselves to this unhappy state. We are unconsciously exhausting our physical, emotional and mental resources to the breaking point. To the primal brain, this resignation to the status quo is a grave and ongoing threat.

Spiritual Stressors

It might be a stretch to think of spiritual issues as stressors, but as spiritual beings, failure to acknowledge this essential part of ourselves results in an imbalance affecting our mental, emotional and physical bodies through the stress response. Faulty perceptions of ourselves and our relationship with God can set the tone for everything else in life.

~ Believing in a God who sits in judgment of our every thought, word and action relegates us to the position of sinner. From here it's not difficult to feel unworthy of the peace and happiness we seek to find and fear is the natural reaction.

~ An existential crisis where we believe we have no purpose for being, or our lives matter little, or we aren't powerful enough to make a difference can all foster feelings of fear.

~ Feeling angry with God or blaming Them for situations in our lives originates from the erroneous belief in separation that results in a sense of powerlessness and fear.

Social Stressors

We are social beings, even those of us who prefer our own company most of the time. We live in communities and to varying degrees we must rely on others for things we need, like access to power, water, food, housing and safety. We interact with members of our community for important functions such as jobs, companionship, guidance, validation, love and support. Though we may give little thought to the importance of community, inherently we know there is safety in numbers and our individual survival is best served by the survival of the group. This has been etched into our DNA since we huddled around fires and built forts to keep out two-legged and four-legged threats to our safety. It's still true today with public safety programs for waste, fire and crime as well as agencies to deal with national security, health and climate change. Threats to the integrity or sustainability of communal or global priorities necessarily affect our sense of safety and survival. This means they are stressors just as real as any of those mentioned above.

The pull to belong to a community and have a sense of "tribe" is innate. It's also a double-edged sword. Belonging increases the chances of survival, but wanting to belong can cause us to make choices not always in our best interest. Living successfully in family and community implies the need to be accepted. We have been indoctrinated that being accepted means living up to standards set by the group, whether, family, peers, bosses or society in general. These standards for acceptability come from so many sources we scarcely recognize the impact they are having on us; well-intentioned family and friends; stated and implied codes of conduct in social networks such as work places, institutions and communities; marketing, advertising and all forms of social media. Each of these, in some way, is attempting to pull us into line with *their standard* of acceptability and force compliance with their ideology. This could sound familiar as "sin's desire for you."

Such pressures to conform to group specified norms or expectations could influence life choices in directions not always consistent with who we are and what we need to be happy, healthy and satisfied as unique individuals. Some of these pressures and the choices they encourage are bad ideas from the start. Some may sound reasonable and worthy, but if the acceptable standard is out of synch with your nature, gifts and intuitive knowing, they can take you down a path not in alignment with the true you. A choice, made in an effort to make someone else happy or comply with a standard contrary to your true self, becomes a stressor for as long as you continue that particular choice. Whenever you abandon yourself in an attempt to conform to the wishes of others, no matter how well intentioned, you are telling yourself, "I'm not good enough as I was created." As long as you continue act in ways inconsistent with your heart's call, you remain in a state of imbalance. If you pay attention, you can feel your message alert systems calling out to you, "Just be your own unique and magnificent self."

Chronic Stress Becomes Chronic Disease

From the examples of stressors listed before, we can see that stress comes in many different forms. Stressors that impact one person will have minimal affect on another. Some stressors, like financial difficulties, losing a job or working while going to school can be temporary. If we look at the listed examples again, we might see that acting differently could eliminate some of them. How we think and feel about our stressors could alleviate their impact. Further, learning from stressful situations can help us grow toward more empowered beliefs, improved attitudes and coping patterns and better choices. The difficulty we encounter when trying to make changes we know will be for the better is caused by the patterns we developed over the course of our lives. No matter how uncomfortable we may feel, our sense of familiarity and safety with what we have always known seems to win out over the sense of discomfort we feel when it comes to pursuing options that are unfamiliar and the outcome uncertain.

We live putting one foot in front of the other just trying to get by. We may hear or feel our intuitions and instincts urging us to make changes, but we imagine our options are not possible or practical. When we actually feel distress, we often dismiss it as unimportant, transient or something we can do nothing about. We press on, business as usual, trying to ignore the way we feel. At this point, we are making a choice to keep moving in the same direction without any adjustments to relieve the discomfort we're trying to ignore. Continuing to live this way freezes the stress response into the permanent "on" position. As long as we continue in the same manner, we're manufacturing more adrenaline and cortisol for the sustained survival mode. If we stay frozen in this way of perceiving, thinking and behaving, the increase in circulating cortisol causes alterations in the brain's monitoring system, affects the other hormone levels and contributes to the erosion and long-term damage to organs and tissues throughout the body. *This slow ongoing erosion and damage is the physical mechanism leading to chronic diseases.*

Progressive Erosion of Our Parts and Pieces

From our discussion of the hypothalamus-pituitary-adrenal (HPA) axis and its regulatory function over the other hormones it's easy to see where many of our quality of life problems come from. The stress response affects all hormone levels: its effect on estrogen and testosterone leads to lack of interest in sex and sexual difficulties in both men and women; alterations in thyroid hormones affect metabolism, bodily functions, fatigue, anxiety and depression; changes in growth hormone levels affect the body's ability to heal tissues and maintain healthy bones and joints. Prolonged stress also shifts the balance of hormones and neurotransmitters including dopamine, serotonin, oxytocin and vasopressin, which then disrupt our sense of wellbeing and connectedness.

Let's look at this in a little more detail. The Autonomic Nervous System (ANS) manages the balance of adrenaline and its companion, norepinephrine, to address changes in energy demand. Together they enable the body to immediately respond to any increase in energy expenditure including exercise, heavy labor and the stress response. The systems most affected by the increase in adrenaline level include:

Respiratory — With exercise, manual labor or stress, adrenaline opens the nasal passages wider and increases the rate of breathing. This makes more oxygen available to the brain, heart and muscles. When this is sustained without the actual physical need for more oxygen, the brain signals the muscles around the rib cage to decrease expansion and breathing becomes more shallow. This shallow, rapid breathing, especially with increased amounts of adrenaline can contribute to feelings of panic and anxiety, as in "I can't get my breath!"

Circulatory — Adrenaline accelerates heartbeat and constricts blood vessels to move blood toward the heart, lungs and large muscle groups. This is great for exercise, running and fighting, but if excess amounts are prolonged, it contributes to high blood pressure and other forms of cardiovascular disease. As blood is reallocated to the heart and muscles, its flow is decreased to the gut which then compromises its ability to perform efficiently.

Digestive — Adrenaline interferes with digestive enzymes and secretions necessary to break down food into usable forms of energy. It raises blood sugar levels. Dysregulation of the enteric (gut) neurotransmitters, dopamine, serotonin and adrenaline, contribute to inflammation and digestive issues, and are implicated in such diseases as Parkinson's disease, irritable bowel syndrome, inflammatory bowel disease, leaky gut syndrome and depression.

As part of the stress response, adrenaline is considered pro-inflammatory, which means it's part of the first-line defense to help rid the body of foreign invaders like bacteria and viruses. Its precursor, norepinephrine, stimulates cytokines, which are a factor in the inflammatory actions responsible for protecting and healing tissue...when the system is in balance. Prolonged and elevated levels of adrenaline and norepinephrine could be a partial explanation for why those life-enhancing microbes become disease provoking instead.

Now let's turn our attention to the other part of the nervous system involved in the stress response, the HPA axis. The adrenal gland is at the end of this axis and releases cortisol, and more adrenaline, according to the demand interpreted by the hypothalamus. Cortisol has been nicknamed the stress hormone because of its major role in supporting the body in times of acute and prolonged stress. Beyond its stabilizing efforts during stressful periods, cortisol is a necessary hormone that supports all cellular function. It influences everything from fetal development to reproductive function, metabolism to immunity, inflammation, concentration, learning, memory and much more. Unfortunately, when it circulates in excessive amounts over prolonged periods, every cell suffers the effects. Cortisol is like sunbathing, just a little is needed to synthesize Vitamin D, but too much becomes a painful sunburn.

Researchers are still working to unravel the mysteries of the human body, including the brain, but there are some things we know to be true and others that are highly suspect when it comes to elevated cortisol and its damaging effects:

Circulatory — Cortisol constricts blood vessels, preferentially sending blood, and the nutrients and oxygen it carries, to certain organs and tissues and diminishing the supply to others. This prolonged blood vessel constriction causes high blood pressure and plaque build up. Prolonged blood vessel constriction contributes to many common medical conditions, including but not limited to erectile dysfunction, kidney disease, heart attacks, strokes, peripheral vascular disease and some diseases of the eyes. Chronic stress and its prolonged elevation in cortisol contribute to clot formation, which can be part of the pathology in diseases such as strokes and blood clots.

Renal/Urinary System — Cortisol works in the kidneys to help regulate the fluid and electrolyte balance critical to optimal cellular functioning. High levels of cortisol shift kidney function to retain sodium and water. This can alter the body's chemistry to a less balanced state compromising the function of every single cell. This fluid retention also contributes to high blood pressure.

Metabolism — Cortisol plays an important role in maintaining sugar levels for energy expenditures. In long-term stress, it pushes the liver to convert stored glycogen (energy) into usable glucose (sugar) thereby increasing the amount of sugar circulating in the body. It increases appetite and food cravings. Along with raising the blood sugar, cortisol decreases the pancreas' insulin production, interfering with the cells' ability to get the fuel they need to do their work. This in turn fosters feelings of fatigue and the onset of metabolic syndrome, obesity and diabetes. The unused sugar supply is stored as fat, mostly in the abdominal area. These fat cells contribute to the storage of ingested toxins, increased cholesterol levels and an increased circulatory demand on the heart.

Immune System — In healthy states and in acute stress, cortisol has strong anti-inflammatory properties and protects the body's tissues. Researchers are still trying to fully understand what happens during periods of chronic stress, but it's clear that cortisol is a dominant force and works largely through the nervous, immune and endocrine systems and the expression of genes. In chronic stress, cortisol becomes dysfunctional and detrimental. According their article, Chronic Stress, Cortisol Dysfunction and Pain, published in the journal *Physical Therapy*, Hannibal and Bishop inform us that cortisol becomes a strong inflammatory stimulus and is being implicated in many different psychological and physical diseases including over 200 autoimmune diseases, such as fragility, aging, various bowel issues, atherosclerotic diseases, Parkinson's disease, various types of dementia and depression. It also increases susceptibility to all viral and bacterial infections and the risk of cancer.

Endocrine System — Increased cortisol levels negatively affect every gland in the endocrine system contributing to erectile dysfunction, male and female fertility issues, menstrual irregularities, issues with metabolism, heat regulation, skin and digestive problems and much more.

Nervous System — Prolonged elevations in cortisol can interfere with many of the processes within the brain itself. It contributes to impaired cognitive ability, learning difficulties and memory problems. It negatively impacts cell growth and regeneration and the function of the "thinking" prefrontal cortex. But possibly the most far reaching problems associated with prolonged elevations in cortisol are the interference in nerve cell connections affecting structures of the primal brain. This interference decreases the size and alters the function of the hippocampus, which we remember as essential to emotional temperament, memories, learning and concentration. This then alters the balance of all hormones regulated by the HPA axis. Once this happens, the HPA axis holds the body in an even more sustained stress response creating greater potential for new onset of diseases and the worsening of existing disease. Additionally, severe stress suffered in early childhood, or repeated exposure to severe stress in adulthood, changes neuronal connections in the hippocampus, amygdala and prefrontal cortex, potentially exaggerating an individual's response to future perceived threats. Post-traumatic stress disorder (PTSD), depression and anxiety are among the diseases caused by changes in these neuronal connections and the subsequent changes in the circulating hormones and neurotransmitters regulated by the HPA axis. In this way, chronic stress becomes *a vicious circle of progressive deterioration*. There is no way to separate chronic stress from disease.

Epigenetics—The Impact of Environment on Genes

Based on the discussion of the brain, the stress response and the effects of excessive adrenaline and cortisol, it's not difficult to see how we can become uncomfortable, dis-eased and unhealthy. So what do our genes have to do with health and disease? In his book, *The Biology of Beliefs: Unleashing the Power of Consciousness, Matter and Miracles*, Dr. Bruce Lipton informs us that DNA is simply coded instructions telling cells how to build the proteins they need to do whatever job they do. Genes are smaller structures within the DNA that dictate the code building those proteins, but genes and DNA are not the sole determinants of health, aging and illness. Our genes, and the genes of our resident microbes, are tools the body uses to adapt and respond to the environment and changes in it. It's an interactive process by which the environment can change the behavior of genes—the behavior of a gene is known as gene expression. Thus, whatever is circulating in the blood constitutes the gene's environment and will affect how it behaves to either support health or foster unhealthy processes; this process is called epigenetics. In response to its environment, a gene directs a corresponding coded message into our DNA, which then builds proteins responsible for every minute structure and function in the body. Changes in the environment, dictate changes in gene expression, which alter the structure and function of cells to support health or disease… depending on the choices we have made. This becomes the cycle we formerly attributed to the genetic inheritance of diseases.

When you are happy and healthy, the balance of chemistry and

Spiral of Dis-ease

Fear is the basis for all negative thoughts, words, feelings and actions; it is the trigger unleashing the spiral of decline that becomes mental health problems and physical diseases.

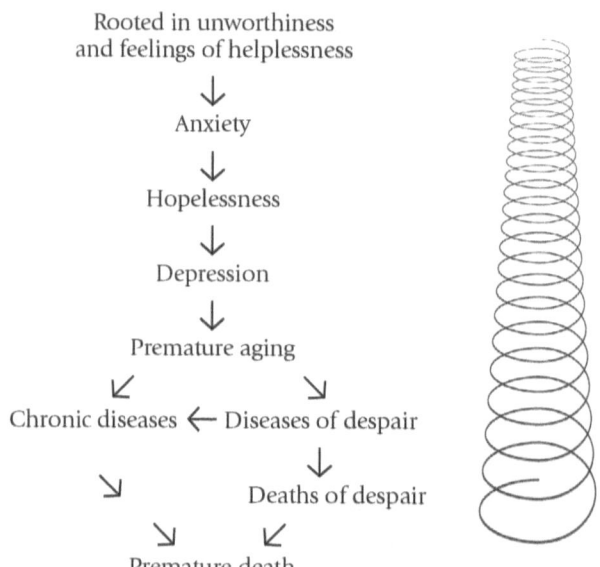

Rooted in unworthiness and feelings of helplessness
↓
Anxiety
↓
Hopelessness
↓
Depression
↓
Premature aging
↙   ↘
Chronic diseases ← Diseases of despair
↓
↙   Deaths of despair
↙   ↙
Premature death

Unresolved emotional pain sustains imbalance in the body, damaging physical structure and functions that become disease.

Disease can appear at any point along this spiral.

Healing the root causes of negative emotions shifts the energy to higher vibrations and back up the spiral in the direction of health and happiness.

hormones circulating in your blood activates genes to behave in a way that builds proteins for optimal functioning, maintaining healthy tissue and warding off diseases. Conversely, if you are chronically stressed, excess cortisol changes the balance of hormones and chemistry and increases the inflammatory factors circulating in the blood. This imbalance, increased inflammation, and the increase in circulating cortisol creates an unhealthy environment around the genes and causes them to express differently than they would in a less stressed environment. In response to this unhealthy environment, beneficial genes can be switched off while genes that contribute to disease can be switched on. This is the mechanism by which our inherited genetic potential can become the diseases that "run in our families."

According to epigenetics, there are no specific genes for high blood pressure, depression, diabetes or most other diseases; rather it's the unhealthy environment surrounding the genes that ultimately determine disease. In a detailed synthesis reported in the *Journal of Molecular Endocrinology*, Xiang Zhang and Shuk-Mei Ho's article titled, Epigenetics Meets Endocrinology, suggests that many diseases seem genetically determined and irreversible due to the probability that epigenetic adaptations [changes] take place during times of rapid development, specifically, *conception to the first few months of life, puberty and pregnancy*. And so, traumatic events and chronic stress during periods of rapid growth have life-long consequences. Studies that don't appear in a quick Internet search, reveal there is a tremendous amount of work being done to find answers for environmental links between health and disease. In another research article, Epigenetic Pathways in Human Disease, published in *EBioMedicine*, Argentieri et al. compiled numerous studies offering hope through science and the greater understanding of the relationship between stress and disease. They reported that there are factors in our internal and external environments which can cause genes to mutate and become cancers and other diseases. Some of these factors include radiation exposure (external) and oxidative stress from things like toxic diets and tobacco use (internal). Chronic stress and the effects of imbalance may also cause mutation. Diseases caused by mutations are difficult to manage and curing them comes under the realm of miracles, though they *are* possible. Fortunately for us, many diseases are caused by changes in gene expression rather than gene mutations. This means that most of our diseases are *reversible, or better yet, preventable*. Even some genetic mutations are preventable. But once gene expression has started adapting to the effects of chronic stress, shifting it back toward health and wellbeing requires concentrated effort…to change our minds, thoughts, feelings and behaviors.

CHAPTER 8

Why We Get The Diseases We Do

"Before you heal someone, ask him if he's willing to give up the things that made him sick." – Hippocrates

As discussed earlier, the amygdala's alert system is altered by the emotions of love and fear—threat to survival. The nervous systems respond by modifying the balance and flow of hormones in the body. Diseases are the end product of prolonged wear and tear caused by excess cortisol, imbalance and over-worked nervous systems. So, why do some of us get heart disease, some fibromyalgia, some cancer and some depression?

It's not uncommon for diseases to run in families. Diseases such as heart disease, diabetes, breast and colon cancers appear to have a strong family predisposition. We also know that people of certain ethnicities are more plagued by some health problems. As an example, African Americans appear to have a higher incidence of high blood pressure and diabetes than do Caucasians. The explanation for family inheritance is the effect of epigenetics and the environment on genetics.

On a deeper level, our bodies, DNA and genes are molecules made up of space and the energetic vibration of love and light behaving according to our belief-biased observations. This is the process by which we become the architects of our own biology. Whether or not we are consciously aware, we are the constant observer of ourselves. Whether we believe we live within in the Mind of God where the Word is made flesh, or we believe we live within a collaborative quantum field of endless possibilities, our observations are weighted by what we have come to believe as true about ourselves and our world. This weighted observation becomes the force directing the photons that shape the events and reality of our life.

As we observe our lives with our own unique of beliefs, thoughts and feelings, the photons of the quantum field—Mind of God—respond according to our will—the power of our mind. The Mind/Field reflects back to us what we create with our thoughts, words, feelings and actions. We continue to see the same thing and perceive life as essentially the same every day. In this way, we create a cycle of projecting and receiving the same image of reality we observed yesterday and the day before that. This is the mechanism reinforcing our belief in separation across all levels of our being and all planes of existence—collective consciousness. This is the repetitive cycle based on our entrenched past now taking hold as disease. This is why it's difficult to cure and why some diseases come back after they've been treated with traditional methods alone. The power of our minds directs our observations to hold the same, broken patterns in place, and this is how our past becomes the present and our future.

People in families and ethnic groups not only share genetic coding, they also share many of the same beliefs, coping patterns, emotional expressions, cultural understandings, traditions, life experiences and worldviews. These are handed down and reinforced to future generations through word of mouth, behavior modeling, parenting, teaching, expectation setting, norms and repetition. All this becomes the matrix of our perceived reality and the bias informing our observations—observations that change the behavior of photons. What we have in common with our ancestors' beliefs and view of reality, we stand a good chance of sharing in our genetic expression. This is not the same as thinking our DNA and genes are the sole cause of disease, though such a belief, with the power of the mind, could certainly increase the likelihood of developing a disease. The unique view and perceptions we have about ourselves determines which disease we will deal with during our lifetime.

In earlier times, the Earth was believed to be the center of the universe and it was known to be flat. Energy and matter were understood as two completely separate entities. These truths were ardently embraced until a few alternative thinkers used inspiration, observation and contemplation to challenge convention, sometimes at great peril to reputation and life. Eventually science proved them right. While science strives to find the precise mechanisms by which health is maintained or disease takes hold, we can use what scientists have learned to think outside the box of conventional medicine. We can blend what has been proven with what appears to be true and accurate based on the insights, understandings and experience of alternative healers to form greater understanding, support healthy choices and improve the quality of life for ourselves.

That said, this is a good time to begin including alternative perspectives regarding the origins of disease and their corresponding treatments, as we move beyond the limits of conventional thinking and what science and technology currently have the instruments to measure.

Chakras and Health

Chakras are energy centers that govern the flow of energy in, around and through the body. They connect our physical body to external energetic forces such as our personal and ancestral history. They extend through all layers (spiritual, mental, emotional, etheric and physical) weaving together internal and external energies to affect function and wellness at all levels. This is also how the energy of others affects us. If there is imbalance in a chakra's energy flow, there will be dis-ease in the organs related to it. Chakras are common concepts in Eastern and Western religious and esoteric philosophies. Most recognize the seven chakras on the body and may imply the presence of additional chakras in their teachings. This list details the areas of influence ascribed to each of them.

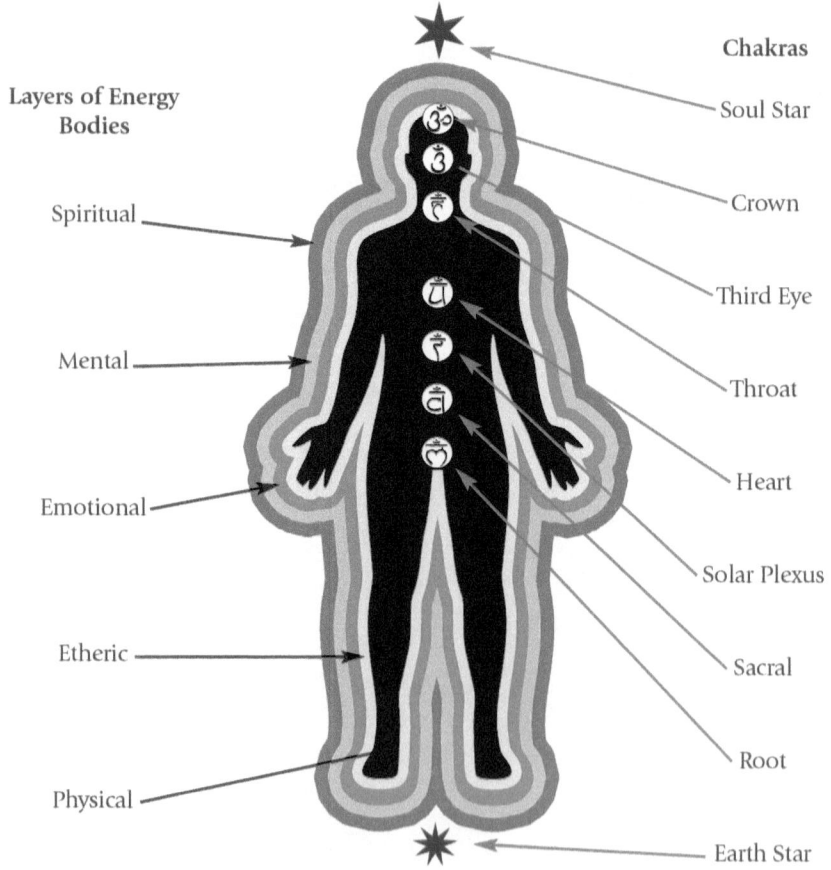

Soul Star Chakra (White)
~ Our higher consciousness and connection to Universal Intelligence
~ Access to higher vibrations commonly referred to as our Angels and Guides
~ Knows all there is to know about us, providing guidance along our true path

Crown Chakra (Violet/Purple)
~ Opening to the larger mind, allowing access to knowledge we otherwise could not know
~ Guides our consciousness to the higher vibrations of love and ascension
~ Affects the pineal gland, which facilitates sleep and wake cycles on the physical level and awakening consciousness on the spiritual level

Third Eye or Ajna Chakra (Indigo)
~ The higher heart; receiver of intuition and transmitter of thoughts
~ Center for the various forms of clear vision (clairvoyance, clairaudience, clairsentience)
~ Affects the organs and glands in the head, notably the hippocampus, amygdala, hypothalamus and pituitary, thereby influencing overall health

Throat Chakra (Blue)
~ Power of voice and power of silence; projects intention through the spoken word
~ Broadcasts your beliefs about what you think others think about you
~ Affects thyroid and parathyroid glands (metabolism) and health of cervical spine
~ Expresses creativity generated by the sacral chakra

Heart Chakra (Emerald Green)
~ The middle heart; receiver of Divine Love and transmitter of love
~ The space where intuition is received as heartfelt knowing
~ Clear heart energy is the key to the Kingdom of Heaven; be still and know that I AM God
~ Affects the heart, lungs, thymus gland and breasts, influencing health in the circulatory, respiratory and immune systems

Solar Plexus Chakra (Yellow)
~ The seat of the emotions
~ Influences the state of balance and health through the autonomic nervous system (ANS)
~ Affects the immune system and abdominal organs related to digestion and metabolism

Sacral Chakra (Orange)
~ The lower heart; center for creation; the place we give birth to our purpose
~ Home for our inner child
~ Affects the organs of reproduction, influencing desire, fertility and creation on physical, emotional, mental and spiritual levels

Root or Base Chakra (Red)
~ Center of stability and survival
~ Grounds us to earth for our journey to transformation
~ Affects kidneys (flow and balance), adrenal glands (fear/ANS), spine, (support) hips, knees and feet (flow, movement and courage)

Earth Star Chakra (Brown)
~ Like the Soul Star, this center is a channel bringing the nurturing energy of Mother Earth into our energy fields
~ Imagine this connection as roots of a tree drawing energy up through your feet, legs and spine to infuse you with vitality, stability and support from higher levels of vibration

Interpreting The Message of Disease

All disease has a common origin; the original sin of separation from Spirit, ourselves and each other. Separated from the Source of love, wisdom and power, we collectively decided and agreed that we were unworthy of the good life has to offer. Our individual life experiences morph the original sin into other beliefs of unloved/unlovable, unsafe, unimportant and not enough. Our faulty beliefs create the negative emotions common to many of us, including fear, anger, shame, hopelessness and despair. There are others, but the root of them all is fear—the inherent fear we are not worthy of love, peace and harmony. Though the origin of disease is common to us all, the many different disease possibilities are the result of our individual lifestyles, experiences, stories and family and cultural tendencies traveling back through generations. All these factors become the environment surrounding our genes and affecting our biology in ways that are specific to us as individuals.

As you consider the different examples being offered, please remember that each person is on a unique life path of self-healing and spiritual growth. What is going on spiritually, mentally, emotionally and physically is an individual experience and can't be understood with simplistic thinking and reasoning. What is being presented with these examples is a different way of looking at health issues than has been previously considered. It's a more empowered way of understanding what disease means to us.

If you have any of the conditions discussed in this section, or any conditions at all, you came by the thoughts, emotions and physical conditions naturally. They are part of your unique journey and though you may not be aware of it, this is the perfect life experience. It allows you opportunity to know and love yourself and to move forward toward greater possibilities. There is no place for shame, blame or guilt in mental and physical health problems. There are only opportunities for the healing powers of compassion, acceptance and love so you can discover the power you have to transform your life through surrender, forgiveness, release and remembering the Love and Light that you are.

If you know someone with one of these or other conditions, it's important to remember they're on their own journey to self-discovery. They may not interpret their situation from the same vantage point as you. Your love comes through respecting and honoring their unique journey and allowing them to live life as they choose…intervening in only rare and desperate situations. The most appropriate response to another person's choices is compassion.

The Emotional Foundation of Chronic Diseases

Obesity — Obesity is one of the major health concerns of our time. We have dismissed the causes to genetics, depression, medication side effects, poor food choices, character flaws and an imbalance between calorie intake and energy expenditure. While some of these factors may contribute to obesity, the problem did not start there nor will modifying those factors remove all the excess weight. The problem started long before the weight appeared. It started as an entrenched state of mind grounded in fear. The fear of being unsafe with no one we could count on and with this, we decided we were unlovable. In effect, our weight creates *a protective barrier to insulate us from the pain* caused by our beliefs and perceptions. If we look back over time, we may recognize experiences that confirmed the world as unsafe, unloving, and possibly cruel. Specific underlying events causing such beliefs are too numerous to list completely, but include domestic and sexual abuse, unsafe neighborhoods, bullying and neglectful or demeaning parenting. If food and beverages were used as rewards, apologies, consolation or bribes, this association with food can become a destructive and life-long habit as we continue to use food as proof we are loved or to ease our distress. In this pattern, fear, self-protection and insulation become the emotional matrix of obesity. This is the primal brain, early learning and cortisol holding our reality and our weight in place. Once the long-held beliefs and entrenched thoughts and feelings have turned the stress response to the sustained "on" position, diet and exercise alone will not take the weight off. Effective methods will require addressing the core belief of unworthiness and the perceptions of being unsafe, unloved and powerless.

Heart Disease — In esoteric philosophies and holistic practices, the heart is governed by the Heart Chakra and is the organ of love, compassion and hope. Those of us struggling with heart disease tend to have a sad demeanor and perspective on life. Our sadness is caused by fear and the underlying belief that we are unloved, unlovable and unworthy. Though we may be productive and active, some of our efforts may be based on the need to prove to ourselves and others that we are lovable and worthy. Despite the beauty, love and success we do have in our lives, we are never quite satisfied with such proof, allowing the undertones of sadness and fear to continue. Taking time to follow the "feelings of heartbreak" in all its forms, will allow us to release the beliefs of being unlovable and inadequate so we can let love and happiness penetrate and heal the heart.

Breast Cancer — Regardless of the anatomical parts we were born with, we all have feminine and masculine traits that contribute to our unique expression of self. Breast cancer is a disease mainly affecting women, but men are not exempt. In esoteric healing modalities, the breasts are the organs of nurturing and they are connected to the Heart Chakra. People who contract breast cancer may be very good at giving to, caring for and nurturing others, but rarely ask for or accept gratitude, caring or nurturing in return. Our relationships tend to be out of balance because the flow of energy is broadcast out from us, but it's not returning. Either the receiver is not reciprocating or we are blocking the loving energy others are trying to send. We judge our worthiness by how well we care for others and often consider self-care as selfish. We may get our hair done, have lunch with friends or take a bath with candles, but beneath the surface of such activities is the learned belief that we are unworthy of being loved and cared for, just for being our unique and wonderful selves.

While many chronic diseases and cancers are grounded in the belief of unworthiness and inadequacy, the way we cope, reason and think about ourselves and our world is what gives direction to malignant cells and processes. Breast cancer is different from lung or colon cancer because in this disease the coping pattern has to do with the lack of self-care and nurturing. The problem is we are not good at caring for ourselves in deep and meaningful ways that nurture our hearts and souls.

Being told you have cancer is one of the most monumental and breathtaking events to ever enter a person's reality. It's a major trauma. A cancer diagnosis rips us out of the stability of patterned thoughts and routines like nothing else. In dealing with the condition and all the tests and treatments required, we enter a world of self-focus in a way we never imagined possible before this point. In this cataclysmic state, all entrenched patterns of thoughts and reality that have held our world in place are suddenly and traumatically scattered across the landscape of our minds. It's not uncommon to withdraw to an inner space and ponder questions such as How did this happen? Why me? What does this mean? What now? And many others. As we emerge from this contemplative journey, it is possible to have a different understanding of self, our priorities and our relationship with the world around us. This change can be for the better. If we arrived at a place of self-knowing and self-love and we continue to live in this new understanding, we will be ever closer to beating the odds of cancer returning at some point in the future. In other cases, we may not beat the diagnosis, but we may come to the gift of surrender and a greater sense of peace, allowing us to embrace the beauty of life in the moment. Either way, we have changed our beliefs and shifted our perception of reality for the better.

Diseases of the Digestive System—Repressed Emotions

There are many conditions and diseases that affect the organs of the digestive system and the enteric nervous system...the gut brain. At this point science suspects, but has not proven definitively, that feelings we experience can be generated from memories held in the heart brain, gut brain or head brain. We know memory plays an important part in our experience of emotions and we also know memories are held in different body tissues. Gut reactions are our instinctual signaling system; the recognition of information being communicated from our internal and external mind through our gut brain to our head brain. In esoteric and holistic healing modalities, all organs of the digestive system are under the influence of the third energy system, the Solar Plexus Chakra, considered the seat of the emotions.

Diabetes — Diabetes is a condition caused by insufficient amounts of insulin (type 2) or a complete lack of insulin (type 1). Insulin is a hormone that moves glucose—sugar—into the cells so they have the fuel to do their jobs. Diabetes type 2 is the more common form and is thought to be the combined result of lifestyle, environment and genetics. Diabetes type 1 is an autoimmune disease in which the blood sugar is elevated because the pancreas is not making any insulin.

In esoteric healing, the pancreas is the organ of joy. In either type of diabetes, the emotional dilemma is a lack of joy or the belief that there is no reason to be joyful or possibility of experiencing it. Feelings of joylessness or chronic unhappiness can happen to anyone, but we can better understand how this state of mind contributes to diabetes by considering ethnic groups with higher incidence of this disease. These groups include African-American people, Native-American people and Asian-American people. While there is much cultural diversity between these ethnic groups, they share deeply rooted trauma across many generations. They belong to multitudes who have been displaced from ancestral homes because of slavery, terrorism, wars and disasters. In part or in whole, many have relinquished their cultural heritage as a necessary act of self-preservation that required blending into new cultures to mollify discrimination and abuse. The cultural traditions and beliefs that brought their ancestors a sense of belonging and joy have been stripped away and replaced with isolation, alienation and feelings of unworthiness, hopelessness and fear. Even as members of these ethnic groups are able to have meaningful and purposeful lives in a new country and culture, they still carry the energetic fragments of an unhappy existence and the molecular biology associated with the pain their ancestors experienced. The perceptions and beliefs shaped by their ancestral history are only a few generations away, thus they remain a significant influence in their mind/body connection as it continues to affect their health and happiness. Sadly, much of the isolation, alienation and fear are still a daily reality for the people of these ethnic groups because the society they currently live in is egregiously behind the curve in accepting and treating them as equal members of society. This perpetuates the long-held beliefs of separation, rejection, hopelessness and most of all, a life with little reason to be joyful.

Many people from these ethnic heritages also struggle with obesity and heart disease. Based on their ancestral histories and the emotional context of these conditions, it's not difficult to see how even if their ancestors were lean and healthy, the life they now live has shifted the environment of their genes to express the health concerns common to them. It's also not a leap to see how obesity, diabetes and high blood pressure are the triad for the ever more common condition known as Metabolic Syndrome. Going a step further, depression is a distinct possibility in the lives of marginalized ethnic groups and people of color, which also contributes to diabetes. This is the gut brain under the influence of chronic stress.

Anger — Anger is a huge emotional factor in many physical and emotional conditions so it bears its own discussion. It is probably the most pervasive of all emotions because it accompanies and obscures many others. Anger is an integral part of any grieving process. And for some of us, anger is a state of mind, a current running swiftly beneath the surface of our awareness. It's a warning signal that all is not well and change is needed. Anger is the feeling that can motivate us to action…for better or worse depending on the choices we make. It triggers the survival mechanism giving us the resources to puff up verbally or physically and creating a fierce exterior we hope will make others leave us alone.

Anger is easier to feel and deal with than other more frightening emotions hidden deeper in our psyche, feelings like violation, rejection, betrayal, hopelessness or desperation. Because these feelings are so painful, anger serves as a proxy while it creates a smoke screen hiding our true feelings from our awareness. Acknowledging anger is the first step to finding the deeper emotions that are keeping our survival mind and stress response in chronic overdrive.

Learning to recognize our anger as the smoldering volcano lurking beneath the surface of our pleasant demeanor and ready to erupt at any little thing is a vital tool for achieving health. For many of us, we *think* everything is just fine…until something happens. Things like traffic delays, spilled milk, cancelled dates or unexpected expenses will open a hidden valve and we explode. Often, our eruption is much greater than the situation warrants. When we can quickly recognize anger as it rushes to the surface, we can ask the question: Who am I angry with? If we're honest, we discover we are really angry with ourselves. This is the most beneficial and empowering realization because it puts us in control of changing whatever lives at the bottom of our smoldering eruptions.

Because of our ability to suppress our emotions including anger, we think we're managing just fine. When anger flares, we blame the situation or another person for how we feel. In reality, they are only the trigger. Often times, that person isn't aware of us, but even if they are interacting with us directly, what they said or did wasn't intended to hurt or anger us…we just took it personally. Even in situations when there is intent to slight or be hurtful, their behavior is about their own problem, but again…we took it personally. Either way, this external event is the trigger setting off our explosion. If we had a more loving and empowered perception of ourselves, minor disruptions and other people's weaker moments wouldn't register a blip on the screen of our emotional wellbeing. Learning to recognize anger, find the place where it hides and the reasons for it will help us become more calm, clear and able to heal our deeper pain.

Cirrhosis — This condition is described as scarring of the liver. As it progresses, the scarred and non-functional area becomes greater than the working portion to the extent it can no longer perform effectively or repair itself. The liver has several important jobs, but the main function is detoxification. It continually filters the blood for the entire body. In addition, everything we swallow moves through our stomach and intestines to be broken down into fuel and nutrients the body can use. These very fine compounds then pass into the portal circulation, which flows directly to the liver so it can remove the toxins and harmful chemicals we put in our mouths. Dealing with excessive amounts of toxins and chemicals strains the liver's ability to do its work. Viruses that cause hepatitis, chronic alcohol ingestion and fatty liver disease attributed to obesity are also damaging to the liver. And, the stress response diminishes the liver's ability to heal itself.

In esoteric healing, the liver is the organ of anger (detoxifying). Unresolved anger is detrimental to our physical, emotional and mental wellbeing. Whether suppressed, acknowledged or demonstrated through ballistic behavior, unresolved anger perpetuates destructive behaviors. Overeating, drinking to excess or risky behaviors that increase the likelihood of contracting some form of hepatitis are just three ways anger can impact the liver. These health problems can also be a pre-condition contributing to liver cancer.

Addictions — Since overeating, excessive drinking and risky and habitual behaviors are all forms of addiction, this is a good place to talk about them. Addictions are not associated with any one organ. They are based on fear; an extreme expression of being unsafe, unimportant and powerless in the world. Those of us who struggle with addictions may be aware of other emotions such as anger, anxiety, despair, sadness or hopelessness, but beneath all of these is fear.

The origin of all addictions is our wounded child. The inner child is our source of innocence, joy, curiosity and unconditional love. S/He is also the wise one who knows our deepest pain and is keeping our attention riveted on healing it. As we reach for a cigarette, or some other form of habitual behavior, we are attempting to silence the restlessness and distress caused by the wounded child constantly calling out for attention and love. The core belief in addictions is that we are not important or powerful enough to make a difference in our lives.

We have discussed how we came to these faulty beliefs and the importance of the inner child in earlier sections, so we can appreciate that this perception of ourselves and the way we cope with the resulting distress is a natural consequence of our lives to this point. Many of us experienced something in our early lives that could be identified as an Adverse Childhood Experience (ACE); for some of us the event(s) was more traumatic than it was for others. No matter what happened or how long it went on, our inner child only remembers that s/he didn't have the power to fix the problem and this faulty perception is following us into adulthood. The child needs to be recognized, protected and loved.

To feel safe, we learned long ago to "keep ourselves in control" as not to bring unfavorable or painful attention to ourselves. Controlling our feelings of distress become more difficult as the wounded child screams louder for the recognition and help s/he needs. Until we heal our inner child, s/he is the one calling the shots in almost every aspect of our lives. The demands come in messages we have long ago muted, so now we just feel jittery, restless, anxious or uncomfortable. To soothe our increasing discomfort, we light a cigarette, have another glass of wine, smoke another joint, buy another dress, have sex with a stranger, snort or shoot some chemical…the list of addictions is very long. Two other common forms of addiction are more difficult to identify as such. One is our addiction to our story where we continually replay the reasons we feel justified in our feelings or behavior. Whether repeating the litany of symptoms our diseases cause us or recounting the misery of our lives, we cling to the story like others pick up a cigarette or drink. The other less recognizable form is the addiction to distraction; of keeping ourselves so very busy with projects, commitments or diversions that we can "honestly" say, we have no time for ourselves and therefore, no time to get to the bottom of our obvious distress in life. But no matter which addictions we employ, the need to quiet our distress becomes more compelling as time goes on. Our individual addictions are unique to our own experiences and personalities, but make no mistake, they are symptoms of the inner child's fear that s/he is unsafe, powerless and helpless in her/his own skin and in the world.

Addictions are a vicious, cyclical trap of being afraid, feeling uncomfortable, quieting the discomfort, feeling at ease for a short while and then repeating as the effects of the balm wears off. Replacing the faulty belief at the core of our misperception is essential. Taking the time to find the inner child and assure them in effective ways that they are safe and important is a vital and ongoing effort. As we work through the pain and mistaken beliefs our inner child took on, we can replace the erroneous perceptions causing our own destructive behavior. With devotion and dedication, we can nurture and love our inner child into a happy, capable and loving adult. This individual effort is a great accelerator we can use in conjunction with the expertise of support groups and recovery programs. Breaking out of this trap is not easy but it can be done with love and support. 12-step programs offer recognition, acceptance and support that are instrumental in acknowledging a Higher Power whose Presence will aid us in taking control of our lives.

Diseases of the Alimentary Canal

The alimentary canal is the tube running from the mouth to the anus. It's the processing channel for everything going into the mouth. In esoteric circles, it is within the governance of the Solar Plexus Chakra...the seat of emotions. Problems occurring along this entire tract have their origin in the question, "What's eating you?" Erosions and eruptions in the mucous membranes of the mouth and lips can result from mechanical or microbial causes, such as acidic food or viruses, but the emotional precursor allowing this invasion to occur is anger. Anger causes eruptions. An example of this process can be seen in the chancre sores and herpes simplex outbreaks which occur more frequently in people who have a pre-existing history of those conditions. People prone to chancre sores or who have the simplex virus in their bodies usually experience outbreaks when they become more stressed. As discussed earlier, stress compromises the immune system and interferes with the protective and healing mechanisms of the body, allowing for such outbreaks.

Heartburn, indigestion, esophageal reflux and gastric ulcers have anatomical, mechanical and chemical causes. Conditions like hiatal hernias and incompetent stomach valves as well as irritating foods, alcohol and drugs can cause or aggravate the burning sensation and erosions attributed to these problems. They can also be caused or aggravated by the stress response and the resulting inflammatory actions that damage the lining of the esophagus, stomach and intestines. This happens because the stress response is held in chronic "on" position by the underlying emotion of fear and the gripping feeling that something is not right in our world...it's "eating at you." Life-long struggles with these physical and emotional conditions can give way to gastric and esophageal cancers.

Irritable Bowel Syndrome — IBS is an intestinal condition that can cause constipation, diarrhea, abdominal pain, bloating and gas. Medical science recognizes a strong emotional component associated with outbreaks. Louise Hay and Mona Lisa Schultz, M.D. explain the relationship between anger and constipation in *All Is Well: Heal Your Body with Medicine, Affirmations and Intuition*. They link negative emotions to constipation as an act of "holding onto the past" by repeating negative stories in order to justify clinging to feelings of anger, resentment, jealousy and fear. It's about holding onto old baggage. For those of us who bottle up our feelings, diarrhea is the body's way of blowing out anger and resentment. According to Hay and Schultz, it signals our desire to run away, rather than deal with issues causing our pain.

People who suffer with IBS can exhibit either constipation or diarrhea or move back and forth between the two. As with many other afflictions, the origins of this disease are the unresolved emotions held over from adverse childhood events and the subsequent inflammatory effects of chronic stress on the intestines specifically.

Leaky Gut Syndrome — Leaky gut syndrome is a condition only recently coming into the spotlight of medical attention and research. Because scientists are still working on the biological mechanisms of this disease, tests to confirm a diagnosis and treatment protocols remain elusive. This makes it difficult to identify and treat, even when suspected. However, ongoing research indicates this is an emerging and important problem worthy of our attention. As we consider this syndrome, it's important to remember the gut functions to provide energy for every cell, protects our internal environment from detrimental toxins and microbes and is the gut brain that makes neurotransmitters which have a major impact on the HPA axis and the balance overseeing our health.

Leaky gut is a condition that appears when the protective "tight junctions" between the cells lining the intestinal walls lose their ability to keep larger molecules in the gut where they belong. The gut is where food is broken down into usable compounds and chemicals and harmful microbes can be detoxified or eliminated according to the wisdom of biological structure and function. When compromised by an overload of toxic chemicals or inflammation and decreased blood flow caused by cortisol and chronic stress, these protective and functional tight junctions become loose and the space between the cells becomes wider. As the tight junctions are compromised, harmful bacteria, viruses, chemicals and food particles too large and complex to be used for fuel and nutrition pass through the wider spaces into the blood stream where there is no mechanism to utilize or eliminate them properly. Since none of those compounds or microbes belongs in the circulating blood stream, the immune system identifies them as foreign bodies and launches an attack against them. This innate defensive mechanism creates an inflammatory response and the body develops antibodies as part of the natural immune response. As the body works to manage this continuous stream of orally introduced invaders leaking out through the gut wall, the immune system continues to ramp up its protective process thereby creating more inflammation throughout the body. Leaky gut syndrome is being implicated with an increasing number of autoimmune diseases including Alzheimer's disease, lupus, multiple sclerosis, diabetes type 1, heart disease, Hashimoto's thyroiditis, premature aging, osteoporosis, rheumatoid arthritis, Crohn's disease and cancer to name just a few.

Leaky gut syndrome is the quintessential "What's eating you" condition caused by a sustained inflammatory response. It's the result of prolonged stress and immune responses triggered by unresolved emotional states. It also has physiological origins which are worth paying attention to given their association with a growing number of autoimmune diseases. It's caused by what we put in our mouths on a regular basis, including alcohol, sugar, molds associated with stored grains, chemical and food additives, highly refined carbohydrate and processed foods, antibiotics and various other prescription medicines including non-steroidal anti-inflammatory drugs such as ibuprofen and naproxen. Dairy and grain products have been implicated as well. Harmful microbes such as bacteria, viruses and parasites that slip in with improperly prepared food can damage the intestinal wall. Another significant cause of damage to the tight junctions is the proliferation of harmful bacteria and fungi that occurs when toxins and stress compromise the gut's balance of beneficial and protective microbial residents.

When we consider that all things have molecular and atomic make up, we might also ponder how things manufactured in laboratories and introduced into our food supply might affect the delicate balance of our own biology. Herbicides, pesticides, genetically modified foods and heavy metal contamination should be suspect. Since chemicals are a major causative factor, we might consider the toxic petroleum-based plastic bottles, wrappers and food containers that such things are stored in for extended periods. These chemicals can leach into the food and liquid they contain. The safety of all chemicals continues to be contentiously debated, so we must each decide for ourselves how much exposure is acceptable.

The list of damaging agents is large, but once the tight junctions are damaged, they are difficult to repair and there are no medicines to treat it. Once leaky gut develops, the problems it causes are many. Food intolerances and sensitivities have their beginning in leaky gut syndrome. As larger food particles leak through to the blood stream, the immune-initiated inflammatory response causes food intolerances and uncomfortable symptoms when we eat them. Some of those symptoms include diarrhea, nausea, pain, headaches and feeling yucky. This inflammatory response is also a contributor to the inappropriate up-regulation of immune factors that result in the *immune system's attack on healthy tissue*. This is the underlying cause of autoimmune diseases.

Avoiding or healing leaky gut syndrome may be one of the most important health priorities of our time. It will require a combined and integrated approach of healing emotional trauma and chronic stress and eliminating as many of the ingested sources of toxicity and immune-initiated reactions as is possible, as we attempt to restore the healthy balance of our gut microbiome. Healing our natural environment as we heal our minds and bodies may also have major implications for our world and for future generations.

Autoimmune Diseases — These are caused by an overactive or dysregulated immune system. The immune system is responsible for keeping us healthy through complex processes including identification, inflammation, and elimination. It maintains the protective linings of several organs including the stomach, intestines and kidneys, rids the body of mutated and cancerous cells, eliminates harmful microbes and participates in healing strained tissues and broken bones. In autoimmune diseases, the protective immune system begins attacking healthy tissue. Researchers are not certain why, after offending infectious agents and toxins that trigger the immune response have been eliminated, the inflammatory response remains elevated to such an extent that it destroys tissue in other body systems.

If leaky gut is the common pathway for autoimmune diseases, why do some people get multiple sclerosis, some get dementia and others get thyroiditis? The answer has to do with the individual's emotional makeup and their perceptions about life.

Thyroiditis — The thyroid gland is governed by the Throat Chakra, which influences how we put ourselves out in the world; how we speak our truth and purpose. Emotional dilemmas in thyroiditis are related to the perception that we are not recognized, valued or taken seriously. Speaking our truth, living our purpose, standing up for ourselves and taking our power back is part of the journey to wellness. This is part of a combined approach that includes being mindful of what we ingest to avoid inflammation, as well as seeking medical help.

Dementia — Dementia has its emotional roots in fear and anger. It's a form of giving up as we perceive a world we can't deal with and we don't want to participate any more. It's effectively withdrawing from the chaos and pain we believe is controlling our lives. People with long-standing depression, a condition also rooted in anger and hopelessness, are at more risk for developing dementia. Diet, exercise and social engagement are important factors for preventing and slowing the progression of some forms of dementia. Prevention is preferable to management as there are no treatments to reverse dementia. Recognizing fear and anger and releasing the stories of hopelessness and resentment allow us feel safe, connected and loved. As we do this, we can appreciate that we have the power to make a difference in our lives.

Multiple sclerosis — This is a progressive disease that damages nerve cells. As it progresses, it diminishes the speed of nerve impulses governing many bodily functions, especially muscle control. Profound disabilities affect walking, standing and caring for oneself. The emotional context of this condition is fear, especially the need to manage this feeling in a way that others will not recognize it. According to Louise Hay and Mona Lisa Schultz, M.D, we can become "excessively forceful, stubborn or hardhearted." As an autoimmune disease, food is an important factor. Healing the source of our fear, lack of trust and vulnerability, and remembering that the source of our power resides within us and our connection to God, is a combined approach that will support healing and improve our quality of life.

~~~

The more researchers learn about the body, the more the underlying processes of common diseases are being linked to dysregulated inflammatory responses and their impact on human tissues. The more they know about the molecular damage, the more they can see the role stress and inflammation play in the early stages of disease. Even as an increasing number of medical conditions move into the category of autoimmune disease, it will take science time to *prove the causal link* between inflammation and disease in such a way that conventional medicine, education and popular thinking can be shifted to prioritize lifestyle alterations aimed at prevention above symptom management. In the meantime, we can use what is known to move forward with our own wellness programs.

Regardless of the organ or system affected by an inappropriate immune response, all autoimmune diseases share some commonalities. On the physical level, autoimmune diseases are caused by a dysregulated or overactive immune system that is attacking the body's own healthy tissues as if they were foreign invaders. This shared physical pathway also suggests the nature of the emotional dilemma holding chronic stress in place and adds another dimension to the "What's eating you" associated with all gut problems. No matter what autoimmune disease we contract or the coping patterns we have adopted to survive in our world, the underlying belief is that we aren't good enough as we are. We think we must maintain rigid control and behave in some very specific way in order to be deserving of love, respect and belonging. We have spent our lives struggling to be something we were never intended to be and we became more inauthentic, stiff and untrusting. Since we've been acting in the same manner for years, chances are good that we long ago dismissed the internal warning system screaming, "This isn't me!" On an esoteric level, the immune system is doing its best to rid the body of the foreign invader it doesn't recognize as the true you. Since we have devoted our lives acting in a way that is out of synch with our true selves, it's reasonable to imagine the immune system is having trouble recognizing us as belonging in our own skin. Healing the faulty beliefs and behavior patterns handed down from parent to child for generations can restore the "real me" that our immune systems can recognize as belonging. Healing requires loving yourself, embracing what makes you happy and living life as the unique and beautiful being you are.

Fibromyalgia — Fibromyalgia is a chronic and debilitating disease that affects many body systems. It has a myriad of symptoms including muscle pain, fatigue, memory and concentration problems, bladder and bowel irritability, insomnia or non-restful sleep, anxiety and depression. It is not classified as an autoimmune disease though it is linked to leaky gut syndrome, stress, infective agents and trauma. More women than men suffer with this condition and there is a tendency for it to run in families. The emotional context of fibromyalgia is self-rejection grounded in the beliefs of unworthiness and being unimportant. People who suffer with fibromyalgia may be those who gave up on their own dreams, aspirations and heart-felt purpose so they could become what others thought they should be. This includes accomplished people who gave up rewarding careers to support spouses or care for families because they believed it was expected, according to traditional thought paradigms or cultural standards. They may have felt pressured into this decision by well-intentioned family and friends. People who altered the pursuit of their dreams because of family tragedy, unexpected pregnancy, financial considerations or other life-changing events are also at risk for developing fibromyalgia.

To heal the emotional root of fibromyalgia, we need to follow the thread of self-rejection to the place where we didn't feel worthy or important enough to stand up for ourselves and our dreams. We allowed others to influence our choices and in so doing we muted the voice of our inner wisdom and the heart's desire that guides us on our true path. We rejected our own desires and quest for meaning and replaced them with someone else's. Healing fibromyalgia means reconnecting with our inner wisdom and locating the place where we hold unworthiness as the faulty belief. As we release this error message, we are able to reclaim our dreams, step into our power and pursue the things that make our hearts sing and bring us joy and health.

Osteoporosis and Osteoarthritis — These are conditions affecting bones and joints. On the physical side, they have many causes or risk factors including diet, anatomy, wear and tear, genetics and age. Our bones and joints are about strength, support and flexibility. Diseases or conditions affecting bones and joints are about feelings of being alone, unsupported and unable to be flexible on our journey through life. Just like rusty gears, we are grinding to a halt. Healing our beliefs and perceptions about being loved, cared for and supported, and trusting ourselves and God as our source of support, strength and flexibility are the roads to preventing and healing our bone and joint problems.

Stress Incontinence and Overactive Bladder — These problems result in urine leaking from the bladder as an "accident" caused by pressure (coughing, sneezing, laughing, lifting weight) or not being able to hold urine long enough to get to the toilet. These conditions affect many more women than men. Situations such as obesity or pregnancies can weaken pelvic floor muscles and certain foods and drinks can exacerbate the occurrence and severity of accidents. Research suggests that women who were spanked as children are much more likely to develop these conditions than those who were not. This association makes it easier to see the role of emotions. According to Louise Hay and Dr. Schultz, the emotional context of incontinence is that of "being so pissed off we can't hold it." Coming to terms with controlled or suppressed anger and applying forgiveness with a greater understanding of ourselves and those involved can go a long way in literally taking the pressure off.

Post-traumatic stress disorder — PTSD is a mental health concern that is life altering and can be life threatening. It is such a life-disrupting problem that we really can't discuss it properly here, but I feel it's too prevalent and important to leave out. PTSD can affect anyone who has experienced or witnessed events so horrific that they are difficult to describe in words and nearly impossible to move beyond. It affects people with little discrimination for age, gender and socio-economic status. This includes children who have witnessed domestic violence and sexual assault or are victims themselves, people of any age who have witnessed or experienced the inhumanity and atrocities of social injustice and war, survivors of natural disasters, victims of violent crimes, rape and human trafficking and survivors of mass shootings. The list is long. Traumatic memories, unresolved emotional pain and chronic stress dictate health and quality-of-life issues that are life long. PTSD can present in many different ways including insomnia, anxiety, depression, headaches, flashbacks, addiction, memory and concentration issues, accelerated aging and more as the unresolved emotional pain continues to gnaw at the physical body. Those of us who suffer with PTSD have often lost hope and trust to the extent that we alienate family and don't seek the help we need, if such help is even available. We may become homeless as an expression of the depths of our despair.

The emotional basis of PTSD is abandonment and hopelessness. Shame, blame and guilt can also be present. For some, early childhood trauma, beliefs and coping patterns set the stage for how we will be affected by traumatic events that come later in adulthood. Later trauma then serves as reinforcement for the negative beliefs and perceptions we have long held. If the emotional pain and hopelessness become too severe, some of us may think suicide is the only way out of the hell we are living. Dealing with this devastating pain means dealing with the experiences that caused the trauma and the learned beliefs of abandonment and powerlessness. PTSD is a complex mental health problem requiring intense compassion, support and professional help. Early recognition, acceptance, effective treatment, forgiveness and compassion are important components of healing necessary to return to the peace that accompanies trust, connection, hope and love.

The increasing numbers of people suffering with PTSD tells a chilling story about the world we live in. Many of the events triggering PTSD have become too common in today's society, including wars, domestic abuse, community violence, inequality, injustice and hate. There is little hope for those suffering with PTSD if they believe the situations that created their pain are still an ever-present possibility and that they are helpless to prevent these situations from happening again, to themselves or to others.

Depression — This is a mental health disorder affecting a growing number from all age groups and an estimated 265 million people worldwide. In recent decades, an imbalance in brain chemistry was thought to be the cause of chronic depression. The chemical imbalance link lifted depression out of the "human failing" category to its full recognition as a disease requiring treatment. This ideological shift opened the door for many people to come out from the shadows of shame and get the help they needed. The medications now available to treat depression work on the hormones and neurotransmitters in the brain and they can offer relief. Electrical Pulsation is also being used with some success. While these treatments are necessary to lift people from their despair, they do not cure the problem at its origin. They don't change the behavior of the gut brain and the neurotransmitters signaling the head brain, neither do they alter the stress response activated by negative and unresolved emotions of sadness, helplessness and hopelessness.

Sigmund Freud defined depression as "anger turned inward." This explanation fell into disfavor as the field of psychological sciences advanced. However, if we look at what we know about anger and the suppression of emotions, it could be that suppressed anger devolving into hopelessness and despair really does have a major role in depression. We naturally experience anger when we feel our lives are not going well. Whether we suffer from health issues, injustice, inadequate financial resources or the pain of feeling under-appreciated, unloved or unsafe, we can become angry about our situation. When we feel helpless to make a difference in the things that really bother us, we often bury our anger. We feel there is no solution, so why bother trying.

Depression, treated or not, is an expression of pain. All pain is the body's way of saying there's a problem that needs attention. The appropriate attention is to search for the original cause and make meaningful changes to resolve it. More and more of us feel trapped in our lives, thinking we are helpless and hopeless to make a difference. We suppress our anger with increasing levels of depression, and frequently with addictions to further numb the pain. As depression worsens, prescription medication may be needed to lift the darkness enough that we have the emotional and physical energy needed to get through our day. These treatments, while necessary, do not cure depression nor do they fix the beliefs that brought us to this place of hopelessness. These treatments are the bridge allowing us to explore necessary changes that will lead us back to happiness. If the origins of anger, sadness and hopelessness are not addressed appropriately, depression can worsen, requiring changes in prescribed therapies.

Suicide — Suicide is a disastrous exit strategy for a person who is dealing with incapacitating despair. In these situations, we have given up all hope of finding a way out of our situation. We believe we have no power to make a difference in our lives…we just want out. Approximately 800,000 people die by suicide annually. *It's the second leading cause of death in people ages 15-29*. When we look at this alarming age-related statistic, we need to ask, "What is going on here?"

There are "black box warnings" on most anti-depressant medications stating that this medicine could cause worsening depression and suicide in children and young adults. Why is this? No proven explanation has been offered. But, what if we asked a different question? What caused a child, teen or young adult to become so depressed that suicide became their only answer? Why are they in such a desperate state when they should be the most carefree and adventurous of any time in their lives? Maybe it's a state of extreme imbalance created by their innate knowing that life should be peaceful, harmonious and loving juxtaposed to their reality of conflict, abuse, disregard or despair. Situations that can contribute to their depressing situations include parental depression, domestic violence, unsafe neighborhoods, isolation, bullying, school shootings, world affairs, climate change, disabling student debt compounded by lack of meaningful opportunities, and so on. In a life overwhelmed with one or more factors such as these, this age group understandably feels angry and hopeless. Society is leveraged so they have little control over their environment and at least at this point, no possibility of fixing the problems affecting their lives and the world around them. When we, the responsible adults in their lives, do nothing but fret and take them to a professional for a pill, we are saying to them, "You are the sick one that needs help." If we don't help them uncover the cause of their anger and hopelessness, listen to the real source of their pain, and then actually work with them to make appropriate changes in a positive direction that has meaning for them, we are, in effect, giving them very little hope and too few options.

But, It's Not Just Young People

Addictions, depression and suicides, death from unintentional overdose and PTSD are on the rise in our society. They are grim health concerns affecting more and more of our brothers and sisters of all ages. The cost of this burden adds up to billions of dollars in economic loss annually. Beyond financial considerations, the loss of human potential is staggering and incalculable, not just in death but also its impact on the living. As discussed, all these diseases have their roots in unresolved emotional distress making them a very personal dilemma. It will require a great deal of devotion to self in order to overcome the struggles that contribute to depression, addictions and suicide. Beyond the individual impact, these tragic human losses are the canaries in the coalmine of society. The escalating numbers of people suffering with these diseases are flashing neon signs for all of us. People experiencing the kind of anger, betrayal, abandonment and hopelessness that bring them to this point are living in a society they deem unsafe, unjust and unloving. These beliefs and the conditions perpetrated by them have been going on for long enough that there are now generations who share the patterns and diseases that hopelessness conveys. As nothing changes for the better, the patterns deepen and the hole that is being dug for many of our brothers and sisters is becoming too deep for them to extract themselves…without help from the rest of us.

Addictions, depression, suicides and PTSD are also society's diseases. Society's diseases are caused by fear, greed, hate, isolation, war and corruption which are all misuses of God's Love and Power. As individuals, we must work diligently to heal and love ourselves so we can effectively contribute to changes needed in a world where too many are struggling under burdens created by the actions of others. We are all connected as One and together we must fix the conditions that are creating our collective mental, emotional and physical pain and suffering.

~~~

The diseases presented in this section are a small sampling of common conditions afflicting too many people. The discussion of the underlying beliefs and emotional distress associated with these diseases are not intended to be absolutes in a one-size-fits-all approach. Because we are each unique, these examples are best viewed as a starting point to ponder the underlying spiritual, mental and emotions discomfort that in time became physical and mental conditions. It's the deeply hidden beliefs, the resulting perceptions and unresolved negative emotions that allow diseases to take hold in the physical body. Clinging to entrenched beliefs make it difficult to prevent, resolve or even manage diseases effectively.

The information presented is an integration of insights from alternative philosophies and medical intuitives. This adds a valuable dimension to scientific discoveries even as science has not yet been able to delineate the exact mechanisms of the mind/body connection. Both holistic practitioners and conventional medical practitioners are working to promote health and heal disease. In truth, they are working the same problems from different directions. In time, the insights of one will dovetail into the proofs of the other and we all will benefit from a more complete understanding of health and disease. In the meantime, we can use both medical science and the wisdom of intuitive healers to stay healthy and reclaim our sense of wellbeing.

Coming to the understanding that pain and disease start as a spiritual, mental and emotional dilemma in no way suggests you do not need to seek medical assistance to manage diseases once they occur, or even when you suspect there may be a problem. A more broad understanding of the origins of disease is neither a suggestion nor a recommendation to self-diagnose and self-treat disease. Once disease takes hold in the physical body, the downhill spiral becomes steeper and more debilitating if not managed properly. It requires the expertise of medical practitioners who are educated, trained and licensed to provide that level of expert care. The more broad understanding of disease and its hidden origin means you have more tools to enhance the necessary medical treatment ordered by your medical practitioners. They want you to heal, feel better and not need those medicines any more. After all, that is why they went to school…to help people.

That said, a holistic approach can only be accomplished through individual introspection and effort. No one can know you better than you can know yourself. No one can feel your emotions the way you do. No one can hear the call of your heart or feel your gut reaction. No one will react to life the way you do. Because of your uniqueness, you may bear witness to the same dilemma as two or three hundred other people, but the meaning it has for you and the way your respond to it is all about you and who you are. Ultimately, you are mental. It is your mind that will process the messages of your emotions, the signals of your physical body and the thoughts that come into your awareness. It is your powerful and magnificent mind in eternal connection with your Divine Spark and the Mind of God that will bring you together in balance, health and wellbeing.

CHAPTER 9

Healing Is a Life Changing Experience

"We cannot solve our problems with the same thinking we used when we created them." – Albert Einstein

The key to healing is the *experience* of being healed. Self-help books, seminars and retreats plant seeds that will germinate in time though they rarely produce the major life shift we were looking for when we made the purchase. Even if the book made complete sense or the retreat experience felt so illuminating and life altering, it's difficult to sustain the magic as you return to life's usual routines. This is because your usual routines are entrenched in your subconscious mind. You take them with you wherever you go. A great experience, even if it embodies exactly how you want your life to be going forward, is too short-lived to change your long held beliefs and perceptions, and *to change the neuronal connections programmed into your brain*. Only changing your beliefs and perceptions and *how you live and experience yourself differently* will alter the connections in your brain and shift your reality to one that is healthier and happier.

Tools for Healing Spirit, Mind and Body

Ultimately, healing means learning to love yourself. The purpose of this three-dimensional life experience is to find love, happiness and meaning. For most of us, it has been an elusive and somewhat frustrating journey. Moving onto an easier path is a matter of finding the most effective tools and using them consistently in order to create a better life experience. This may feel like a mid-life career change but, as with most well thought out life changes, it will produce great benefits a short way down the road.

These tools are not new or even difficult. They've been offered as part of "the way" by wisdom teachers, philosophers, religious leaders and many in the helping professions. It is up to each one of us to decide how we will use them to enrich our lives.

MINDFULNESS is a state of mind where you are fully present to yourself. It's an experience of living in the holy moment of now, where the ruminations of the past and future do not occupy space in your mind. You do this by being intentional and paying attention to whatever you are doing in the moment. You focus on the task as if it was the only thing in the world. This can be done while washing dishes, driving a car, eating a meal, bathing a child, listening to a friend or making love...anything. Being present with yourself allows you to be aware of the thoughts as they pop into your mind. As you are aware of them, you can engage them in a way that gives you a better understanding of yourself. You can also do this with emotions and bodily sensations...focusing on one at a time. The more you practice being present in the now, the more you become aware of the feelings and thought patterns pulling you off course, and the more opportunity you have to self-correct for happier thoughts and a happier life. In mindfulness, you open space in the congestion of your mind and you are present to receive the magic trying to find its way to you.

RENUNCIATION is a rather archaic concept that has several meanings; the rejection of creeds, beliefs or rights; self-denial of comfort and abandonment of the pursuit of happiness. The Old Testament makes several references to renunciation that appear to support the notion of shame for bad behavior such as idol worship and include the perception of a judgmental God. I believe these more common understandings of renunciation have caused us to distance ourselves from the benefits we could receive from the practice if we understood the intent better.

First, we can't reject a belief if we have no knowledge of it. We can reject injustice or prejudice, but only to the extent we are aware that they exist. We can't reject our beliefs in unworthiness and inadequacy if we're not aware we harbor them deep inside. The true spirit of renunciation is found in relinquishing the pursuit of false idols such as wealth, fame, addictions, distractions and material possessions, so we have the time and attention to pursue the true purpose of life, which is learning to love ourselves as God loves us.

For our purpose here, renunciation is the practice of self-denial that comes in the form of not partaking in excesses and the various ways we attempt to comfort ourselves and quiet the restlessness or distress we feel. These excesses and distractions are different for each one of us, but they're easy to identify. When you feel distressed and attempt to soothe yourself by doing something you know you probably shouldn't do—behaviors like purchase, pursue, eat or drink—you are in effect worshipping a false idol. From the story of God's discussion with Cain in Genesis 4, the things that quiet your dis-ease are "sin's desire for you" and in relenting, you are giving them power over you. When you deny yourself the comfort of this temporary balm, you will feel even more distress rising up inside. In this moment, you can use your mindfulness to ask, "What am I feeling?" and "Why do I feel this way?" This was the intention of renunciation, to refocus priorities and get down to the truth of who you are and what's important.

In my own life, I experience daily opportunities to step away from habitual comfort-seeking behavior and dig deeper into the patterns cluttering my life. Renunciation has nothing to do with shame, guilt or punishment. It's the practice of understanding what makes us tick so we can rise above the issues jerking us around.

DEVOTION is a heart-felt sense of commitment. Loving yourself and being whole require self-knowing and self-appreciation that can only happen with a committed devotion to yourself. Just as you give all of your heart, mind and soul to a new relationship, a new baby or a purpose that's precious to you, this is the degree of devotion you must have for discovering the true you and learning to love yourself as God loves you. Devotion implies a sense of reverence and honoring. Chances are good you were not taught to honor yourself as the loving, creative, important and powerful human being you are becoming along this journey. Now is a great time to observe your life with an aura of reverence and honor.

DEDICATION is similar to devotion but it includes an element of doing. Dedicate yourself to being mindful and exploring every thought, word, emotion and experience as you reveal the unknowns of your life. These are directional indicators guiding you to true happiness and peace. Be focused and unwavering in your curiosity and desire to know everything there is to know, taking every opportunity to discover the nuggets of truth that will be revealed through your experiences. You may not remember how persistent you were when you learned to walk—trying again each time you fell and delighting in every successful attempt. You may remember how focused you were in learning to drive a car, earning your black-belt, climbing a tree or accomplishing whatever was so very important at some point in your life. You were relentless until you were successful. So be relentless now as you reclaim the magnificent and unique you and learn to love yourself completely.

DISCIPLINE is even more doing than dedication. Discipline is the grit and the practice of change. It's sticking to the commitment you made to do something different. It's doing it even when you're too tired or stressed to step out of your comfort zone just now. It's the "fake it till you make it" determination that makes you scream and cry, but you do it anyway because you promised yourself and your inner child that you would always be there, no matter what. It's keeping the promise you made to yourself, even when you must call out for help from a Source you may not be sure of, but "Please God, give me the strength to do this now."

Discipline is the consistent practice of paying attention and being in the moment. It's taking the time to listen to your thoughts and emotions and following them where they take you. It's making yourself look at your pain and ponder the history, the stories, the beliefs and the choices holding your suffering in place. It's the practice of letting go of faulty thoughts and beliefs each time you find them, no matter how often they show up. It's changing the thoughts, words and actions that create your reality and choosing more positive beliefs, thoughts, feelings, words and actions to put in their place...in every moment. This is this *disciplined practice of doing things differently that changes the neuronal connections in your brain* until you have rewritten the operating programs for health and happiness. Discipline holds your focus on the practice that allows old error messages to be pruned away—because you're not using them anymore—and supports and reinforces the growth of new connections you are practicing. This is where learning to walk becomes walking and learning to brake, turn and steer becomes driving. This is where the seeker finds mastery and lives in peace and harmony.

DISCERNMENT is defined as the ability to judge well. Long ago, our ancestors began dismissing the Still Small Voice Within in deference to the knowledge promoted by authorities and the information that could be validated according to society's sanctioned standards. You are thousands of years downstream from this separation from God and self. Conventional wisdom and experts have become the dominant source of available information, acceptable ways of thinking and the final word on truth and reality. Reclaiming your abilities to be still, to listen, to receive, to interpret and to trust the inner knowing that was always present will take devotion, dedication and discipline. It will also take discernment. You may see yourself as a discerning person, but as you begin to examine some of your past decisions, you may discover they were driven more by unconscious thought patterns than by a well thought out choices. Remember, about 95% of your thoughts, words and actions are automatic or habitual. Even your conscious analysis and reasoning are prejudiced by early learning and therefore can interfere with true discernment.

Chances are good that you didn't grow up learning how to do listen to your heart, trust your intuition or follow your gut. You may have been persuaded to dismiss your intuitions and that Voice Within as "just your imagination." As you grew older, you joined the rest of us in accepting the conventional wisdom dictating truth and you forgot about your imagination and your inner voice. Like most of us, you spend a great deal of energy grappling with messages that justify immediate gratification, like: another cookie (glass of wine) won't matter; I deserve a new phone because I work so hard; I really want that new pair of shoes because it will go perfectly with my new outfit...for work of course. There are so many habitual thought patterns and little messages playing in the background of your mind. These in turn lead you to make decisions that are ultimately based on the belief that you are incomplete as you continually seek happiness and fulfillment outside yourself. Learning how to break out of the life-long patterns created by entrenched beliefs and habitual thinking is a process that will take time, practice, patience and compassion.

Obviously, remembering and relearning something that was forgotten long ago will take time to re-establish connections that have been lost through lack of use. It will require devotion, dedication and discipline to retrieve the latent tool of true discernment. It will also require patience and compassion with yourself as you move through the process of relearning.

You will need patience and compassion because this process involves the same trial and error routine used by children and our ancestors. At this point, you're probably so comfortable following the habitual messages popping into your conscious mind that you think these messages are coming from your heart and inner guidance. How could they not be true? Just the anticipation of having what you really want makes you feel so much better! Unfortunately, this is a hormone rush caused by anticipation...it will disappear quickly. Chances are, in a very short time, you realize that you feel no happier or fulfilled than you did before you secured the prized item. Complicating this realization is the possibility that there will be payments or other weighty consequences to deal with even after the excitement has worn off. Oops, it turns out the choice was a mistake and not the answer to a prayer.

Mistakes are only opportunities to learn and grow. From the beginning of time, evolution has progressed through trial and error. If something worked, we lived and learned. If it didn't work we died, or we lived to try a different way. Many great discoveries are the results of this process. At this point in humanity's evolution, you are no different in this regard. You will make choices that, in the perfect science of 20/20 hindsight, you will wish you had chosen otherwise. This is an important revelation and it's learning. Sometimes, your life journey presents you with a hard experience you may interpret as a mistake. Some of the toughest experiences come because they offer much more insight than you would have gotten without enduring such an experience. In the moment, it might be difficult to appreciate the learning that comes with a mistake, but there is always a lesson to be learned when you take the time to reflect. Mistakes open the door of discovery so you can find your powerful, loving self and use your gifts to grow in understanding. These gifts include forgiveness, compassion, humility, vulnerability, responsibility and acceptance.

Just as a child learns to walk or ride a bike, so it is with learning discernment. As you practice listening and trying to understand the messages you hear, sometimes you will get it right. Take time to recognize that you got it right, appreciate your successful use of this skill, and bask in the wonderful feeling of getting it right. Like a child, commit your success to memory so you can do it again soon. Sometimes you will *not* get it right, and that's okay too. Take time to see how you got off track, recognize the feelings and thoughts that might have been behind the decision to make one choice over another. Maybe it's time to release the belief that takes you down this same path time and again. Have compassion for yourself as you would for others who stumble. Have patience for the process of your own growth and take time to imagine, *visualize and feel* yourself choosing differently when this opportunity comes up again, as it surely will.

Learning to listen to your inner wisdom is a process that expands with practice, so go slowly, honoring gut reactions, heart calls and inspirations. Follow the guidance they offer. The more proficient you become at discernment, the more you will trust the guiding messages you receive. The more you trust yourself and follow your inner guidance, the more success you'll have at bringing peace and balance to your life. The more you appreciate yourself for achieving this valuable life skill, the stronger you'll grow the neuronal connections that allow this to be your new habitual way of life, leading you to the happiness and health you seek.

Practicing Discernment

Your days are filled with opportunities to become more aware of the subconscious messages you use to make the choices you do. If you set your intentions to be aware of your thoughts, words and actions, you will discover that they emerge from habitual patterns rather than actual choices. With this insight you are exposing patterns of behavior that are actually obstacles to health and happiness. This then allows you to recognize these habitual patterns as decisions that could have been made otherwise and this is the insight that enables you to make significant changes.

When you go out to dine with friends, what choices do you make? Did you select healthier items from the menu? Did you stop eating when you are satisfied, or did you clean the plate? Did you order that second or third glass of wine? Why did you choose one way over another? Could you sense the battle between good and evil in your mind? Did you follow your inner guidance or did you make the same choices you usually do? Did you succumb to the pressure of friends? When the evening is over and you reflect on your choices, you may remember the little voice urging better choices. If you disregarded these messages and did as you normally do, there is a good chance you will be struggling with disappointment, guilt or some negative emotion making you wish you had chosen differently. Now is the time for forgiveness and compassion. If you did make better choices based on those inner messages, be aware of how good it feels to be successful and self-honoring. Take time to appreciate the power and joy that comes with being in a place of power and harmony with yourself. Celebrate your success!

Shopping is another opportunity to grow. Some times you really need an item of clothing or a new phone, computer or car. But many times, these things are purchased in an attempt to feel better, especially when you're in a slump. A new purse, pair of shoes or the newest phone upgrade may make you feel better in the moment and for a few more moments, but that feeling wears off in a relatively short time. If the voice coming from your head—often countered by your heart or gut—is saying things like, "I deserve this" or you cave to instant gratification, then your desire is being directed by faulty beliefs and you are looking for happiness outside yourself. Paying attention to the internal dialogue as you justify acquiring something you think will make you happy gives you important clues that this choice may not be in your best interest. When your justifications don't match the intuition of your heart or your gut feeling, you are in conflict with yourself and chances are good there is a better choice.

What about your friends? Are you lifted up and supported by them? Do they encourage wise choices and support your potential and growth? Do they respect and honor your choices even if they don't agree? Do you do the same for them? Being with friends affects the way you feel about yourself. Do you feel accepted, loved, safe and happy? Are you honest with yourself about how you feel when you're with them? Do you stand up for yourself and expect to be treated with respect and kindness? Or, do you diminish yourself by acting according to their expectations instead of your own? If you have great friends (and family) who are loving, supportive and respectful, do you appreciate them and thank them for the blessings they add to your life? Do you appreciate yourself for your excellent choices and express gratitude for the good fortune of having such wonderful friends? The answers to each of these questions offer opportunities to change patterns that don't serve your happiness and also to recognize and reinforce the good you *do* have in your life. Either way, you are growing happier and healthier.

Practicing discernment means you are mastering the art of separating your truth from the truth of others and you are making choices based on your unique understanding of yourself. It means you honor and trust yourself, and you're making choices that demonstrate self-love as you pursue your dreams and passions on your own terms…as your authentic self.

Response-ability

Your Seed of Divinity expressing as inner wisdom and intuitions is who you are. This wisdom comes to you through the Mind of God/Field of Possibility where you live, move and have your being. You have as much access to this amazing source of knowledge as you are willing to invite in and use for your purpose. You are the master of your destiny. You have also been given the gift of free will. This is the ability to choose your thoughts, words, attitudes, emotions and actions in every moment. Free will means you are free to choose alternatives to your usual patterns. To choose differently asks you to step into your power and make changes to the beliefs and preprogrammed thought patterns no longer serving your happiness and health. This requires you to acknowledge that you alone are responsible for making the necessary changes.

Responsibility often sounds like a burden; a drudgery that comes with ownership and obligation. Thinking this way is someone else's truth and it's a handicap slowing progress. *Response-ability is claiming your power.* It's not only believing you have the power to respond to situations in your life in positive and life-enhancing ways but, more importantly, it's stepping into your power and making those changes.

The repeating cycles of restlessness, poor choices, misery and failed attempts at happiness that we experience over the course of our lives are simply unrecognized learning opportunities. We keep repeating unproductive patterns over and over again because we don't understand the messages they're bringing us. We view the mishaps and struggles like being adrift on the sea of life, at the mercy of the waves and wind without paddles or clear sight of land. Breaking out of these repetitive cycles is easier when we remember that our discomfort is a signal for change, and that our Spark of Divinity means we have everything we need to make appropriate changes. As we add mindfulness, intention and discernment, we uncover the faulty beliefs and habitual patterns creating the repetitive cycle of disappointment. With a better understanding of what is going on, we are able to change anything that doesn't bring happiness into our lives. When we know our feelings and patterns are clues, we can start asking useful questions.

The question, "why do I keep doing this the same way?" embraces a sense of responsibility. It says I am responsible for how I'm feeling and the course of events that brought me to this place. This opens the door to self-discovery, revelations and replacing the hidden error messages. When we ask a question like, "Why does this keep happening to me?" we are in effect blaming someone or something else for our situation.

One of the biggest stumbling blocks obstructing change is *our story*. Our story is the narrative of our tragic event(s), and how deeply we were affected by it. It's the reason we feel and act the way we do. We tell it to friends and to family and to therapists. Because they care, they listen…every time we repeat it. Beyond listening, there is nothing they can do to help. We also tell the story to ourselves when we feel bad and wonder why. And, we repeat it in the subconscious messages holding our patterns in place. We're not aware of this but our story has become our identity, a crutch and the excuse we somehow believe justifies not taking responsibility for changes that would improve the quality of our lives. We are trapped in and addicted to our story.

Claiming your power is to be response-enabled.

When we reflect on our story, was the event tragic or traumatic? Yes, absolutely! And yet, we must decide if we will let this event define us for the rest of our lives. Is this who we truly are? Should we let this event limit our potential for success and happiness forever more? When we choose to cling to our story, it becomes our default identity. As we stay stuck in this place, we are giving our power to those who harmed us. When we identify with and repeat this story we are allowing the perpetrators to define and limit us. Through this choice, we are in effect giving them permission to continue hurting us. The only way to stop the pain of the past is to step into our power and claim responsibility for how we will move forward. With compassion, forgiveness, and sometimes with the help of others we can let go of the story, quit rehearsing it and redefine ourselves as capable, powerful, loving and worthy. As life altering as the event and its story was, holding onto it is a limiting choice. The choice to let go leads to our release from bondage and is the beginning of a whole new level of freedom to define ourselves as healthy and whole.

Never Look Back

"Do not dwell in the past, do not dream of the future, concentrate the mind on the present moment." – The Buddha

Everything you have experienced in your life including your hopes, dreams, disappointments and struggles are a reflection of your past. Your past includes your eternal nature as a spark in the Mind/Field, your ancestral heritage and genetics, your early learning, life experiences, thoughts, words, feelings and actions. All this bundled together is your unique journey and it's what propels you along the path of survival and your quest for peace, love and fulfillment. The Laws governing energy in the Mind/Field hold you in patterns of reality and attract every life experience to you so you can learn and move forward into the fullest expression of who you are. You are a quantum being of light and love interacting with the Mind/Field. You are the image and likeness of your Source.

This truth affirms you have the power, capacity and opportunity to make conscious choices in order to think, feel, speak and act differently. You have the power to capture and release the beliefs and stories no longer serving your happiness, purpose and fulfillment. The more you choose to live in the higher vibrations of harmony, peace and love, the more you change the circuits in your brain and the more this becomes your default way of being.

As you move forward on this beautiful journey of self-discovery and self-love, it becomes easier to continue making the choices and changes that serve your unique expression of Love and Light. You are creating a happier and healthier reality for yourself. Stay mindful in your daily journey and reinforce your progress with appreciation and gratitude for each positive step you take. Be vigilant for old entrenched patterns that will pop up and tempt you back to the familiar ways. Friends, family and situations will provide you with opportunities to test your resolve, strength and commitment to yourself. The most important choice you can make in any moment is the choice to move forward. Fill yourself with positive feelings of love and self-appreciation, thinking, speaking and behaving as if your new beliefs of worthiness and being good enough are the only ones you have ever had. *Never look back.* Looking back to things from your past or falling into old patterns means you are creating your future from the past rather than the beneficial patterns you are adopting in the present. Choose to move forward creating your future from a place of self-love and appreciation. Step into your power and walk in the higher vibration of love.

> *"When you come to the edge of all the light you have, and must take a step into the darkness of the unknown, believe that one of two things will happen. Either there will be something solid for you to stand on - or you will be taught how to fly."* – *Patrick Overton*

PART THREE

Love Is In Everything

"Someday, after mastering the winds, the waves, the tides and gravity, we shall harness for God the energies of love, and then, for a second time in the history of the world, man will have discovered fire."
–*Pierre Teilhard de Chardin (1881-1955)*

CHAPTER 10

Love Is the Elixir of Life

"All You Need Is Love."
– Lennon–McCartney (1967)

Love is the magic potion.

Love is the healing balm that soothes all pain and heals all wounds.

Remember how enchanted you felt when you first fell in love? In those early moments of love's magical embrace, you may have felt so whole and expansive that the edges of yourself seemed to disappear; time was limitless; everything was beautiful; all things were possible. Everything in your world shifted to a higher vibration, just because you were filled with love.

What is it about love that makes all things perfect, if only just for a moment?

We believe this magical feeling is caused by our intimate connection with another person. In reality, the awe-inspiring feeling of love comes from deep inside as we recognize our own loving essence being reflected back to us through the eyes of another. The ecstasy we feel is produced by the flood of hormones washing through our entire body triggered by the emotion of love. At the atomic level, it's our electrons vibrating and resonating with the truth of who we are. In these fleeting moments, we are experiencing ourselves as love...*a being of love and light created in God's Image and Likeness.* Our full body experience is the Love of God reminding us that this is who we are and calling us back home to harmony, peace and joy...Paradise. In those serene and giddy moments, everything is in perfect balance. Even as we perceive this feeling as coming from a connection with someone outside ourselves, this whole-body sensation is a powerful message reminding us, "This is your perfect state of being! This is your essence."

What a glorious feeling it is! It's like crack; mind-altering, compelling and addictive. Once we experience this powerful high, we want to feel that way all the time. Whatever brings us to this magical and compelling experience, we're hooked on it. It feels so right, so perfect and so true. As the feeling fades away, we are back on the hunt for more. Our yearning for the peace and joy of love's expression is built into us; we were created with it. We rightfully believe on a very deep level that we could and should feel this incredible all the time, but conventional wisdom and life experience tells us that living in such endless bliss isn't possible.

But, what if it *is* possible? What if you could learn to release the pain and suffering and replace it with the higher vibration of love, peace and harmony? What if you could experience that bliss-filled state of love more regularly; so regularly that it became the stabilizing current moderating all the events in your life? What if you could raise the vibration of your consciousness with the empowering belief that you are love and live your life from a perspective of peace and harmony? Such a state would allow you to respond to all situations from a place of loving kindness and a better understanding of who you are. This is not only possible; it's your magnificent potential and your destiny. Since you were created with the irrefutable desire to be joy-filled and loving, your growth toward that goal is the purpose of your life. Because you were created with this desire, it also means you were created with the power and tools you need to make this reality happen. It's your choice to use these inherent gifts for your purpose.

Loving yourself whole means you are healing on all levels, spiritual, mental, emotional and physical. It means leaving no stone unturned as you move forward in your quest for happiness, peace and fulfillment.

Your body, mind and spirit are integrated and working together to bring balance and harmony into your life. The unrealized love of self and the wisdom of your inner knowing are literally magnetizing you to the people and situations that will give you exactly what you need to identify the faulty beliefs and messages causing you to stumble and stay stuck. At times you may think these people and situations are the source of your pain and struggles. In reality, they are your teachers. Recognizing learning opportunities as they appear in your life and using them to heal the wounds of the past are the tools you need to become more happy and healthy. Woven through the trials and lessons of life will be bright moments of love and joy to remind you that you are being supported and encouraged along your journey. It's important to recognize and seize these uplifting experiences and learn to use them to replace the struggles you are releasing. It's all about you and the choices you make. And, you're never alone as the Love of God manifesting through you is always with you as your guiding force.

The fast track for effective and lasting change comes from using every experience as inspiration and guidance on your quest for peace, joy and fulfillment. Engage every happiness to its fullest. Absorb every drop and commit it to memory. Experience your painful emotions and follow them to the wounds and lies you've been living with for too long. Listen to your thoughts and words, and be aware of your actions as they speak to you of the beliefs and messages that may not serve your highest good. Sit in stillness with your pain, discomfort and disease asking it what you need to know so you can move forward in health and peace. Do this for yourself, as you would be present and attentive in this same way for someone you truly loved.

Experiencing Love Requires A Relationship

From the very beginning, you learned love came from outside yourself. If you acted a certain way you received attention, kindness and love. Whatever your life experiences up to this point, you have reinforced your beliefs about love and your lovability through relationships. You've come to believe the magical state of love is dependent on finding the right person—or situation—so you can experience that awesome feeling we are all drawn to and spend our lives chasing.

Relationships are critical for surviving, learning, growing and evolving. You need them to discover who you are, find your gifts and uncover the faulty messages; they illuminate the path of healing. While relationships with others are absolutely necessary, the most essential relationship is the one you have with yourself. It is the relationship you have with your own Spark of Divinity, the God-Self, who is guiding and supporting you that matters most. This is the only relationship that will bring you to the love you long for; the love you know deep down inside is possible.

You may be asking, "If this is so, why do I only feel the magic of love in relationship to another?" When you experience the magical rush of love, it's like a pinball machine lighting up as you hit the jackpot. What did this person or situation do to you or for you that made you feel so incredible? Maybe you answer, s/he made me feel loved, appreciated, whole, complete, important and worthy. In reality, you have *attracted a mirror image of your loving self*. Looking into her/his eyes is like looking in a calm clear pond. In that moment, you see the reflection of yourself as whole, complete, important, worthy and loving. In this magical rush you identify as love, you are feeling the essence of all that you are. In this moment, you are experiencing yourself as the integrated whole of body, mind and spirit, complete as one.

Life is filled with moments to experience ourselves as worthy, loved and complete. These moments come frequently, but we are so wrapped up in the chaos of life we rarely recognize our opportunities. We trudge on unchanged by the beauty, wonder and possibilities surrounding us. In truth, our blessings come in all shapes, sizes and colors of emotion. The positive ones, the negative ones, the little quiet ones and the earth-moving ones are all sending us messages, if only we would learn to listen and interpret them correctly for ourselves.

Just as our discomforts and dis-eases came to us through the process of human evolution and missed opportunities to recognize and make changes at our spiritual, mental, emotional and physical levels, so too do our opportunities for understanding and healing come at those same four levels. The good news is that love and truth are much more powerful than our default settings of fear and misperception. When we open to the possibilities and use our tools and gifts, we can heal at multiple levels simultaneously. As the light of self-love grows stronger, the more brightly we illuminate the places calling out for love and healing. With this awareness, it's easier to recognize what we must do to reach the place of balance and wholeness we always wanted for ourselves.

Loving yourself whole and healing on all levels requires building a conscious connection with each of the four planes of your human experience. This means understanding and strengthening your connection with your *spiritual* nature and allowing the power, wisdom and love available at that level to guide, encourage and empower you. It means understanding and strengthening your connection with your *mental* nature so you can actually hear the thoughts as they dawn on your conscious mind and then use your growing discernment to determine if they are in cohesive alignment with health, happiness and your highest purpose. It means understanding and strengthening your connection with your *emotional* nature so you tune in to every information-bearing message as soon as it arrives, using it to heal your pain and evolve to your highest potential. Lastly, it means understanding and strengthening the connection with your *physical* body. You may not have been taught this, but your body is communicating with you all the time. What you *have* learned is how to place it on mute so you can't hear the body's wisdom telling you exactly what you need.

CHAPTER 11

Loving Yourself Whole

"Life isn't about finding yourself. Life is about creating yourself."
– George Bernard Shaw

You are one with God.
God is One with all, every person and every thing.
Therefore you are one with every person and thing.
This is simple logic, and it's Universal Truth reminding you that no matter what's happening in your life and no matter what your reality appears to be, your power, health and happiness are *all about you.* When you look in the mirror, you see a three-dimensional image of the electromagnetic field that makes up your material self. What you don't see is the much larger reality you are an intimate part of. Just as the quantum field and the Mind of God contain all possibilities, so too do you. You are complete and whole just as you are and within this wholeness you have everything you need to be all you wish for yourself. The answers reside within you.

Connecting With Your Spiritual Nature

"You are not a drop in the ocean. You are the entire ocean, in a drop." – Rumi (13th Century Mystic and Poet)

Just as an acorn contains everything it needs to become a mighty oak tree, your Spark of Divinity contains everything you need to find your way back to harmony and oneness. As a Spark in the Mind of God you are eternally connected to the Absolute Source of Wisdom, Love and Power. "Be still and know that I AM God" was the enduring wisdom of the Masters. By being still and listening to that Still Small Voice Within, you are strengthening the connection with your spiritual nature. When you do this, you open your conscious awareness to profound possibilities enabling you to create a better reality for yourself and the whole of humanity. As you strengthen this bond, you are reconnecting with your innate gifts of wisdom, power and love; you are opening the door and allowing the power of Love to burn away and transform the original sin of separation and unworthiness. In this connection there is a growing awareness of God's Presence providing moments of love to remind you of who you are, moments of struggle to help you appreciate and strengthen your gifts and synchronicities that move you ever closer to the joy and contentment you seek. Once you understand that all of this is actually originating inside you, you have greater access to the high vibration of love—in all its forms—as it offers encouragement, healing and quick infusions of happiness. With this understanding, you are transforming yourself into a living, breathing expression of God's Love.

The surest way to strengthen and empower the connection with your spiritual nature is to embrace the knowledge that you are a Spark in the Mind of God; that God is with you, unconditionally loving you through every thought, word and action…no matter what! This may take time and practice, but it's worth every moment you give to making this realization your own. Prayer, contemplation, meditation and listening to that Still Small Voice Within are all ways to grow this connection and make it fundamental in your pursuit of happiness. Find the practices that speak to you and make them a regular part of your life.

Our lives are filled with blessings, gifts and tools to help us move through the density of our struggles and reach higher vibrations of love. As we consider these gifts of guidance and encouragement, it is good to remember the Universal Laws presented earlier. The Law of Cause and Effect positions us as the masters of our destiny and the creators of our reality. The Planes of Correspondence remind us that the wisdom and vibrations from higher planes flow through to the lower and more dense levels. It also promises that no matter what level we seem to be operating on, we can petition and receive help from higher dimensions. "As above, so below" guarantees the peace, love and harmony of God-likeness when we open ourselves to receive the blessings of higher vibrations. Our *blessings* include the innate *gifts* we have been given to use as the *tools* we need to create the life we desire. I will use these three words interchangeably as they are one and the same.

MINDFULNESS is one of many form of meditation. Sitting quietly and bringing attention to your breath or a body sensation allows you to clear your mind in such a way that you may access higher realms than you might in your usual state of mind. In Chapter Nine, I discussed mindfulness as a tool—a state of being present in the holy moment of now—where we can better appreciate our thoughts, feelings, words and actions. You can use mindfulness as both a meditative practice and as a state of present-centered awareness to accompany you throughout your day. However you use it, mindfulness brings peace as you release the clutter of repetitive thinking and the worries of the past and future. In the quiet of the moment, you may sense divine wisdom and guidance coming to you through insights, intuitions and awareness as they provide answers that otherwise could not find their way through the noise produced by your conscious mind when left unattended and undisciplined.

SURRENDER is among the most powerful tools we possess. It's a gift because it requires the strength and courage that can only come from a power greater than ourselves. It encourages us to restore faith and trust in the Higher Power with whom we have lost touch. It's a tool because, while rarely used, it is a mechanism for changing what's no longer working. Surrender means letting go of control and the beliefs that hold our world together in its present form, even as we are sure our lives will completely fall apart if we let go. This is the meaning of trust. Surrender isn't about quitting and walking away; it's about release. Surrender is the heart of profound and life changing insights, spontaneous healings and miracles. It's the Phoenix rising up from the ashes of our despair and brokenness. It's the place where we let our connection with God lift us to a new level of being without setting conditions that would limit God's ability to assist.

There are no step-by-step instructions for the art of surrender because opening to this gift and learning to use it as a powerful tool is part of our journey.

> With permission from my family, I offer this story as an illustration of the power of surrender to heal the pain of a lifetime:
>
> My father, Frank, was a depression-era child born fourth in a family of five children. His heritage included German, Catholic, Caucasian, lower socio-economic and rural, farming community. When his father died, he was sent to live with an aunt and uncle as his mother believed this would give him a better life than she could provide. He was about five years old when he was dropped off there, a few small towns away. Both his family of origin and his new family defined love as providing for the necessities of life. Hard work, responsibility and heavy-handed discipline served as guidance for behavior and future choices, and those were the characteristics impressed upon him as he grew up. During his first year of seminary, he dropped out and joined the Navy. He married in his mid-twenties and had six children in keeping with the guidance of his Catholic faith.
>
> His life was defined by struggle and torment. He was addicted to tobacco and alcohol, suffered with anxiety and depression, and had multiple nervous breakdowns. He talked incessantly to himself. Sometimes he was so agitated, his words were audible to those around him. For a few years, his burdens seemed so heavy he would disappear for days at a time, leaving his wife to manage her job and six young children. He did the best he could to raise a large family, sacrificing much

to make sure his children all had a Catholic education, music lessons and discipline.

In time, therapy, medication, Alcoholics Anonymous and a tobacco aversion program helped him gain some control over his life. Most important to him was his devotion to God and the Mother Mary, in the tradition of his Catholic faith and upbringing. He was an avid supporter of an Indian Mission School and the church parishes he belonged to over the years. He did his best to make amends, be happy and find peace according to the 12-step program he espoused. But he could never let go of the fundamental beliefs that he was unworthy, unloved and inadequate. Even as he remained dutiful and available to his mother, aunt and uncle, he believed that he had been discarded by his mother and abused by a harsh aunt and a complicit uncle. After 42 years of sobriety, business successes and the love of his family, my father still struggled with abandonment, worthiness and lovability issues that hampered his happiness for all of his 86 years.

Despite being a non-smoker for over 40 years, his years of smoking caught up to him. After several years of declining health, he was once again in the hospital struggling to breathe; not enough breath to eat, turn over in bed or get to the bathroom. With no effective treatments to improve his breathing, he sat in his hospital bed with a look of terror on his face as he attempted to communicate with his children and the hospital staff. As I walked into his room early on the fourth morning of his hospitalization, my dad said to me, "Call the priest Pat, I'm ready to die. I'm done struggling." The priest came to minister to his spiritual needs and then he was discharged to the loving home of my brother and his wife. Hospice met us there with all we needed to keep him comfortable.

Only Frank knows what happened during that night, but as he left the hospital and went home with family to live out his last few weeks, it was obvious a transformation had taken place; he was a changed man. Always proud and independent, he now asked for help with everything he needed and he accepted all help graciously. He was wheeled everywhere he went, bathed by hospice staff, catered to by family, and he always responded with a broad and appreciative

"Thank you." He let his children help him with decision-making, even relinquishing major decisions to them. Over a period of a week, he met privately with each of his children and our mother and took full responsibility for the mistakes he had made and the hell he had put us through. To the best of his knowledge, he made amends for his transgressions. He called old friends across the nation to say his good-byes, and when asked how he was managing, he would declare, "We're having one big love fest here, and it's *just wonderful*!" This became his mantra. There is no doubt that the medications provided by hospice eased his breathing and anxiety, but the sense of peace, joy and love he felt was of a quality that drugs could never provide. His eyes were bright with peace and love. His words were caring, gentle and gracious. His actions welcomed and acknowledged the gifts and talents of others, allowing them to reach him in ways he had never known before and he was demonstrably grateful. He was, at long last, experiencing the love he had tried so hard to find throughout his life.

He continued to pray every day until just a day or two before his death. He transitioned peacefully with family and angels lifting him up. Frank lived out his last three weeks in what can only be described as a State of Grace; the Peace that passes all understanding; that place where control and struggle are surrendered and where the Love of God becomes known.

Surrender is a powerful tool even when our struggles are not big or life threatening. We surrender in each moment we practice Mindfulness, surrendering one moment as we open to the next. We practice surrender in meditation as we let go of our thoughts and concerns and open ourselves to possibilities held for us in the Mind of God and delivered by the Still Small Voice Within. We practice surrender when we give ourselves over to fully experience our joy, our gratitude, our pain and our struggles. In each of these experiences, there is a blessing and a message if we let go and become open to new possibilities.

Mindfulness and surrender are tools that greatly accelerate your efforts to strengthen your connection and support your efforts at each level of being—spiritual, mental, emotional and physical. As you refine and empower these tools, you open the door of awareness to the love, beauty and synchronicities that exist as possibilities within the Mind of God/Field of Possibilities. Living in the present strengthens your Divine connection as you become more cognizant of the splendor and miracles happening around you. Surrendering to those experiences allows the healings, blessings and grace to raise your vibration, change your perceptions and observations and in so doing, you change your reality, one magnificent heartbeat at a time.

More Blessings and Gifts

The heart-warming and expansive moments of awe, appreciation, gratitude, compassion, forgiveness, courage and all other positive emotions are simply variations of the expression of love. They all originate from the same place...inside you. They flash into your consciousness to be identified as a feeling based on what you *think* caused you to feel this way. You *feel* these profound moments of joy because the interface of your brain is flooding your body with hormones and neurotransmitters that literally light you up as loving energy vibrates through every part of you. This feeling is the important message of connectedness being delivered to you. When you surrender to the full experience of these moments you expand into oneness. As you relinquish your struggles and woes to the magic of such moments, you are transformed. The more transforming moments you search out, welcome in and are grateful for, the more whole, happy and loving you become.

If moments of gratitude, awe, love, compassion and other such blessings seem to be rare events, you have reason to celebrate! Your path has just become more clear than ever before. You only need to recognize that in the Mind of God where you live, move and have your being, you are surrounded with opportunities to experience love in all its manifestations. Give yourself permission to recognize and fully embrace these opportunities and allow them to affect you deeply. Imagine breathing them into you like the oxygen that supports every cell in your body, for they are all of that and more.

GRATITUDE joins surrender as one of the most powerful tools and it's easier to define and use. Opportunities to be renewed, rejuvenated and changed by gratitude are endlessly available once you set your intention to recognize them. A home, a family, a job, a dependable car, a close friend, a warm meal, a loyal dog, a blossoming flower, a good book, a warm greeting, a stranger opening a door, a hot bath at the end of a busy day, and the list goes on. Learning to experience gratitude in your day-to-day life is a simple and effective way to raise your vibration and feel lighter, no matter where you find yourself. Whether you are thankful for the sunshine that brightens your day or your ability to create happiness in your life, gratitude is *an experience* that originates in you the same way love does. In the Universe of oneness and synchronicity, these experiences are present in every moment when you're open to the awareness. On the other hand, you can take things for granted, not recognizing the blessings of life. Imagine what life would be like if you believed there was no reason to appreciate anything. Gratitude can transform disenchantment and struggle into peace and contentment simply by shifting your perception in the moment.

You know how gratitude feels, but you may not be aware of the blessing you are receiving. Gratitude is an inspired feeling reminding you that you are so very worthy of wonderful things coming into your life. The full expression of gratitude requires a willingness and intention to accept (cause) beauty, grace and goodness into your life and then embracing them as the natural outcome (effect) of your worthiness.

The daily practice of writing down three things you are grateful for and why you're grateful for them will help you identify even more blessings as you open to the possibilities. This practice is magnified when it's done while simultaneously *experiencing the feeling* of gratitude. The more often you experience gratitude, the more opportunities you give your brain to set up nerve pathways that will allow you to live in a state of acceptance and thanksgiving. You are growing happier as you embrace each experience of gratitude as an expression of the loving relationship you have with yourself and All That Is.

Gratitude is acceptance of your worthiness.

Gratitude is also a powerful catalyst. When you set your intention to reach a goal and petition God to help you get what you desire, ask with the attitude of gratitude, as if it has already come true. Feel your joy and thanksgiving for having the very thing you are asking for. This projects your powerful thoughts and intentions into the Mind/Field with the knowing that it's already starting to take shape...and you're grateful for it. This is the Law of Cause and Effect in action.

AWE is the blessing of experiencing your own beauty and magnificence. Consider the way you feel when you see a stunning sunset, powerful waterfall, majestic landscape or witness the birth of a child. You're mesmerized; you can't look away; there are no words to capture the magic of the moment. If you allow yourself to be immersed in this experience, you may feel your heart expanding, your muscles relaxing and your mind quieting as your body, mind and spirit rejoice in unison at the splendor before you. As with love and gratitude, the interface of your brain is lighting you up with hormones and neurotransmitters as, on a higher plane, you are observing your magnificence being reflected back to you. Never look away. Stay right there with this sensation allowing it to grow and expand until you *know that you are one with this breath-taking experience*. No thinking required, only allowing and being present with the feeling. Miss no opportunity to let the experience of awe flood your immune and nervous systems. Imagine, just for a moment, your brain hardwiring that feeling into your memory so you can easily retrieve it when you want or need it. The easier it becomes to recall such feelings, the more useful they are as tools; summon the feeling of awe and imagine projecting it like a blanket of love, throwing it over the problems of your day or the pain in the world. There is so much good you can do with this feeling of magnificence once you learn it's a reflection of your own essence.

Opportunities to experience the healing gift of awe come to us in big and small ways; from the blossoming of a flower to a perfect performance after months of planning and practice. Unfortunately, some of us will miss our chances to be awe-struck. We might notice, but we are unable to let go of our suffering long enough to appreciate the beauty or be even momentarily affected by it. Others among us will come away renewed and rejuvenated. How is it that the same situation can affect people so differently? Our personal perception of life is one reason. Another is the belief, and the illusion, that we are separate from the reality we perceive. Because of this, we think such beauty and magnificence can only exist outside ourselves. You see beauty and magnificence unaware that you are part of it. You are the cause of your feelings, good, bad or indifferent, and what you experience is a reflection of you. The truth is, these heart-expanding moments of awe can only come from *inside you*. Your recognition of magnificence is you projecting magnificence as an observation and it returns to you as your reflection. In this experience you are interacting with the Mind of God/Field of Possibility in a celebration of Oneness. In moments of awe and splendor, you are sensing your own radiant beauty, magnificence and power being reflected back to you. Surrender to that moment and just breathe it in!

COMPASSION is the love of God expressing through you. And, the world is filled with opportunities to be all that. You may think of compassion as an act of reaching out with caring and empathy to someone who is struggling. Within the belief system of separation, this is what it seems to be. In truth, the heartache you feel as you imagine or sense someone else's pain is the experience of oneness with another human being. The pain you perceive in them is a reflection of your own pain, because somewhere in your life, ancestral heritage or cosmic consciousness you have known that pain as well. As you reach out with caring and empathy, you are loving your neighbor as yourself in the fullest sense.

Just as with the sunset or the love of a friend, this person's pain appears to be the prompt opening your heart to extend compassion. Like love and gratitude, the experience of compassion originates in you. You are the Love of God expressing as you, each time you act with compassion. As you express compassion for another, you are projecting love into the Mind of God/Field of Possibility, and it's being reflected back to you as the love that you are. The heart-warming sensations you feel in your compassionate acts are actually the experience of yourself as both the giver and the receiver of your own loving kindness. It's the complete circle of wholeness in an invisible yet palpable form, as once again, you are flooded with the hormones triggered by love. This is also true when you extend the gift of compassion to yourself as you work through your own struggles. It works exactly the same way. Compassion is a high vibration energy that lifts us all up. Its healing and rejuvenating powers are without limit.

FORGIVENESS is a gift of healing *you give yourself*. This is true whether you're forgiving yourself or someone else. Forgiveness is letting go of the pain you feel as the result of a perceived mistake, harm or injury. The interpretation of an injury, how it makes you feel, how you cope with it and respond to it are all determined by early learning. Living in persistent emotional pain and repeating your story of personal injury are chronic stressors. This is also a choice. With forgiveness, you release yourself from the bondage of suffering that keeps you attached to a person or event. Forgiveness has nothing to do with consequences that may result from poor choices or hurtful behavior. Indeed, it may be necessary to take action and make changes so such behavior is not part of the future; however, forgiveness only has to do with letting go of the pain. It's an outward projection of your loving nature and an expression of the divine power you have to heal yourself and create harmony internally and externally. The peace you feel with forgiveness is the reflection of you using your innate gifts of love, power and wisdom to restore balance in your life.

COURAGE is inspirational momentum swelling up from somewhere deep inside when you're faced with a situation that seems to overwhelm your usual coping patterns. It's your Spark of Divinity reminding you of the innate power and love that is you. It's the secret knowing that you have what it takes to stand up for yourself and others. It's the power to run into burning buildings to save lives; the love over fear that stands between a bully and a friend; the determination to take a stance against an authority or system that belittles you and tries to steal your dignity and honor. Courage is the connection with your divine self, supporting you in moments of uncertain outcome and fear. We are rarely called to burning buildings or face offs with bullies, but life is full of moments to stand in your truth and radiate your beauty and natural talents. When situations feel out of balance and cause distress, it's your call to action. Whenever you summon the courage to act according to the guidance of your heart, you are actually connecting with your inherent gifts of love, wisdom and power and then projecting these gifts into the Infinite Mind/Field, allowing your magnificent potential to be reflected back to you. The expansive feeling some call pride is you in connection with your divine nature. In your courage, you are experiencing just how amazing and powerful you are.

Life is blessed with many opportunities to connect with your divine nature. No matter what word you use to describe the heart-expanding feeling, it's an important message originating within you as an expression of your essence. The events that trigger these feelings are gifts from the Loving Mind of God/Field of Possibility, Who are participating in your life and encouraging your journey back to Heaven on Earth. When such opportunities come to you, you have choices. How will I respond? Will I open my heart and mind to this opportunity? How will I let it make a difference in my life? Will I take time to nurture and grow this feeling until it becomes the overarching perception influencing the quality of my life?

No matter what triggers your heart-expanded state of being, the sensations you feel are all about you and your connection to yourself. They are your Spark of Divinity rejoicing as you access your innate gifts and respond with recognition and appreciation. Without being conscious of it, the heart-expanding sensations you feel is your mind acknowledging you are so much bigger than you believe yourself to be. It's the feeling of Oneness; of being connected to something magnificent. On a deeper level, it's the knowing that you are complete as both the giver and the receiver. You are receiving the gift of opportunity to experience your magnificence and access your innate gifts of love, wisdom and power. You are the giver as you choose your response to the opportunity. The expansive feeling you experience is affirmation that you, as the receiver, have connected in perfect resonance with the

Mind of God/Field of Possibility in complete oneness.

When you choose to respond to opportunities in ways that reflect your true essence, your mind signals your heart and gut brains telling them all is in balance. These two independent brains then communicate with your head brain, which showers you with the neurotransmitters igniting your pleasure, reward, bonding and contentment receptors. On an emotional level, you are filled with joy, oneness, peace and love. *You feel it.* In this state, negativity has a difficult time getting your attention. On a physical level, you may feel bubbly, breathless, lighter and brighter. All of this is because you are vibrating at a higher frequency than is your usual. What a delightful and health-filled environment your genes are living in and taking instructions from! How would it be to feel like this most the time, or even *all* of the time?

Humanity may not yet be wired to walk around in such a state of self-generated euphoria, but our Seed of Divinity is firmly planted to keep us focused on expanding into that potential. As we strive to get there, it's important to know we are definitely wired to be happy. The only obstacle to realizing our goal of being truly happy is our personal belief systems holding separation, unworthiness, scarcity and pain in place as we project those erroneous beliefs into the Mind of God/Field of Possibility. As we spend more time embracing our opportunities to experience beauty, love, courage, forgiveness, gratitude and compassion, we are hard-wiring joy, peace and love into our nervous systems as our new default.

Connecting With Your Mental Nature

Ancient Wisdom taught us mind and spirit were essentially the same; Source is Infinite Living Mind. Through the Planes of Correspondence, spiritual and mental planes are in intimate and fluid correspondence. The same is true for us; we are mind and through conscious mind and thought, we have access to ideas, revelations, inspirations, intuitions and instincts held in our subconscious mind and in the larger Mind/Field where we live, move and have our being. Our minds, then, are the portals through which we receive blessings from Universal Intelligence in the form of inspired knowing, information and opportunities for growth and greater understanding.

Mind is also the space where we perceive ourselves as I and Me. Mind is where we observe ourselves living our realities, interacting with others and participating in the collective consciousness of humanity. It's the classroom where we become consciously aware of our God-given gifts of wisdom, power and love and where we use our free will to choose how we will respond to each moment. It's also the place where we decide how we will act out the belief that we are separate from God and from our brothers and sisters. Strengthening the connection with your mental nature means you are refining the power of your mind and using it to create a different life for yourself. Your mind, as part of the One Mind, has access to endless potential.

As I describe the gifts and tools available to us at the different levels, please remember that the lines between these levels are fluid. Gifts, such as surrender and compassion may have been discussed in the section on spiritual connection, but they are also operating on the other three levels. This is true in the other direction; the gifts and tools we will discuss at the mental, emotional and physical levels flow through and are part of our spiritual connectedness. This is especially true of mindfulness, which we are going to explore in more depth now.

MINDFULNESS opens the door to the power of your mind; the power to change, grow and evolve. When you are aware of your thoughts and take time to ponder where they're coming from, you give yourself the opportunity to discern their validity and usefulness in your life. Thoughts floating through your conscious mind are like a breadcrumb trail you can follow back to old beliefs that may have protected you from harm at one point in your life, but now hold you back from even greater possibilities. As you uncover the origins of these old beliefs and habitual thinking you can use the power of your conscious mind to let go of anything that no longer serves your happiness and then, consciously choose healthy and loving beliefs to replace those released error messages. This is how you reprogram your subconscious mind to project happiness and health into the Mind/Field. As you do this, remember: it took time and repetition to get you where you are and it will take devotion, dedication, diligence, discernment and time to achieve mastery with the power of your mind.

Using mindfulness to be aware of your thoughts in the present moment allows you to communicate with hidden parts of yourself for a better understanding of what is going on inside. The more you do this, the more opportunities you have to gain insights into your thought patterns. Consider the example of being present while driving—beyond the obvious health benefits of paying attention to the road. Most of us drive enough that we occasionally encounter someone who cuts us off, abruptly stops to make a turn without signaling or drives slower than the flow of traffic. If your dismay is short-lived, you are living in the world with the agency of calm, flexibility and response agility. You're not taking other people's behavior personally. Take a moment to congratulate yourself on your sense of peace and balance in the chaos of the world. On the other hand, some of us greet these encounters with mental or verbal expletives and hand gestures. We stew in our justified aggravation long after the event is behind us. This prolonged aggravation is a moment of revelation and insight for the hidden dynamic festering beneath the surface of our awareness. We may be frightened by the near-miss accident or angry at the careless actions of another. But when we stay stuck in this distress and ruminate about the selfishness or recklessness of the other, we are tapping into something deeper. Just like love and gratitude, these thoughts and the feelings they generate are coming from within and they are telling us something about what is hiding beneath the thin veil of "I'm okay."

Recognizing the negative impact such events can have on our health, it has been suggested we assign a positive reason for the other person's selfish or dangerous traffic maneuver. We could imagine they are driving fast to get to the hospital to have a baby or to get home for an important event. When we assign happy thoughts to such encounters, we connect with positive energy and dismantle the negativity with compassion and forgiveness. We immediately benefit from these positive feelings because they originate within us. We are choosing to let go of our distress and feel better. The truth is, who among us have not committed these same hazardous driving blunders? If, in the moment of mindfully encountering such an opportunity we quickly remind ourselves, "Oops…yeah, I've done that too" we instantly connect with both ourselves and the other person on a human level. In acknowledging our sameness, we experience the bond of oneness. In this holy moment, we can feel the positive flow of energy, in the form of forgiveness and compassion, expanding from deep within. As this happens, we have chosen to allow this opportunity to lift us to a higher vibration. We are then free to continue being mindful of the beauty and possibilities accompanying us on our drive.

CURIOSITY pulls us deeper into self-discovery. All emotions, and especially the negative ones, are golden opportunities to ask the question why. Cultivate the tenacious curiosity of a child who constantly asks "why" but with the internal focus on "I." Why do I feel this way? Why am I doing this? Why do I need that? Why? Why? Why? Gently explore your thoughts and feelings with a playful, open, non-judgmental why until you find the place where good choices appear more difficult to make and maintain.

Life is full of opportunities to ask why and follow your thoughts, words and behaviors to their core. Consider the example of wanting to change a diet for the better. You decide you're going to quit eating sweets so you can lose a few pounds. When you were at the grocery store, your favorite chocolate chip cookies were steeply discounted, so you bought them for later…as a reward for losing weight. Two evenings later, after a particularly hectic day, you're watching TV and decide you want a snack. The choices are blueberries or chocolate chip cookies and you head straight for the cookies, consciously aware you are breaking the promise you made to yourself. In this example, the why conversation might look like: Why? Because I've had a very stressful day and this will make me feel better. Why? Because I like sweets and chocolate chips are my favorite. Why? Umm. I don't know. I always had cookies when I was a child. When I was little my mom would give me a cookie if I felt bad or if I just wanted to hang out in the kitchen with her. But why do I need to have a cookie now? Because I feel bad. Why do I feel bad? Because I had a bad day. Why did I have a bad day? Because I feel like no one appreciates how hard I work, even when I'm doing everything they ask and more. Why don't I feel good enough about my hard work to appreciate myself? And why does it matter so much what other people think of me that I should feel bad about myself now? Maybe at this point you become aware that you are judging yourself as inadequate, not smart enough or unworthy based on *what you think* others think of you. It might take a few more why questions to reveal that the lack of appreciation and the feelings of unworthiness are coming from inside and not from the world around you. The cookie is a learned and familiar way to comfort the distress that's asking to be healed. With this conscious awareness and curiosity, you have found the place of your healing. Time to let go of the belief that you are not enough and replace it with self-appreciation and self-love as a conscious and mindful daily practice.

Your curious exploration of thoughts and behaviors can be applied to anything that makes you feel even remotely uncomfortable. Sitting quietly and mindfully present with yourself and asking the why questions will, with time and loving kindness, reveal the answers to your deepest healing and give you the opportunity to perceive yourself as loving, wise and powerful.

> Consider what self-doubt might reveal with this example:
>
> If someone told me I was a bad driver, I would laugh her out of the room. I would know in my heart that I'm a skillful and safe driver and they have no idea who I am. She doesn't know me or my driving ability and has no basis for such a judgment. I wouldn't give it another moment's attention. However, if that same person said I was a bad mother, I would implode into a pile of self-doubt, ruminating over instances were I had performed poorly or trying to find instances that would prove I was a good mom. I would feel inadequate about myself as a mother, which is one of the major ways I identify myself.
>
> The difference between these two situations is that at the core of my being, I know I'm a great driver, period. The possibility of not

being a great mother despite trying to do my best, exposes my wounded place and gets to the heart of my personal growth opportunity…I'm not good enough. For if I truly believed I was good enough, I would feel the same unshakeable confidence in all my efforts, even as I must admit I have made mistakes as a driver.

Accepting ourselves as great parents can be difficult, as raising babies don't come with the specific rules and instructions that safe driving does. However, judging ourselves as inadequate after we do our best is always an opportunity for growth.

~~~

The words and actions of others are rarely intended to be harmful. Often, slights and diminishing comments from others come from their own personal wounding and have little to do with us. But, because of our wounding, we can take the words or actions of others personally. When we are knocked off balance or feel injured by what others have said or done, we are being presented with an opportunity to look for the root cause of our distress and be compassionate with ourselves as we release our struggles from the past. When we have a better understanding of ourselves, it's easier to have compassion for the slights, mistakes and pain of others.

I don't want to dismiss situations where mental, emotional or physical abuse is present and it *is* personal and needs to be addressed with serious change. How we change our situation is important, but how we came to be in such situations is also important. These situations are major growth opportunities coming to shake us out of harmful patterns. For some, broken and abusive relationships seem to be a recurring theme and we find ourselves asking, "Why does this always happen to me?" To bring meaningful insight, the why questions must focus on I and Me. "Why do I feel this way?" "Why am I in this situation?" "How did I get here?" Such relationships and situations are difficult to see as blessings or opportunities, but this is what they are. They're signs that it's time to love yourself more fully and heal the erroneous belief of unworthiness so you can eliminate such negative relationship patterns from your life now and in the future. The why questions guide you to the core issue holding this pattern of misery in place.

These situations also present you with other blessings and growth opportunities. This is where you empower your innate gifts of courage, love, forgiveness and compassion and use them to overcome a negative experience and catapult yourself to new levels of self-knowledge and self-appreciation. When negativity is aimed at you personally (or as part of a group), be courageous and stand up for yourself. Demand respect and declare your boundaries for acceptable behavior in the future, then stick to those boundaries as your protective shield and the promise you make to your own sense of self. It may be that you need to forgive yourself for being in a bad situation or contributing to the negativity that has evolved. Self-love means bringing yourself back into balance by honoring who you truly are. Doing this opens the door for even bigger blessings. Extend forgiveness and compassion to yourself as you would with a child who made an innocent mistake. This then makes it easier to offer forgiveness and compassion to the perceived perpetrator who is also struggling within him/herself. In truth, it is not possible for someone who truly loves him/herself to act in ways that would harm another person.

Allow the curiosity and innocence of the child-mind help you uncover the little secrets you've hidden away for so long. The more you stay mindful of your thoughts and emotions and dispassionately ask the question why, the more skillful you become at finding the beliefs you already know are holding you back from the peace and joy that is your birthright.

NON-JUDGMENT is a state of neutrality, openness and balance where you, as the impartial observer, can follow your thoughts through the trail of whys. Non-judgment opens the door of honest inquiry so you can gain a better understanding of yourself. In a neutral and honest state, you allow insights into your conscious mind that your subconscious mind would otherwise obscure and reject. This is because you are unconsciously defensive about some part of yourself that you long ago judged as bad or unworthy. A state of non-judgment is a declaration of clemency allowing your darker thoughts and tendencies to come forward for acknowledgement and healing. As a microcosm of the macrocosm, we *all* have dark thoughts and tendencies. It's not our darkness, but the choices we make that define us.

An attitude of judgment means we have already made a decision about the worth and validity of something or someone, including ourselves. On the upside, judgment helps us quickly sort through the chaos of our lives and get on with taking care of what needs to be done. On the downside, it limits our opportunities for discernment, understanding and harmony. How we judge people, behaviors or situations are based on learned and reflexive subconscious programming, which now serves as the basis for our preconceived ideas and prejudices. Judgment is the relatively unconscious measure we use to evaluate all things based on our perception of their value (good/bad, safe/unsafe, worthy/unworthy, etc). Without being aware of it, the pre-programmed judgments we use to measure others are the same ones we use to judge our every thought, word and action. It's why we feel guilty or defensive about our honest mistakes. As part of the internal protection mechanism we use to shelter our wounded child and fragile egos, we have hidden away the parts of ourselves we judged as unacceptable to ourselves or to others. Hidden from our awareness, it becomes easier to see bad behavior in others rather than acknowledge we also share a piece of such negativity. The more strongly we feel about other people and their behavior, the more we are wrestling with some part of that problematic trait in ourselves.

Living in a state of non-judgment is an ideal that promotes balance and response-ability, and we can rise above the wrangling and posturing of good/bad and adequate/inadequate. As an impartial observer with the curiosity of innocence, we can evaluate truth, worth and goodness from a more useful vantage point and then choose how we will respond. Living in non-judgment requires diligent practice, but it delivers the insights and guidance needed for response-ability and change.

> Consider this example:
> Jill was working with a therapist to deal with anxiety and depression. One of the suggested self-help activities was the practice of non-judgment. One morning, she decided she was going to focus on this practice for just twenty minutes. Almost immediately after the deci-

sion, the phone rang and it was Tina, her former roommate of three years. Jill always thought Tina was too concerned about money and spent it foolishly when she had it. Their differences in friends, attitudes about money and shared household duties had put them at bitter odds and caused them to part ways, abandoning a lease and several contracts prematurely. This created even more conflict in their relationship. Now the residual bills were coming to Tina and she was calling again to discuss how this was going to get sorted out. This time she was quite angry.

When Tina called, Jill was in the middle of her practice so she listened quietly and without judgment as Tina complained about how distressed the bills were making her feel. At the end of the call, Jill told Tina she would consider what Tina had said and call her back the next day. As she hung up the phone and started to contemplate the conversation and Tina's preoccupation with money (according to Jill), she began to see her own deeply embedded and broken relationship with money. She realized that she lived in a constant but suppressed fear of not having enough money to take care of herself. This seemed strange because she had always had everything she needed and she had a secure and well-paying job. As she sat quietly, exploring this fear and her relationship with money, a stream of poor financial decisions popped into her mind. She could see how she rationalized spending or not spending based on fear rather than on the merit of the purchase. Jill followed this trail to the origins of her feelings of unworthiness. Since she was in counseling at the time, she made this issue the focus of several sessions until she improved her relationship with money.

Jill's attitude about money was life long and her uncomfortable situation with Tina had been a constant source of strain for months. The combination of the two created a moment where the tool of non-judgment offered Jill a broader perspective on the issue of money in a way that promoted healing of deep-seated issues of unworthiness and feeling unsafe in the world.

Non-judgment lets us see ourselves more clearly and compassionately.

HONESTY is a critical guide on the road to loving yourself. Honesty combines truth, courage and vulnerability into an expansive energy that lifts you to new heights of self-awareness. It takes courage, integrity and vulnerability to look at yourself in ways that can be uncomfortable. If following the "Why do I think or act this way" takes you to an uncomfortable place, it's okay. That discomfort means you are exactly on track. Stay right there. Healing means letting go of anything that no longer serves your health and happiness. If you don't follow the why questions honestly through your discomfort, you can't find the wound calling out for healing and the belief that needs to be released from your subconscious.

SURRENDER is the tool of clarity, release and healing. When you recognize that the pain you are dealing with is coming from inside and let go of your resistance, you can embrace the most fragile parts of yourself. As you do this you are seeing exactly where compassion and forgiveness can be applied. In surrender, compassion rushes in to heal the pain. Release yourself into the arms of your own compassion just as you would embrace an injured child. In this holy moment, you are the doer and the receiver, experiencing union and oneness. This is healing at its deepest level. You are shining your divine light of love into that wound and receiving it, all at the same time.

HOPE comes from the gift of courage. It's the inner strength to pull aside the curtain of fear and hopelessness. It allows you to see the light at the end of the tunnel of darkness engulfing your world. No matter how faint the flicker of light, keep focused on it. Hope is the light shining from your Spark of Divinity and illuminating the path to a better way. It's a lifeline in desperate times. Holding onto hope for a better life also becomes the thought you are projecting into the Field of Possibility where the Mind of God waits for your permission to help you create a better life. Projecting an attitude of hope into the Mind/Field can bring you possibilities beyond those you can imagine by yourself.

FAITH is the bridge between uncertainty and an unconditional knowing based on absolute certainty or proof. In fact, proof negates the need for faith. Faith is believing in your heart that something is true even if you have no logical reason to believe it is so. It is the power of your mind in action. You feel so sure something will happen that you can live in a place of calm appreciation because you just know your desire will manifest in due time. In your faith, you are able to think, speak and behave from a place of expectation and resolve. You are living in the outcome realized and you are projecting your thought into the Mind/Field with the expectation that it's already becoming your reality.

> This example shows child-like innocence, faith, hope and intention coming together to manifest a deeply held desire:
> When Joy was eleven years old, she dreamed of having a car that would allow her to be more independent. A car would get her and her friends to places where they could be themselves, free from adult censure and restrictions. She rarely mentioned her desire to others but she held onto the dream in her heart and mind by visualizing all the places she would go and the happiness this car would bring to her one day.
> One month before her sixteenth birthday, a friend of the family told her mother there was an old but gently used car going to auction. According to this friend, the car's owner would sell it for very little money if a buyer could be found before the auction. Joy and her mother went to look at the car and took it for a quick test drive. That same evening, Joy was the proud owner of a 1989 Delta 88, four weeks before she could legally drive it. Joy loved that car, delighting in its reliability and the fact that she could comfortably pack six of her friends and their gear into it for their many camping and climbing adventures.

Faith is the power of the mind to create. It's the Law of Cause and Effect in action. It's the power to move mountains, to heal illness and to create the life we desire. If we consider the healings attributed to Jesus, the stories tell us faith was the critical tool of healing, whether it was explicit, "Your faith has healed you" or implicit, "Rise, take up thy bed and walk." There are no biblical stories or translations where Jesus claimed to be the healer. People who have healed themselves, settled new lands or discovered new ways of doing something were able to accomplish these feats because they had the conviction of their beliefs.

They knew in their hearts, had faith and kept that faith until their thoughts became their reality.

The tools of mindfulness, curiosity, non-judgment, honesty, hope and faith are available at no cost other than the time and dedicated practice required to make the tool your own and then use it for your growth and happiness. You can pick just one a day and practice it for 15 minutes, extending the time as you realize how simple it can be. The more proficient you become at using these tools, the more you are strengthening the connection with your mental nature. You are bridging the theoretical and functional divide between your conscious and subconscious minds and using that bridge to clear out the beliefs, patterns and obstacles holding you stuck in the rut you are experiencing. You are also using that functional bridge to intentionally reprogram your subconscious mind with positive, affirming and powerful experiences that will become your new default, automatically generating productive thoughts, words, feelings and actions. The more you let go of the faulty beliefs and replace them with the truth of your own love, wisdom and power, the easier it will be to follow through on the promises you make to yourself.

Connecting With Your Emotional Nature

The inseparable and integrated nature of the spirit, mind, emotions and body means that each one can only be known through its interactions with the others. Emotions are divinely inspired messages delivered through our subconscious minds, felt in our bodies and acknowledged and identified by our conscious minds. This is the spirit/mind/body connection working in a synchronized effort to guide us along our paths.

The blessings and tools already discussed come to us as "feel good" emotional sensations. When we allow it, they lift us up to lighter and brighter states of being, if only for a short time. As we move down through our own planes of existence (spiritual, mental, emotional and then physical), our particles move more slowly as we become a little more dense, literally and figuratively. Life becomes more of a struggle and the fact that we are creating our reality becomes more difficult to recognize and accept. Yet, even at these lower vibratory levels there are even more gifts and tools to help us move through our weaker and denser moments.

VULNERABILITY may be one of the most difficult ways to experience ourselves. Vulnerability requires us to be open to the possibility that we are not okay, we are not complete, or even worse…that we are human, saddled with challenges and frailties we might not have the resources to rise above. It requires us to be honest and take deep and thorough inventories of what makes us tick so we can find those places of insecurity and wounding buried beneath the surface. It requires the courage to leap over shame, guilt, self-doubt and fear to bring our struggles into the light of awareness. Even more difficult than our honest admission is acknowledging our frailties and struggles to another human being and asking for their help.

Vulnerability is a virtue that opens the door of our hearts to let in the gifts of compassion, forgiveness and love. In moments of vulnerability, the veneer of pride is breeched and we become aware of greater possibilities than ever before. Asking for help or redemption is the place where loving ourselves truly begins. It demonstrates that we love ourselves enough to do whatever it takes to fix the part holding us out of balance and peace. Being honest exposes our pain to the healing light it seeks. Vulnerability opens us to the healing power of love that is both given and received. When we ask for help we open ourselves to receiving—an action some of us need more time to practice. The asking offers others the opportunity to give—quite possibly in ways they have wanted to give for a long time. Asking for help says we recognize them as equals and honor their talents, strengths and abilities to help us when we're down and need more than we have in the moment. It demonstrates trust and faith that together we can heal the pain rising to the surface for just such healing.

The miracle of vulnerability is the higher vibrations created by the process of giving and receiving as two or more people work together. The giving and receiving circle of energy pulls us together in ways that allow us to feel united with another, especially when we are open to this awareness. Because we are all one in God, the synergy of two working together is amplified by their intention in concert the power of Divine Intelligence. Vulnerability is a powerful tool that clears away the debris and empowers our innate desire to be happy, healthy and whole.

HUMILITY is a blessing of self-awareness that recognizes *you are gifted beyond your ability to acquire such gifts on your own*. It comes as you witness a person, place, thing or event that seems more magnificent than you believe yourself to be. As you bear witness to the brilliance, creativity or splendor before you, you are energetically connecting to it. The feeling of humility comes through the wisdom of *knowing you are part of something greater* than yourself. You're receiving the support and encouragement of this positive feeling without realizing the larger wisdom informing you that you're not alone and you don't carry the weight of the world by yourself.

The classic definition of humility as "a modest or low view of one's own importance" obscures the significance and power of this virtue. Humility does not detract from your magnificence. It's a state of appreciation for your own importance in the larger consciousness as you connect with and honor what is greater than yourself. It's a state of grace where you don't need to prove yourself. You can let your guard down and just be who you are, knowing you are surrounded by competence, love, compassion, wisdom and power. As with all emotions, the feeling of humility comes from within. As you clap wildly, smile with your whole face or feel expansive and filled, you are feeling the vibration of oneness and reverence beaming through you. In this magical moment, you are receiving the reflection of your own magnificent potential. The virtue of humility has been undervalued by its definition and reputation. Its healing powers can be found everywhere; in meditations, a brilliant presentation, a symphony, the birth of a child, the night sky and the blossoming of a flower. You only need to open to the grandeur surrounding you and then experience yourself as an integral part of it.

EQUANIMITY is the feeling of unshakable calm in any situation. It's a state of being where you know you're in balance and have what it takes to respond to whatever presents itself to you. It's a state of grace that evolves as you acknowledge and refine your other tools and honor yourself as the resilient, wise, powerful and loving person you are. It's the balance and harmony equalizing your response to life as you appreciate you have the power to rise above any situation, the wisdom to see yourself and life from a more holistic and beneficent perspective, and the love to respond with compassion, agility and commitment. Equanimity grows with you by degrees as you deepen your connection to your Divine Spark and clear away the faulty and disabling beliefs. It's a gift you receive—because you give it to yourself—as you rise above the perceived duality of good and bad and rest in peace with your divine nature and oneness with God. You will know this blessing when you feel calm in the eye of any storm. Restlessness and distress signal its absence and alert you that there is good work waiting for you.

Our desire to be happy, loved and satisfied is the driving force propelling us through life, and achieving that desire is the ultimate determinant of our health, happiness and overall survival. Our happiness is not diminished by our painful emotions nearly as much as our growth toward a more loving and satisfying reality is hampered by our lack of appreciation for the important revelations they bring. Strengthening the connection with our emotional nature means being open to all feelings and letting them rise to the surface so we can receive the messages and respond appropriately to the wisdom and guidance they offer. Our emotions are calls to action, whether it's to stop and take in the majesty we are part of, or to search honestly for the source of our discomfort so we can make appropriate changes.

Embracing the transformational power of love and all the ways it manifests in our lives is the illumined path to health and happiness and ultimately to Heaven on Earth. The more we use the blessings, gifts and tools we have, the faster we reshape our brains, lives and reality into the peace-filled and loving existence we are compelled to find. This is our most important work, for it is the high road to all we seek in this life. Now the question becomes this. If we are innately drawn toward love in all its forms, how do our pain-filled emotions fit into our quest for harmony, peace and happiness?

Part of the answer to this question can be found in the concepts discussed earlier. Each of us is here in this three-dimensional reality with a specific purpose, which we will accomplish in a manner that is unique to us as individuals. We are also in this collective experience together, as one, because at our current level of understanding we need each other to help separate the truth of who we are from the erroneous beliefs and misperceptions we have accepted for too long. It's up to each of us to choose how we will participate in the redemption of our collective mistakes and the evolution of our collective consciousness. As I mentioned earlier, each of us was born into a body and circumstance that would provide us with the best opportunities to heal the wounding held in our individual consciousness and in the collective consciousness. We don't recognize that we actually chose to incarnate as the person we are, but if we could see the larger reality, we would realize this was the agreement we made. We made it with the loving intention to participate in humanity's evolution to the highest vibrations of love.

Because you are one with God, *you are whole and complete already*. You hold within you all that is…past, present and future…and the knowledge of good and evil. Just as your feelings of love, gratitude, compassion and courage rise up from the essence of who you are, so too does your sadness, grief, guilt, shame, fear, doubt, hopelessness and unworthiness. These feelings rise up not because they define you, but because you are part of the collective consciousness that still believes we are separate from God and each other and therefore we are only capable of much suffering and little joy. Whatever situation or condition you find yourself in, take a moment to consider it as an opportunity to heal the pain and misconceptions you have about yourself. As you heal and love yourself, you are making quantum leaps in the Mind of God/Field of Possibility and as you do this, you are contributing to the higher vibration of the collective human consciousness. Take a moment to be both amazed and humbled by your own magnificent contributions to our ascending evolution.

All Emotions Illuminate the Path of Healing

"The wound is the place where the light enters you." – Rumi

How you honestly feel about yourself indicates the level of trust you have in your capacity to love and support yourself through life's experiences. How you feel about your capacity to love and support yourself is also a direct reflection of your trust in God's love, wisdom and power. Individually and collectively we are still an evolutionary work in progress, and so we all struggle, make mistakes and have healing work to do. For the most part, we didn't learn to accept our emotions as messengers and roadmaps to self-love. We are adverse to experiencing and *re-experiencing* the discomforts that come with our negative emotions, so we push them from our awareness, doing our best to camouflage them in a way unique to our beliefs and life-long experiences. Unrecognized and unhealed, they ride along in the background of our subconscious contributing to our 95% preprogrammed thoughts, words and actions. To flush them out of hiding, we need someone or something outside ourselves to push our buttons and fire up those uncomfortable feelings in an undeniable way. Without any awareness of how we do it, we attract a person or event into our lives to help us expose our emotional pain. When this happens, our default response is to blame the person or event for our disappointments, struggles and pain. We repeatedly attract people and situations that will help us feel our pain until we change the beliefs holding these patterns in place. The divine guidance offered by our negative experiences and feelings are recurring opportunities to learn something valuable about ourselves so we can decide what changes to make in order to heal the old wounds crying out for redemption. Each experience offers us an opportunity to choose a different perspective, approach and reality.

We live within the Mind of God, an Infinite Cosmic Consciousness that provides everything we need to find our way back to the Everlasting Love from which we were created. Within this much larger Consciousness, we attract people and situations to help us realize our potential as loving, wise and powerful beings. In intimate relationships, we attract our mirror image as a beautiful reflection of the love we are. Our inner knowing recognizes this person as the perfect partner for our journey to self-awareness and it leaps for joy...we fall in love. This magical and energetic pull locks us on course for learning about ourselves so we can heal and grow.

The magical wonderment of new love may feel like it's wearing off as a relationship becomes more familiar. For some, what was cute now seems annoying as patterns of speech, behavior and attitude emerge from hidden places. Sometimes our love and happiness becomes tainted with inconsistencies, anger, resentment or betrayals we didn't sense earlier. The most difficult thing to acknowledge is that this person is still our perfect mirror image and we, with the support of the Mind/Field, drew them to us for just this reason. The knowledge and growth possible from our relationships comes with the courage to look at the wounding being exposed in difficult moments so we can acknowledge and heal it. And, before you blame God for a pain-filled relationship, look again. Chances are very good there were signs suggesting that the problems cropping up now were foreshadowed by early behavior you chose to ignore for many reasons.

Consider this: After the intense feelings of love subside into the familiar and every day patterns, we begin to sense the innate longing that compels us toward happiness. As we wonder what happened to the blissful feelings we experienced at the start of the relationship, we may think the other person is not as invested in the relationship, that we are being taken advantage of, or we think we're giving more than we're receiving. This could be happening because we failed to set appropriate boundaries in the relationship, a sign of our sense of unworthiness. Another possibility may be that we are unconsciously rejecting or devaluing what we are being given, again an indicator of unworthiness. No matter how we process our discomfort, we end up feeling angry, sad or resentful. These negative emotions are telling us we're out of balance and changes need to be made. Too often, our faulty perceptions include blaming the other person as the cause of our pain. We are certain they are the one who needs to change. While that is indeed possible, this is not the first step on the personal path of healing and growth. Blaming others for how we feel is a dead end leading to more separation and distress. If we don't address the wounded part of ourselves being exposed in this situation, we'll continue the same patterns of thought and behavior that brought us to this point. We can abandon this relationship, but before long we'll attract more of the very same learning opportunities that are making us miserable in the current one. Blaming others is a place of powerlessness and repetitive patterns.

Healing starts with acknowledging the uncomfortable feeling and asking the why questions. But the question is not, "Why do I feel this way when s/he does this or that?" This or that behavior is simply piercing an existing wound, one that has risen to the surface and is calling for your attention. Healing comes when we find the source of our discomfort and release it from our own hearts and minds. When we ask the right why questions, we can get to the core issue, "Why do I feel unworthy—or inadequate?" As we find the place where this lie is held, we can release it and replace it with self-love and acceptance. As we release our fear and sense of unworthiness, we discover we're not as angered by those same words and actions as we once were. This is because we are releasing the faulty belief maintaining our biased perception and attracting the same types of learning opportunities to us. We are healed. From our new perspective, we are empowered to stand up for ourselves and set new expectations for our relationships. This is also part of our growth process. In turn, how others respond to our evolving process then becomes the stage for even more interaction, understanding, compassion, forgiveness and growth.

How we interact with and respond to the people in our lives is a clear indication of how we are honoring and loving ourselves. This is the purpose of and the blessings realized through relationships. When we heal an issue all the way back to its origin, we no longer attract this learning opportunity to us. When we walk our journey without the baggage of faulty beliefs and old habits and patterns, we experience a profound sense of gratitude for the lessons that brought the healing and for the freedom and balance we are living as a result. Our gratitude is an emotional sign of great understanding and wellbeing.

Emotions and Past Lives

As we follow our emotions back to the source of our erroneous beliefs and thought patterns, we will inevitably find ourselves dealing with family and ancestral traits and the misconceptions handed down through the ages. It's part of our spiritual, mental, emotional and genetic endowment. We are made of the same molecules as the stars, and the same hydrogen, carbon, oxygen and nitrogen elements that Buddha, Jesus, Hitler and the authorities of the Spanish Inquisition were made of. But, we rarely consider the effect this may have on our reality and our potential. Since we exist in the same cosmic consciousness and share the same molecular components of the best and the worst of humanity, we are one and contain all possibilities—the good and the not so good. We may reject being any part of the debauchery of our ancestors, but it's part of our collective consciousness. In our deepest darkest molecular structures we carry its memory, even as we block its possibility from our awareness. As we do this, we stay stuck in its painful history by holding its low vibration in the collective field. This shows up in our lives in different ways… unique to our own journey and agreement.

According to ancient wisdom, we are a microcosm of the macrocosm. This means, as Rumi offered, we are "the entire ocean, in a single drop." Within our individual potential we contain all possibilities. Because we are eternal beings living in an evolutionary time-space continuum, we are blessed to have just a few of our many possibilities to address during this lifetime. The possibilities we are dealing with as individuals are based on that agreement we made when we incarnated into this life and they are influenced by the choices we make as we move through life. Denying the dark shadows held in our energetic field is what holds our struggles in place. When we intentionally confront the remnants of our darkness as they show up in our lives, we can see the errors, abuses of power and misuses of love that we, and all of humanity, have been involved in for eons, right up to the present. When we acknowledge our mistakes and the pain they are causing, we can release them and fill that space with forgiveness, compassion, love and gratitude. (Recall the example of being cut off by a reckless driver. When we acknowledge we too have pulled such a maneuver, we find forgiveness, compassion and peace.) This is how we heal ourselves and it's how we contribute to the healing of the collective consciousness.

Our inherent strengths and weakness are natural outcomes of ancestral heritage, familial tendencies, society's influence, life experience, and of course, connection with our divine nature. As we use emotions to guide our healing, we may discover that our exploration into the core of our discomfort take us deeper into our ancestral legacy than anything we could have imagined. Our life experiences may be providing many reasons to feel the way we do, but ultimately we are attracting these experiences so we can heal very old beliefs and errors imbedded in our ancestral heritage. Knowing our family history and thinking about our struggles as programmed outcomes resulting from that history can aid our understanding somewhat, but it doesn't take us to the core of our distress and recurring problems. More often, it just keeps us in the story, explaining how we got where we are and justifying why we feel the way we do. All this happens on the analytical level of conscious mind and it isn't discernably connected to the suffering entrenched in the subconscious mind. When we embrace our discomfort and follow the why questions to the source of our pain and problems, we are connecting our conscious and subconscious mind in a way that makes recognition, release and healing possible.

Past lives are three-dimensional constructs for our linear perspective on reality. They are a way to visualize the struggles held in our molecular structures and DNA so we can understand why we feel the way we do. It's not necessary to believe in reincarnation to use the idea of past lives to gain insight. A "past life experience" is simply an understandable conceptualization. It's like a story or movie allowing us to see the imbedded nature of pain and a way to appreciate great gifts, talents and wisdom that seem to come from nowhere. When we can see the story and the pain running back through time, we can appreciate that we came to our place of pain naturally. Visualizing a past life helps us recognize we are still holding pieces of our ancestral heritage; a heritage that has been causing distress for many generations and is now causing pain in *our* lives. When we acknowledge our struggle and the deeply seeded origins of it in ourselves, we can then consciously apply the healing gifts of forgiveness, love, compassion and gratitude. From this place of release, it's easier to make different choices and live a more peace-filled life.

Emotions Are Guides To Our Healing
— Examples —

The array of human emotions appears to be large, but they essentially boil down to either love or fear in the way they affect us mentally, emotionally and physically. Because life is a unique experience for each of us, it isn't possible to discuss how to follow each emotion to the hidden error causing the imbalance. Consider these real life examples of how relationship issues can trigger our emotions and how we can use those events to get in touch with our shadow issues. (These are actual accounts of individual journeys. The names and details of those involved have been modified to protect privacy and confidentiality.)

Anger

Cindy and John were life-long friends, having grown up in the same neighborhood and attending the same church and schools. In high school, they had even gone steady for a short time. They stayed in touch during college and returned to their hometown after graduation. They shared many of the same friends from the old neighborhood and would get together regularly for hiking, skiing and after work gatherings.

In their mid-30's, John became involved with a woman from outside their usual circle of friends. Cindy *wanted* to like John's new partner Crystal, but she just didn't think Crystal was the right person for her friend. As the months went by, Cindy tried to avoid interacting with Crystal when they were at gatherings. When she did interact with her, she found herself increasingly angry. Heading home from a particular event where she had spent considerable time listening to Crystal's thoughts about politics, religion and family, Cindy found herself in a rage. As she drove, she felt like she'd lost her mind as she screamed out the window and pounded her fist on the steering wheel. This reaction was, admittedly, out of control...even irrational.

When she got to her apartment, Cindy put on meditation music, lit some candles and lied down on her bed to ask the question, "Why do I feel this way?" Staying focused on her intent to understand her own emotional reaction, the words "manipulator, liar and whore" appeared in her mind. The next question became, "What do those words have to do with my anger?" As she stayed with her uncomfortable feelings and negative words, Cindy saw herself mirrored in Crystal. Cindy now had to look at the shadow side of herself that somehow resonated with a manipulator, liar and whore. As she stayed with her efforts to understand where all this was coming from, she remembered instances in her own life where she had told white lies and half-truths to get what she wanted; situations where she had manipulated narratives or circumstances to hide her deep sense of inadequacy or give her an advantage over others; and ways she had over extended herself or used sex in an attempt to be more accepted and loveable to others.

As she observed the string of life events that seemed to prove she was indeed all of those unacceptable awful things, she saw her mother, her grandmothers, her great grandmothers and all the women before them lining up through history, their shoulders slumped and heads hung down. She literally felt their regret, shame and sorrow in her own body. She became aware of the lie many women have lived with and handed down for so many generations. Not worthy of equal status, not good enough and strong enough to stand up for themselves, they believed they had to act in these demeaning ways to get what they needed for a decent life or just to survive. She felt their rejection of themselves. She felt their anger at men for having made a society where such behavior was considered necessary and normal for so long. As she witnessed the line of ancestors and experienced each emotion as it came up, Cindy could see how long this belief had endured and she was able to appreciate that she had come to this place naturally. Her feelings of anger, resentment and rejection were replaced with forgiveness, understanding and compassion for herself. Feelings of forgiveness and compassion seemed to radiate from her heart to all of her ancestors. As she stayed focused on the images of her ancestors, she noticed her heart opening with compassion to both the women and the men who had perpetrated this paradigm of unworthiness and struggle for so many generations. Staying with the experience until she felt calm and peaceful, she became aware of a sense of gratitude for the understanding and healing this insight had brought to her.

As a result of this meditative journey, Cindy was able to spend time with John and Crystal without being angry or annoyed as in the past. She was also able to see that her own relationships with men needed some exploration, understanding, forgiveness and compassion. The revelation birthed from her anger with Crystal made a dramatic impact on her personal and professional relationships, and equally important, Cindy made a big step towards becoming a more authentic and happy person.

Disdain For Authority — It's probably obvious that this example is my own experience, so I'll own it from the start.

I grew up in a large patriarchal, Catholic family with what I considered to be an average amount of dysfunction. I attended a strict, heavy-handed parochial school through the eighth grade. I became a well-regarded intensive care nurse in a community hospital. I married at thirty and was divorced by forty. I had a good life and wonderful friends but always felt restless, anxious and somewhat depressed.

Through daily practice of journaling, I became aware of a growing sense of contempt for all forms of authority, especially male authority figures. According to my way of thinking, people in authority were untrustworthy, self-indulgent and abusive of power. At times I even saw myself as a helpless victim. As my distress started to have a greater impact on my personal and work relationships, I became even more aware of these feelings and thoughts. I realized I had a fear of speaking up to those in positions of authority. When I did speak up, it was usually an ill-conceived explosion rather than a calm exchange of ideas. As I spent time with my feelings, I realized they had been with me for most of my life, remembering episodes with my father, my elementary school teachers, boyfriends and superiors at work.

As part of my attempts to bring happiness into my life, I attended a Tom Campbell Consciousness retreat. Following Tom's instructions to take an inquiry into meditation and expect to receive insights and information, I put on the headphones and let the binaural beats take me deep into an altered state. My question was, "Why do I have such a contempt for authority and men?"

The first thing I noticed was an erotic feeling flowing through my whole body. The first image that came to my mind was of 16th Century Rome. I saw myself as a high-ranking male official attending an event in a large and extravagantly ornate room. In this vignette or past life experience, I was a man and an active participant in the orgies held in this place. I saw myself raping a young boy and I felt it in my body as if it was actually happening. As I observed this scene, I wanted to stop the experience, but remembered that following the why is a necessary part of getting answers, so I asked the question, "Why am I raping this child?" The answer came back, "Because I can. I have the power to do whatever I want." As the scene closed, I saw blood spray across the room as I slit someone's throat with a large double-edged knife. In the interval between this and the next vision, I saw myself wrapped in a cocoon secured with brightly colored threads, which I was given to understand as strands of DNA.

The next scene started in a remote medieval village. I was a sad, bent woman struggling to survive. I had three small children who were playing in the dirt outside the hut. There were no men here. The thunder of horses came racing through the village. Soldiers were burning huts and scooping up children to take as slaves. I saw myself hiding behind a tree, as I made no attempt to save my own children. I was frightened and angry, but what I felt most strongly was shame. As this scene closed, I found myself in the same cocoon with bright colored threads. This time it was gently opening as I transitioned to the final vignette.

Exhausted and filled with shame and guilt, I was lying on an altar surrounded by many people. They were speaking so quietly I could only hear a musical hum. I recognized this as a healing. Each healer brought a different gift to the ceremony. They brought light, warmth, herbs, gentle touch and some whispered loving and kind thoughts into my mind. Each of them reached out with compassion and gently honored the pain I was experiencing and the road I had traveled to get there. There was no mention of the past or of the future. All I felt was peace and calm as their love and compassion washed my pain away.

As part of acknowledging my problems with authority and dealing with the shame of not being my own advocate or speaking up for myself in this current life, I shared my experience with my fellow retreat participants. Their respect, compassion and outpouring of love in the form of hugs and kind words completed my healing. I felt tenderness and compassion from both men and women in a way I never had before.

In the months that followed, I continued to journal about this new self-understanding and I gained further insights and healing release. I remembered times when I used my own position of authority to manipulate group decisions, and situations where I used my power in ways that were not balanced with wisdom and love, and this had caused pain to others. As I continued to work with the insights from this experience, I realized that those authority figures I had had such disdain for were reflections of myself asking for recognition, forgiveness and release. As I worked with these insights in meditations and later experiences, I was able recognize the ancestral memories of abuse, shame and fear and release them to the understanding of forgiveness, compassion and unconditional love.

As a result of this experience, I'm more mindful in my interactions with others, especially those who represent authority to me. If I sense familiar patterns of distrust or disdain, I take a moment to explore, "Why am I feeling this way?" If it feels like old patterns trying to pop through the veneer, I ask myself, "How can I respond to this situation from a more powerful and loving perspective?" As time goes on, I am less distrustful and I feel more free to be authentic and express my thoughts in more loving and powerful ways which better represent the gifts I have to offer.

Regardless of the message presenting for recognition, the process for following emotions to their source and receiving the healing is the same. We must feel our emotions strong enough to follow them where they lead. As we receive images or thoughts, we must courageously stay the course and accept what we are being shown, asking questions that will take us deeper into our own mystery. When we search with honesty and non-judgment, the answers come because we are ready to accept the message and the gift of healing. No matter what form the answers come in, the experience and the understanding will take us to a place of forgiveness, compassion and love. This is the blessing offered by our emotional guidance.

Not all emotions are cataclysmic or awe-inspiring, but they are all messengers. Along with your patterns of thought, words and actions, emotions offer valuable information about how you are growing in the mastery of loving and valuing yourself and how free you feel to be your authentic powerful self. Recurrent patterns of self-deprecating and self-sabotaging behavior or constant feelings of anxiety, dread and depression are all indicative of hidden darkness pulling you out of balance. No matter how legitimate these emotions seem to be or how long the beliefs supporting them have been part of your life and ancestral heritage, now is always the right time to let them go.

Healing yourself is a process of loving yourself so much that you will walk through the valley of darkness to bring light to your pain. Loving yourself means sitting with yourself and holding yourself in the arms of compassion so you feel safe enough to allow your painful emotions to rise up into your awareness and *feel the discomfort* in your body. It will be uncomfortable, but only for a short while. It can't hurt you like the actual event(s) did. As you experience your feelings, you pass through the layers of pain to the place where the memory and pain are stored. Even if you can't "see" an actual event, you are still, in a very real sense, revisiting the place where it all started.

As you do this, you will become aware that this was not about you. It was not about your worthiness, your lovability, your goodness, importance or power. You may recognize those beliefs as mistakes without foundation. This is the moment you can release the hold they have on you. Just keep breathing as you let the beliefs and pain attached to them wash away. You know you are healing because the negative feelings that were so uncomfortable are draining away as you experience the relief in your body. You may be aware that you are forgiving yourself for the choices you made that brought you to a situation, or for thinking you were responsible for what happened, or for staying trapped in this dark place for such a long time. You may feel compassion for yourself as you would for someone who had been through the same experience. You will emerge with a new understanding of yourself...a more powerful, wise and loving sense of self.

Interdimensional Healing Is Your Purpose and Your Gift

Each time you choose to think, speak and act from a higher vibration of love, understanding and compassion, you are contributing to a higher vibration within the collective consciousness of humanity. When you follow your emotional pain to the source of abuse or misunderstanding to forgive and release the hidden darkness that has been part of humanity's struggle, you are also contributing to the higher vibration of the collective. This is known as ancestral or interdimensional healing. This is your contribution and the gift of love you bring.

It may be difficult to grasp the idea of interdimensional healing, but science can help where Ancient Wisdom remains cryptic. Einstein told us reality is an illusion; the double slit experiment demonstrated how we shift outcomes with observation and the power of our minds; and quantum mechanics informs us that time is not linear. These concepts are difficult to put into the context of our day-to-day experiences but all we really need to know is this: all of eternity exists in a single moment. The present moment is our only reality...*it is as we observe it*. Because time is not linear, what is forgiven and released in the moment is also forgiven and released from the past. And, the past is only a different dimension of the continuum in which we exist. If we forgive and release something in the present moment, we no longer observe life with the past perception of what reality seemed to be, and we no longer create reality from the brokenness of our ancestral heritage. When we move forward from such healings with a more enlightened and loving sense of self and continue to make choices grounded in love, understanding and compassion, we are creating a better future for ourselves and for humanity. The future is also just a different dimension that exists in the eternity of the present moment. Interdimensional healing—healing the past in the present—is a possibility in the Mind/Field because it is the Universal Laws of Cause and Effect, Vibration and Correspondence working in unison to guide us all back to the Love of God.

> *All of eternity exists in this single moment.*

If you have followed your pain to the place where you have "seen" the heritage of pain, suffering and abuse and then experienced forgiveness and compassion for your family and ancestors, you are doing very important work. You're shifting the collective consciousness to a higher frequency as you transmute the negative energy of unworthiness and fear to the higher vibrations of love. Such an extraordinary act of compassion and service can only be undertaken by someone with the wounds to guide them to such dark places, and who also has the power to bring light and love to that darkness. As you break the bondage of lies, suffering and addictions that have existed in families for generations, you are healing yourself, your family and future generations with your magnificent and God-given gifts of power, wisdom and love.

These healing *experiences* are often completed with a sense of heart-felt relief and joy. We know we have healed something major when we feel calm and peaceful in situations that once caused us distress. We can also be assured of healing when we experience a sense of gratitude for the pain-provoking events that brought us to the place of healing and the peace we are now experiencing. There may be times when we might need to look at this again for a deeper understanding, but we will know we have healed the biggest piece of our misunderstanding. Because of this healing experience, we also know we have the wisdom, grace and strength to finish digging out any remaining pieces should they come to our awareness.

NOTE: This healing journey can be done with physical symptoms, painful memories or destructive thoughts or actions. You can start this leg of your journey whenever you feel like you've had enough of the struggles and discontent that mark your life. It does involve confronting the pain and darkness hidden deep inside, but you have what you need and there is always help available when you choose to ask for it. You do *not* need to go through this alone. There are many modalities and skilled practitioners to assist and support you through healing the wounds of the past, especially if trauma is severe or you are new to the healing process. Not all therapists will use this particular method, but they can help you work through the revelations you receive from such a journey in their own compassionate and productive ways.

Modalities include but are not limited to hypnotherapy, therapeutic counseling, bodywork, acupuncture, meditation, Shamanic Journeying, energy healing, Yoga, Tai Chi, Breathing Techniques and plant medicine. Not all healing modalities work for every person. You must find the ones that speak to your uniqueness. Always remember your life is a journey of healing and you are worthy of support, kindness, compassion and love along the path.

Connecting With Your Physical Nature

Many of us learned to think of ourselves as a physical body having a physical experience with little thought to other planes of existence. We have also learned to treat our bodies as an expendable commodity instead of the precious resource it is. Loving yourself whole includes developing a profound respect and adoration for the physical vehicle that carries you along this journey. Your body is the place where spirit, mind, emotions and body come together. In this three-dimensional reality, it is your only means of communicating with your internal and external environment in order to accomplish the things you came here to do. As both a receiver and transmitter, the body allows you to experience and interact with your environment so you can learn to appreciate yourself as the cause and creator of your reality.

Strengthening your connection with your physical nature means paying attention to all the information your body is receiving through the sensations and thoughts coming to your awareness. Respecting and honoring yourself implies you are listening to those messages and responding appropriately. Like pulling your hand from a hot pan or putting on a warm coat to go out in freezing temperatures, health-enhancing behaviors become reflexive when you love yourself and honor the body enabling you to experience life to the fullest.

Your physical body is as unique as your mind, perceptions and experiences. People come in all shapes, sizes, colors, interests and desires, and thank God they do. The world would be stagnant and very boring if we were all the same. None of us fit into one-size-fits-all recommendations or protocols for health and happiness. Books, magazines and the Internet are a cornucopia of health recommendations, diets, exercise routines and the like. They offer research, information, opinions, insights, and guidance in all manners of health and wellbeing. Most of them will be helpful to some people, but not to everyone. As you look for ways to respect your body and support your health, it's important to embrace your uniqueness and follow your instincts, intuitions and intelligent mind. Develop healthy lifestyle behaviors that work for you and make you feel good while doing them. When you find what works, make it a regular part of your life. Continue to explore new possibilities as they spark your interest and serve your intentions. Your body will always let you know when you are on the right track because you will feel good; nagging little problems may disappear. This is the wisdom of the body speaking to you. If you have trouble following through with your lifestyle changes, take some time to look for the "I'm not worthy" belief sabotaging your strategic plans to be happy and healthy. (Reminder: This is not permission to disregard seeking or following medical advice as it is warranted.)

Supporting Your Physical Health

There is no way to overstate how the treatment of your body will impact your health, for better or for worse. Everything you think and do affects the balance and function of your body. You are pure energy made up of subatomic particles and waves moving in open space and interacting with other waves and particles. That is true of every person and every thing in your environment. Absolutely everything you do to and with your body is an interaction within electromagnetic fields...fields of possibility that become your reality. As you consider a plan for maintaining the health of your body, it's important to remember that whether it's the food you eat, the liquid you drink, the air you breathe or the positive or negative energy in the space you occupy, your particles and waves are interacting with it all. Things that support your health bring you into balance, increase your vibration and improve function across all systems. Things that are not so healthy and supportive have the opposite effect.

NUTRITION is the food you eat. What you eat and the stress you live with are undeniably the two greatest self-imposed determinants of physical health. (Part Two went into great detail on stress and its detrimental effects, so I won't repeat it in this section.) Food contains calories and calories are simply the fuel providing energy to the body. In addition, food contains many but not all of the necessary nutrients we need to function, grow and stay well. The imbalance between calories and nutrients is where many of our problems begin.

Our ancestors found the food they needed in their local surroundings and moved if their supply became scarce. For them, convenience foods were literally low hanging fruits. Fast food was grubs found by turning over a rock. As they learned to cultivate and preserve, their food supply became more reliable. Domestication of animals helped with farm chores and increased their sources of protein. These advances in food procurement served humanity well for thousands of years.

Several things have come about in the last hundred years to dramatically alter not only our relationship with food but what we consider healthy and nutritious. First, food has become so plentiful that we can use it as an emotional salve. We eat for comfort when we're upset. We use it to pacify boredom. We offer it as an enticement or reward for good behavior. We can even become addicted to it. Secondly, some of us are moving so fast we take little time to plan or prepare meals and we don't consider the nutritional value of the food we consume to fill the void. Next, the quality of our food has changed. We've moved from food that was mostly locally sourced, organic and whole—with a rare sweet treat—to a diet filled with modified, sprayed, processed, sweetened, chemically laden and prepackaged "food." Not surprisingly, alongside these shifts in emotional association and food composition are the rise in asthma, allergies, autoimmune diseases, obesity and related illnesses. Lastly, the quality of food and these unfortunate health consequences have been fostered by corporations presenting faulty or misleading information, misguided government approval, medical endorsement and marketing campaigns. For example, some of us grew up in an era when science and health experts informed us that margarine, a hydrogenated oil, was healthier than butter, a naturally occurring dairy product, and zero calorie artificial sweeteners like aspartame were touted as healthier than the calorie-dense cane sugar. It took decades before there was sufficient evidence to disprove these two well-accepted health advisories. The truth is, both hydrogenated oils and artificial sweeteners have more negative health consequences than their naturally occurring alternatives *consumed in reasonable amounts.*

In very recent times, there is a revolution in nutritional awareness causing more of us to consider food as medicine, or at least a worthy adjunct for health. As you consider making changes in your dietary choices, take time to explore anti-inflammatory diets and the diet-related causes of leaky gut syndrome and autoimmune diseases. Having a better understanding of common diseases and their relationship to the food you eat may help guide your choices. If you're not interested in a deep dive into nutrition, here are a few simple thoughts to keep in mind as you shop and eat:

- ~ If it doesn't look like it was plucked from a plant, pulled from the earth or taken from an animal then there is probably a much healthier choice.
- ~ If you can't pronounce the name of an ingredient then chances are good it was produce in a laboratory. Chances are also good that your body won't recognize it as an absorbable nutrient and will then need to figure out how to deal with it as a foreign substance.
- ~ Processed and packaged foods necessarily have chemicals binding the ingredients together and preserving them in a wrapper or box. Most of them contain incredibly high amounts of sodium and sugar or other sweeteners. Whether due to excessive calories from sugar or the use of artificial ingredients, these choices are worse

than not good for you for the same molecular reasons. High sodium contributes to water retention and high blood pressure.

~ As you consider governmental stamps of approval on the safety of food additives, you may enjoy this. The FDA has approved Castoreum, a secretion from the anal glands of beavers, as a "natural flavoring" for foods and beverages. (Hats off to the individual who discovered this.) So when you read "natural flavoring" on the ingredient list, it's a safe bet the vanilla, strawberry or raspberry flavor you taste didn't come from those plants. If it had, the manufacturer would have proudly named that ingredient. This doesn't imply that Castoreum is unhealthy as such; it does after all come from a natural source before it's processed. If you consider this sleight of hand government approval alongside others such as the margarine and artificial sweeteners, you may begin to think these agencies have other priorities. Labels and advertising can be quite misleading when it comes to the actual state of "natural" and the health benefits claimed by the manufactures of such products.

~ When it comes to chemical additives and genetically modified organisms (GMO), there are volumes of conflicting information regarding health effects. Consider this: these foods and additives are molecular compounds and substances held together at least in part by laboratory engineered bonds that don't occur in nature but can impact nature and the nature of your body. They have an altered or engineered molecular structure with atomic properties that when ingested will interact with your own atomic structures. Occasional contact with such "food" may not have a major impact, but daily and heavy exposure can add up to more permanent consequences. Ultimately, you will need to decide for yourself what makes sense for you.

~ Your gut brain will let you know if something you are eating isn't in your best interest. Heartburn, indigestion, belching, gas, diarrhea, constipation, nasal congestion, itching and headaches are just a few sooner-than-later signs you have eaten something that doesn't agree with you. Better to pay attention to these signs now, than attempt to figure out the source of diet related chronic health problems after they develop.

~ A prayer over your food or a moment of mindfulness and gratitude brings you and the energy of your food into alignment for your health and happiness. It acknowledges that, indeed, you have been given your daily bread and it honors everything from the natural elements that produced it to all those who labored to get it to your plate. As you taste each morsel you are present with the experience of fueling and nourishing your body and honoring your connection to all that is. This fills more than the empty space in your stomach.

WATER is essential because 60–70% of your body is water. More so than food, water is critical to survival and adequate amounts are necessary for your systems and cells to do their work efficiently. As a rule of thumb, the average woman needs over two liters per day and the average man needs more than three liters. The daily water requirement is actually more than this with the extra amounts coming from food and the other beverages you consume. If you are working up a sweat, doing heavy manual labor, breastfeeding or struggling with fever, vomiting or diarrhea, more water is necessary. (In some cases, electrolytes may also be needed, but this should be determined with the help of a professional.)

Most liquids contain water, though not all liquids help with hydration. Carbonation, caffeine and alcohol can be dehydrating. As with your food, the molecular and atomic structure of the liquids you drink and the containers they are stored in will be interacting with your own atomic make up. It's important to drink pure clean water as your primary source of hydration…molecular structures being what they are.

BREATHING is the essence of life. The ancient teachers advised us to take three slow deep breaths to center ourselves. Some of our mothers offered the same advice when we were angry or irritable. They understood the calming benefit of deep breathing. Their wisdom and experience told them what science is discovering now. A nice full belly breath triggers the tenth cranial nerve, signaling the parasympathetic nervous system that all is well. With this message, the neurotransmitters collectively sound the "ahem" as the body and mind relax. Breathing is the life sustaining activity that moves oxygen into the body and carbon dioxide out. If this activity is diminished in some way, all other systems are also diminished, even to the point of collapse.

As with your food and water, the air you breathe has a natural molecular structure and atomic vibration. When the air is contaminated with pollution or chemicals, including artificially scented candles and air fresheners, you are breathing in the molecules of chemicals with each breath. Since these chemicals aren't found in nature, it may be reasonable to imagine that mingling their atomic vibration with your own is less than beneficial to your lungs and your body. Just because it claims to neutralize odors or sweeten the environment doesn't mean it's good for you.

On a spiritual level, breathing and following the breath are methods used in many forms of meditation. Mindful breathing brings your body to a state of calm and balance. It quiets your busy mind so you might hear the Still Small Voice Within.

SILENCE is golden. This truth was also taught by the Ancient Teachers…and by our mothers. Whether quieting your mind in meditation or holding your tongue when you desperately want to share some salient point, silence is often the best approach. You can't hear the Still Small Voice Within if your mind is chattering away about this and that. Listening with presence is the only way to hear answers to the questions you may be asking.

In your communications with others, it's important to note that they are rarely asking for advice. Most often, people are looking for acknowledgement and compassion. Listening in silence is the response that says, "I honor your experience and I am here with you now." This is a gift of self and of love. The same is true of addressing people who annoy you. Angry or snarky comments, verbal or written, only fuel division, misunderstanding and struggle. One of the greatest powers you have is to silently hold your struggling brothers and sisters in the arms of compassion, love and understanding.

SLEEP is the space of time where your body heals and rejuvenates itself. It's where messages in the form of dreams can come to you. Most sources agree the average adult requires seven to nine hours of uninterrupted sleep each night in order to function most efficiently. Some studies suggest the closer you come to setting your sleep schedule with the setting and rising of the sun, the more in synch you will be with nature and the natural rhythm of your body.

If you have trouble going to sleep or staying asleep, you may have too much on your mind. It's possible you're not letting your mind and body power down before going to bed. Investigate "sleep hygiene" and all the different techniques you might employ to help you get those much-needed hours of rejuvenation. If you regularly wake up tired, seek professional help for the possibility of sleep apnea. Inadequate amounts of restful sleep are attributed to many chronic diseases including heart disease, depression and dementia.

EXERCISE is a must. Health experts agree that 150 minutes of aerobic exercise or 75 minutes of vigorous exercise, spread out over a week, is considered a minimum amount. More is better. Aerobic means large muscle activity (walking, biking, stairs, swimming, etc.) that elevates your heart rate over its resting rate. It's important to choose something you love doing because this increases the probability you will actually do it.

Exercise burns off the excess calories. It uses up excess adrenaline pumped into your system by the stress response. It builds collateral circulation for many muscles including the heart. It, along with water, lubricates your joints and increases flexibility and strength. Exercise, especially when you are enjoying it, produces endorphins, which promote a sense of wellbeing. It's also credited with delaying and slowing the progression of dementia. If you plan your exercise just right, it can help you avoid a few negative influences in your life, such as the TV, refrigerator and pantry. All of this for a mere 30 minutes, five days a week.

There are many different forms of exercise and all of them have merit, especially if we don't turn them into an addiction or strain our body's capacity to do what we are asking of it. Less familiar forms of exercise including Tai Chi, Qi Gong and Yoga have been part of health programs in Eastern cultures for millennia and may be more beneficial to our overall health. These forms of movement and meditation may not appear to be much exercise to the uninitiated but they are quite vigorous and beneficial to both body and mind in actual practice. In my experience, these three practices can offer profound release, relaxation and insight.

FOREST BATHING, known to the Japanese as shinrin yoku, is now gaining appreciation in Western cultures. By increasing the parasympathetic tone of the nervous system, it helps return hormone levels and body functions to a healthier balance. Forest bathing is the practice of immersing yourself in nature, preferably but not limited to an undisturbed canopy of trees, with the sole purpose of interacting with nature. It's not about exercise, like a walk in the woods. Forest bathing is the mindful contemplation of a leaf, tree, stream or the whisper of the breeze blowing through the leaves or across your face. Its benefits come through your experience as you interact with nature itself. On a very deep level, the electrons of your body and mind are involved in an energetic exchange with the electrons of those things living in the peaceful balance of nature. Such a practice opens you to the possibility of actually sensing yourself as one with the life force of the tree or stream you are interacting with in the moment. Like falling in love, forest bathing can have profound calming and healing effects.

SACRED SPACE is a dedicated room or corner with a comfortable and quiet place to sit and nurture yourself. It's a place where you can meditate, read a good book, close your eyes and find peace or contemplate how you are feeling. It's a space that encourages you to relax and let go. It is not the space where you work, interact on social media or watch television. What this space looks and feels like is unique to you so create it with the things that bring you peace and joy. This space then becomes your temple, your solace and your refuge from the chaos of life.

MEDITATION has been encouraged across many cultures for thousands of years. The ancient teachers recommended, "be still and know that I am God" as a necessary avenue to higher levels of consciousness and the path leading to enlightenment. Our mothers thought so too.

They sent us to our rooms when we were out of sorts. Possibly hoping we would "get the message" they had been unsuccessful in delivering to that point. Science now recognizes the calming benefit that helps restore balance and healthier functioning to our bodies. Whether for spiritual enlightenment, mental connection and clarity or physical health, the practice of meditation is a most worthwhile daily effort.

There are many different forms of mediation of which Transcendental, Mindfulness, Vipassana, Qigong and Yoga are only a few. Some require sitting still, some coordinate breathing with movement and some use focused awareness on a word, phrase or object to help quiet the mind. The best form of meditation is the one that works for you. You can incorporate more than one form into your life as the benefits are many and each one speaks to you in a different way. Generally, meditating 20 minutes twice a day is a suggested standard. More is better, but even five minutes is helpful. Some forms of meditation are easy to begin on your own, though learning from those with experience can greatly enhance your practice. Meditating with a group also expands the benefits you receive from your practice.

FRIENDS are a must for your health and wellbeing. The most important friends are the one or two you can rely on no matter what comes along; a person with whom you can share your innermost joys and fears knowing they will share your joy, hold you in compassion and maintain your privacy. You can count on them to gently shake you when you're out of control, lift you up when you're down and fly with you when you're doing well. This means you are the same quality of friend in return. Such friendships are based on love and trust. They create a complete circle of giving and receiving that is nothing short of divine in nature and essential to health.

PROTECT yourself from negative energy in your environment. As we have discussed, negative feelings give us valuable information and indicate that a course correction is in order. Some times this course correction simply means removing yourself from the environment in which you find yourself. An environment with negative vibes can come in many forms and some people are sensitive enough to feel the heaviness of it. Whether or not you can sense it, it's affecting your energy in unhealthy ways. Examples include a work environment with many stressed out or angry co-workers, a home with chronic unresolved tension, or places where many people are present, such as an airport or a shopping mall. You may not be able to avoid some of these places so protecting your good energy can come in the form of a prayer or setting an intention to protect yourself. One way to do this is to visualize a bubble of radiant light surrounding you. As you do this for yourself, you can also project radiant light and compassionate thoughts to lift up those around you who may be struggling.

Another potentially hazardous environment is the one you are occupying with social media. Most of the information coming from these sources is bent with the purpose of selling you something or attempting to sway you to their point of view. It's rare that you are getting complete and accurate information which would allow you to fully understand the truth behind the noise filling your space. Limit the time you spent with the TV, computers and smart phones; be discriminating in your use of all forms of media. Evaluate whether this input is making you feel good or bad about yourself. You can stay informed with very little exposure but there is real harm in judging yourself or the world according to the information coming through these sources. Likewise, be discriminating with any information, groups and institutions that imply an "us versus them" mentality or pressure you to conform to a standard that makes you feel uncomfortable. If the information you're getting contributes to feelings of fear, anger, jealousy or inadequacy, they are not grounded in truth or love. They can only decrease your vibration and your ability to be happy.

BOUNDARIES are another important way to protect yourself. They are more specific to the relationships you have with others. Boundaries are like a virtual fence you maintain for your safety and the safety of your inner child. Like a good parent, you know what your child needs to feel loved, safe and secure and you are mindful of these things when you let your child out to explore the world.

Developing effective boundaries means you know yourself well enough to be aware of your needs, desires, priorities and even your tender vulnerabilities. In your relationships with others, you keep this self-knowledge close to your heart so you can feel if someone is potentially encroaching in subtle and inappropriate ways. Many times, feelings of discomfort just need to be explored to determine why you feel uneasy. Once you know why you feel uncomfortable, you can share it with the person for clarification and negotiation as is appropriate for that relationship. There are times when people want something from you, such as time, energy or emotional investment, which you are not ready or able to give…for your own good reasons. Your feeling of discomfort is your inner knowing telling you to "protect the child." Maintaining and respecting boundaries are important elements of self-knowledge, self-respect, self-love and the growth opportunities offered in all relationships.

LAUGHTER is great medicine for mind and body. A good belly laugh releases endorphins and serotonin, which makes you feel good all over and brings your body back into the healthy balance it was programmed to maintain. More importantly, when you feel like you have nothing to smile about, it's even more critical to laugh. Science tells us that a fake and forced laugh has the same beneficial neurotransmitter release as a real and heart-felt one. Laugh yourself back into balance at least once a day. Take two if you are feeling down.

HOBBIES are activities that speak to your unique interests and passions. They are things you make time for because they're important to you. They're important because they make you feel good and give you a sense of peace and purpose when you are actively engaged in them. As you feel peaceful and satisfied, you are resetting your parasympathetic nervous system and restoring balance to your mind and body. Hobbies can be anything that makes you feel good while you do it, including painting, sewing, carpentry work, cycling, hiking, camping, gardening, bird watching, exploring junkyards or walking dogs. The list is endless. The only requirement is that you feel so much better after you have taken the time to do this for yourself.

These are just a few of the many ways you can honor and care for yourself as a physical being and as you can see, they spill over into your spiritual, mental and emotional wellbeing as well. You are in a relationship with your body and as with any intimate relationship, acknowledgement and communication are necessary to keep it strong, lasting and loving. Your body is always telling you exactly what it needs; I feel thirsty (water); I feel hungry (food); I feel stiff (exercise); I feel anxious (breath work, forest bathing, sacred space, meditation). I feel happy, loved and satisfied (continue on the path that keeps you here). When you respond appropriately to the information you receive, you act from a place of power, wisdom and love, and you communicate honor, respect and unconditional love to yourself. If you don't respond, and especially if you repeatedly fail to respond appropriately, the communication becomes distant and muted, even as the consequences of inaction become more compelling. As with any relationship, you strengthen it by paying attention and responding appropriately to the messages you are being given.

~~~

No matter how we talk about the different aspects of our being, it's quite clear that each one is inextricably imbedded in the others. Whether the high vibrational gifts of gratitude, awe, humility and surrender or the lower vibrational gifts of fear, anger and resentment, they all come to us through the physical, emotional, mental and spiritual planes of our existence. No matter what label we use to identify a feeling, each one has the exact same purpose. They are guiding us toward the higher vibration of fulfilled purpose and love, that innate longing which draws us ever closer to our own divinity and our oneness with All That Is.

As you can see, the tools you need to heal the dis-ease and struggles in your life are available to you every day, indeed, many are available in every moment. While there are benefits in joining classes and seeking experienced practitioners to learn proper techniques for some tools, such as Yoga, Tai Chi, nutritional modification and meditation, most are available without financial cost. The investment for adopting these tools is, for the most part, an investment in yourself using the resources of your time and dedication. What is required of you is the same effort necessary to acquire any new skill, such as learning to play the violin, speak a foreign language, change a career or care for your first child. The degree to which you give yourself over to a new skill or life change gives you powerful clues into the health of your spirit/mind/body connection and shows you exactly where work needs to be done. You have all the tools and deep in your heart you have the wisdom and love to use them to find the balance and happiness you are ever drawn toward.

CHAPTER 12

Love and Light—The Essence of All That Is

"Nothing glows brighter than the heart awakened to the unseen light of love that lives within it." – Guy Finley

The All-knowing Mind of God illuminates your mind and informs your growth with insights and wisdom beyond anything you could know were you truly separate from God. The magnificence of this Light is ever more known to you as you open to it and resonate with higher levels of love and acceptance for yourself. The Love of God is as present as the breath that sustains you. It beats in your heart, drawing you closer to the Truth that *you are the Love of God* expressing in the world. Your innate heart knowing is the mind that speaks the wisdom of love and guides you along the path of truth, reminding you that you are one with God and with all. God's Will (Intention) is that you embrace this Truth and return to the State of Grace where you can live in the peace, harmony and love as the image and likeness you were created in.

You are powerful beyond your wildest imagination. You would appreciate this much more if you had learned early on that your thoughts, words, feelings and actions create your reality. Now you know this is true. You are a being of Love and Light; a living breathing expression of God's Love in this world. You know this is true too, because Love is the essence and the energy of All That Is, *and you are all that*. It's time to reclaim your heritage as the image and likeness of God and recognize yourself as the loving, wise, powerful and magnificent person you are. You are an essential light worker in a world seeking a better version of reality than the one we are collectively experiencing. All the answers and all the tools you need to participate fully wait only on your willingness to acknowledge and accept them.

Because you are a Spark in the Mind of God and an essential element in the Infinite Field of Possibility, you contain all possibilities, the good and the bad. This is true of each and every one of us, and as one whole of humanity, we are all contributing to the reality we are experiencing. As we perceive, observe and experience all that is good, loving and beautiful *and* all that is struggle, pain and suffering, we are projecting, reflecting and living the "knowledge of good and evil." The more we focus on one faction over the other, the more energy we give to that side of the equation. Because the Mind/Field contains all possibilities, it contains the possibility of evil. Because this is true of the Mind/Field, it's true of each of us as well. The evil, pain and conflict we are experiencing now are the effects of choices made individually and collectively along the path of human evolution. Coping mechanisms such as denial, ignorance, shame and blame only hold it in place. Our experiences will be perpetuated indefinitely by our perceptions, projections, observations and reflections of that reality, whether or not we are conscious of them as the cause. Shifting from our experience of pain and struggle to one of love and happiness depends on how we choose to consciously and willfully use our knowledge of good and evil now. As we choose to use our God-given gifts of power, wisdom and love to acknowledge, forgive, redeem and transmute the evil and pain we have created, we will participate in shifting our individual and collective experiences back into the higher vibrations of Love.

We are living in a time of great upheaval and change. There have never been greater growth opportunities than the ones that lay before us now. Whether in ourselves or in the world, the pain and struggles we see are simply opportunities to use the power of love and wisdom to make the changes necessary to move all things into balance, health and happiness.

Even in our darkest moments, we have the opportunity to see God as infinitely available and then ask for guidance and support as an expression of free will and the heart-felt intent to heal and evolve to higher vibrations. As we respond with acceptance, compassion and gratitude to the messages we receive, we open the door for greater possibilities than we have ever known. If we use the wisdom and grace that comes from the guidance of our heart and make the changes we wish to see in the world, we are shifting the shape of reality, for ourselves and for the collective.

Being mindful of your thoughts, words, feelings and actions illuminates the changes you can make in order to shift your reality to a happier and healthy way of being. Daily practice using one or more of the blessings and tools we've discussed heals the pain, eases the suffering, supports your efforts and encourages you along your journey. The more you use them, the easier it is to perceive your reality with the blessing-biased observations of the higher consciousness of Love. Devotion and dedication to yourself and the love of God expressing through you strengthens your resolve to stick with the practices that change your thought and behavior patterns to a new paradigm, releasing you from the illusions that have kept you stuck in the same place for too long. You truly have all it takes to be eternally balanced, peace-filled and whole. Allow your Spark of Divinity to illuminate your unique path and create Heaven on Earth through you.

You are the only one who can change your life. You alone are responsible for your experience and responding to the call of your heart and the wisdom that comes from your own Spark of Divinity. The more you communicate with your innate and divinely inspired wisdom with conscious intent and self-love, the more you connect with your higher powers. The more you repeat the cycle of asking, receiving and responding, the more guidance you receive and the faster you move toward the health and happiness you have always wanted. There is no way to understand how much assistance is available through the Still Small Voice Within until you open to the possibility that it's a part of you and give it permission to effect your healing and growth. As you make this choice, mercy and compassion become companions, easing your daily strain. As you move into higher vibrations through intention and practice, even greater possibilities for harmony and peace come into your life. Quantum science tells us that when an electron jumps from one rotational orbit to another, it makes a "quantum leap." And so it is with you as you strive to bring balance, happiness, and self-love into your life. Honor yourself and feel grateful for the quantum leaps you are making in the electromagnetic Field of Possibility and in the Mind of God!

PART FOUR

"Love Your Neighbor As Yourself."
– Mark 12:31

"Anyone who claims to be in the light but hates a brother or sister is still in the darkness. Anyone who loves their brother and sister lives in the light, and there is nothing in them to make them stumble."
– 1 John 2:9-10

CHAPTER 13

We Are Social Beings Inextricably Connected to One Another

"A thousand fibers connect us with our fellow men. Our actions run as causes, and they come back to us as effects." – Herman Melville

When you look in the mirror and see only yourself, it's difficult to imagine being inextricably connected to others. Even if your beloved appears in the mirror behind you, it's still difficult. And it may be even more difficult to imagine how this is so as you spend time with co-workers, friends or social media. But if you remember you are, at your essence, love and light, sub-atomic particles and waves interacting in the electromagnetic Mind/Field, it becomes easier to grasp this truth.

Within the Infinite Mind of God/Field of Possibility that contains all of humanity and our collective reality, there is no separation. We all exist in this sacred space together as one. There is no hierarchy; no pecking order; no discrimination or arbitrary system of valuing human beings and their usefulness. We are all equal, created in Their Image and Likeness with the capacity to love unconditionally and the ability to use our minds to create with wisdom and power. We are all here together learning to use our power, wisdom and love in ways that support, rather than hinder, our collective journey back to Heaven on Earth. We are here to master our unique gifts and use them to return to the Peace that passes all understanding. Toward this Peace, we all move together as one inseparable human effort, whether we are conscious of it or not.

Our collective consciousness encompasses the perceived reality created by the thoughts, feelings, words and actions of every man, woman and child living together on this planet. We each contribute equally to the bias-based observations being projected into the Mind/Field and then reflected back to each of us as our common reality. Whether we agree about religion, politics or cultural norms is not nearly as significant as our shared beliefs in the worth of the individual, the goodness of humanity and the correct use of our God-given powers to love and care for one another as brothers and sisters. The struggles of an individual or a specific segment of society are not just a reflection of that lone entity, they are a reflection of our society as a whole. More importantly, those struggles are reflecting the aspects of our individual selves that we have not yet healed. As a participant in the collective evolution of humanity, the state of the world we live in is a reflection of our individual and collective health and wellbeing.

Consider the metaphor of a diamond:

Imagine humanity as a multifaceted diamond and each person as a facet within that diamond. The Mind of God/Field of Possibility is much greater than the diamond itself. It's the matrix of the diamond, it contains the diamond and it's also the brilliant Light illuminating each facet. The more perfect the facets—qualified by the number of flaws—the more this Light enhances their clarity and color. Just as diamonds flawed with imperfections have less clarity and brilliance, so too do individuals handicapped by negative thoughts, words, feelings and actions. The Light comes in but is limited in its ability to shine through clouded thinking. It doesn't matter if the negativity is a result of fear and desperation from those who suffer the pain of loss, poverty, inequality or injustice, or if it comes from those who let greed and hatred perpetuate such conditions, or even if the negativity flows from those of us who feel distressed and helpless by such conditions. It's all negative energy.

The more clear, happy and whole we make our individual selves, the more Light shines through us and the more we contribute to the overall brilliance of the collective. Our individual perceptions of reality are inextricably woven into the collective human experience. We are as inseparable as the facets of the diamond and so we are all on this human journey as one. This is why our innate wisdom compels us toward harmony and love as the highest order of survival. Our intimate connection with others is why we feel the heart call to reach out with compassion when we see others in pain.

The Golden Rule
Love Your Neighbor As Yourself

The Golden Rule is found in all religions and philosophies of the world. Some cultures extend this doctrine to include the Earth and all her inhabitants—water, air, trees, winged, four-legged and two-legged—as part of this same Golden Rule. The Rule is golden because in simple words it proclaims all you will ever need to know to get to Heaven while on Earth. At a deeper level, it describes Heaven as a place where you love and are loved equally. *Heaven is the experience of unconditional love.*

Over eons, all Masters taught the Golden Rule in the lessons and languages of their societies. They offered no caveats or qualifiers, simply, "Love one another as you love yourself." Implicit in this Rule is that you first love yourself, and then you extend it to others. Master Jesus, social activist and advocate for the Golden Rule, taught this Rule in greater depth; written in Matthew 25:40, "Truly I tell you, just as you did it to one of the least of these who are members of my family you did it to me" Jesus was sharing multiple Universal Truths as he taught that the sick, destitute and imprisoned were images of the King. In this sermon, he acknowledges all people as family. As a function of this essential connection and love, whatever is done to others—thoughts, words and deeds—is also done to him. From other teachings, Jesus understood and taught that he and Father-Mother God were One. Accordingly, anything done to the least of our brethren is also done to God. Jesus didn't teach quantum physics but what he did teach is now being demonstrated through the scientific understanding of our quantum existence. Our thoughts, words and actions create the energy projected into the collective consciousness and reflected back to us. *Love Thy Neighbor as Thy Self is our greatest decree* and it's our only answer to the love and peace we seek.

We Are Our Brother's Keeper

As we create our collective reality, nothing happens to one of us that is not felt by "the all" of us. As with the metaphor of the diamond, there is no separation or barrier protecting one of us from the experiences of others. The mistaken belief that we are separate from one another perpetuates the illusion that we are immune from the pain and struggles of our brothers and sisters. Further, our inherent desire for fulfillment, peace and love is so strong, we are innately compelled to participate in correcting conditions that bring pain and suffering to others. To do anything less than love our brothers and sisters as ourselves is to do harm to our own wellbeing.

We may live in a safe neighborhood where our streets are paved and brightly lit. Our financial situation may be more than adequate for the comforts of life as we define them. Our children may go to good schools where we believe them to be safe and able to learn without the concerns that affect some neighborhoods. But in all of our perceived safety and comfort, are we really safe, balanced and at peace? The answer is a resounding "No." No child is safe in a world where all children are not safe. We are not safe in a world where there is hatred, violence, poverty, pollution and war, and where perceived differences and prejudice serve as a rationale for ignoring the plight of others. One way or another, the pain and suffering of others will be experienced by all of us.

The programming that allowed our ancestors to survive and evolve to the place where we now find ourselves is part of the ancestral heritage locked into our DNA. At the core of our being, we instinctively know we are only safe in a tribe—as One—and we are only safe when the tribe is safe. Though we have turned down the volume on our instinctive and intuitive voices, our inner wisdom reminds us of our connection to all life. Our innate survival instincts are constantly haunting us with uneasy feelings and the intuitive knowing that we are not safe because there are members in our tribe who are not safe.

No matter where in the world a tragedy occurs, we feel the pain, fear, anger and desperation in our bodies. Through our energetic connection with one another, our bodies' survival mechanisms are collectively sounding the alarm of "change is needed." It doesn't matter what it is or where it is; a mass shooting; prejudicial attitudes condoning abuse, inequality and injustice; children suffering the consequences from lead contaminated pipes; corporations being allowed to pollute the environment and trample sacred land; government regulations, policies and programs of enforcement holding injustice and inequality in place; the list is long. But there can be no mistake! We are all negatively affected by each occurrence as it impacts the electromagnetic field and reflects our reality of suffering back to us.

As a participant in the one brotherhood/sisterhood of humanity, we must recognize that the problems affecting us collectively include inequalities based on gender, gender identity, ethnic identity, color, religious belief and the many other ways people may be considered different. Inequality also includes all situations where the profits of a few are more important than the health, safety and equal treatment of the majority. In a world where there is inequality in any form, we as a human species are collectively at risk. In a society where the lower vibrations of fear, anger, greed and corruption amplify the erroneous message of separation and then mutate into hatred, violence, war and death, we as a human species are in extreme danger.

The vast majority of people on this Earth are kind, caring and compassionate. We know exactly what to do when natural disasters strike; we donate money, time and manpower. We send cases of water, diapers, toilet paper and canned goods. We send blankets, clothes, baby toys and toiletries. Firefighters, utility workers, healthcare professionals and cooks rush in to offer assistance, working together to help those who are struggling. We feel good about ourselves, and even wish there was more we could do. It's rare that these generous acts are accompanied by thoughts of "What's in it for me?" Mostly, we are responding to the heart-felt call to lift up a neighbor in need and the compassion we feel is mixed with the hope that we are making a difference for someone whose pain is felt by all of us.

Note: Our ability to respond compassionately is possible, in part, because of the constant stream of broadcast media tracking the devastation of our neighbors, no matter where they live. Please take a moment to consider that this reporting is always limited to the final event but rarely offers much insight into the many factors contributing to the disasters and the post-event desperation we are collectively experiencing. Such "reporting" rarely offers true insight or information that would help us answer the important questions of how and why buried beneath the horrific scenes of devastation and suffering.

What happens when the devastation and desperate needs of our neighbors are not from natural disasters but from man-made disasters? What happens when the forces of destruction are not so well defined or are intentionally misrepresented or hidden? How then do we respond?

Loving ourselves whole requires us to understand what wholeness includes. It means acknowledging our place and contribution in the world. To answer these questions, and as a preamble to Chapters 14 and 15, we need to acknowledge what is really happening in our world. And as with our own self-discovery, we must look beneath the veneer of illusion and the stories we tell ourselves about what is going on. To heal at deep levels requires us to expose the root cause of our suffering; to this end Chapters 14 and 15 are an uncomfortable exposure of society's darkness and pain. Chapter 16 offers the light we need in order to transform that darkness.

CHAPTER 14

Distress Is The Call For Change

"The world will not be destroyed by those who do evil, but by those who watch them without doing anything." – Albert Einstein

Whether or not we recognize the connection, the pain we see in others is felt in our own bodies. The pain we sense is actually our own distress triggering our fight-or-flight survival mechanism, as our innate body wisdom mobilizes resources to deal with the problem causing our imbalance. Just as with personal stressors, unresolved societal pain in all its forms is chronic and debilitating when it's not resolved effectively. Because we are social beings and intimately connected, what affects one of us, affects us all and in this way, chronic social problems become our individual chronic stressors. Since our innate survival mechanism doesn't alter its response based on the internal or external nature of the stressor, our balance and health are negatively impacted just as if we were being accosted personally. This is happening even when we think it has nothing to do with us. Our Spark of Divinity knows better and is prompting us to respond. Just as with natural disasters, if we listen to our hearts (not our televisions), we will hear the wisdom guiding us to participate in change and alleviate the suffering.

When we become aware of injustice and the inhumane treatment of others, we become angry, horrified and distressed. On the surface we see the devastations affecting people's lives, as media inundates us with a constant stream of vignettes evoking our discomfort. But if we step back from the media coverage and check in with our inner knowing, we find that beyond the discomfort of another person's pain is something else that doesn't *feel* right about it all. We feel confused when we see mass shootings, people of color being choked or shot, victims of human trafficking and children going hungry. As we struggle in the chaos of what we are witnessing, we may feel shocked, angry, victimized, demoralized, violated, desperate and helpless, and *in that moment we are feeling what the victims are feeling*. There is no separation. Together as one, we are deeply troubled.

But what can we do? We feel uncomfortable or even a bit overwhelmed by it all. We may try to push it out of our minds and tell ourselves this doesn't really affect us personally, but in our hearts, we know better. We feel our discomfort and we innately know that none of this is okay. Our own survival instincts, chronic stress response and accelerated disease processes move into automatic modes of operation as such events continue to be part of our common experience.

Just as with our individual learning opportunities, when we don't learn the lesson and make appropriate changes, future learning opportunities will be more compelling and attention getting. As man-made disasters recur time and again, the message our distressed emotions are telling us is that *we're not making the appropriate changes* necessary to bring things back into balance. We might identify the perpetrator as a deranged person, a militant hate group or a bad cop, we may even blame the victim, but our dis-ease tells us this isn't the core of the problem, nor does stopping the identified perpetrator offer a real solution. Whether victim, perpetrator or a confused member of society watching in dismay, we are all feeling helpless and powerless to solve our most troubling problems.

In an effort to ease our distress and reclaim the illusion of normalcy, we cluster around those we think are most like us. We identify them as our tribe. They are like us, or maybe we just want to be like them in some way that's been promoted as safe or desirable. To solidify our acceptance into this group and the safety we believe comes with this inclusive affiliation, we endorse the selective mentality of the group. As we adopt the group's specific ideologies, we may become aware of a creeping sense of discomfort arising from within. Through this self-identification with a homogeneous and limiting tribe mentality, we are willfully separating ourselves from the greater whole. More importantly, as we embrace the selective mentality of one group, we necessarily exclude others based on the notion that they are different by some standard ascribed by our group.

We split ourselves into little pieces, *Lonely. Frightened. Little. Pieces.* There are so many ways we can perceive ourselves as different from our brothers and sisters but a few of the more common affiliations include ethnicity, gender identity, religious tradition, socio-economic class and political persuasion. Unfortunately, the more we focus on these labels and what makes us different, the more difficult it is to see what unites us, and the easier it is to feel isolated and misunderstood. The belief that we are different and the world is unjust or unsafe, keeps us huddled in our isolated groups of "otherness," immobilized by fear and effectively separated from the love, wisdom and power with which we were all equally created. With time and indoctrination, this destructive thinking gives way to unfamiliarity, prejudice, entitlement, greed, corruption, social injustice and war in some form. This is the structure upon which all man-made suffering and disasters have come to find firm footing in a society overwhelmed with recurring catastrophic events broadcast 24/7 by media.

It's not that we as individuals have caused these man-made disasters. But we become disabled and disempowered when we don't take the time to fully educate ourselves with accurate information, and when we don't use our intelligence and discernment to uncover the root cause of suffering that threatens the health of our society. We are not taking ownership of the problems we see. We are not standing up and participating in effective ways to eliminate the suffering that is overwhelming more and more people. As long as we continue to look at each unfortunate event as an isolated incident, remaining blind to the root causes of misery and detaching ourselves from the plight of an increasing number of our brothers and sisters, we will continue to be confused, frightened and ineffectual, if not completely hopeless.

Ominous Signs — Growing Hopelessness and Despair

"All that is valuable in human society depends upon the opportunity for development accorded the individual." – Albert Einstein

By now it's clear that our personal emotional state is a critical factor in our ability to be happy and healthy. Negative emotions, specifically anger, fear, hopelessness and desperation, erode the physical and mental underpinnings keeping us balanced, healthy and happy. As these negative emotions find their way into more and more lives, the fabric of society becomes increasingly tattered and fragile. News outlets rarely inform us of the growing numbers of people suffering from the diseases of hopelessness and desperation or give much attention to the identifiable causes of them, but to deny what's becoming increasingly obvious is to keep our heads buried in the sand. We can no longer view the events unfolding around us and deny the reality of their impact on a growing number of us, and therefore all of us.

Many countries struggle with some degree of wealth disparity, social injustice, hopelessness and despair. This is nothing new. What *is* new is the acknowledgement that these societal ills are negatively impacting the health and longevity of specific populations. Nowhere is this more apparent than in the United States; so much so that the U. S. has started investigating recent statistics indicating a significant downward trend within its borders.

In the last few years, the United States has become *the only developed nation in the world* to experience a decline in life expectancy. From 2014 to 2017, the life expectancy of the average adult dropped three times while other industrialized countries saw improvements in theirs. The U. S. decline was caused by the *increasing rates of deaths in people between 25 and 64 years of age*, otherwise known as working age people. As researchers explored the dramatic increase in the number of deaths, they identified a strong correlation between economic hardship and socioeconomic inequality and these increasing death rates. Their findings were so significant that they developed a new category for the deaths and diseases involved in this trend. They are identified as *diseases of despair* and *deaths of despair*.

Deaths of Despair

In the United States, the decline in life expectancy is directly related to the statistical fact that more people, especially of working age, are dying from suicide, drug overdose and alcoholic liver disease than ever before. These three causes of death are now collectively known as the deaths of despair.

Recent studies reveal that middle-aged White men from areas around Appalachia and the Rust Belts are dying from deaths of despair at a disproportionate rate compared to other segments of the U. S. population. The research further identifies that these untimely deaths were *directly associated with the loss of jobs, lack of opportunity and substandard and inadequate education* in those regions. In addition to the deaths of despair noted above, middle-aged White men are also dying prematurely of common chronic diseases caused by chronic stress derived from those very same causes.

Note: I think it's essential to say what seems obvious if we take the time to ponder it. To become part of any solution, it's imperative to consider the root cause of these deaths of despair. If these premature and therefore unnecessary deaths are caused by lack of opportunity and inadequate education, what then lies beneath these deficits for so many? Uncovering the root cause will *require intentional effort*. We have to ask, "Where is the reporting, health alerts and legislative modifications aimed at resolving such a public health crisis?" And, please don't be misled. "Reporting" such as what was offered concerning the recent epidemic of opioid overdose and deaths would have us believe we were getting the full story. We were not! Opioid abuse and deaths are only symptoms of much greater problems; the problems—root causes—are listed above and lay at the feet of government and many corporations.

The *systems* fostering lack of opportunity, inadequate education and inequality are the root causes.

The United States' world ranking for longevity is lower for other reasons. Before the dramatic decline noted in 2014-2017, non-White people had been dying more prematurely and at higher rates compared to White males; the cause of their early deaths were the same stress-induced chronic diseases and diseases of despair now identified by studies. Because the rate of their deaths has been relatively constant over many decades, there was no change in statistical trends. Non-White segments of our population have been struggling under the burdens of poverty, inequality and lack of opportunity for much, much longer. Their health and longevity have been compromised by the same societal inequities *now* creating focused inquiries. This longer suffering segment includes people of color, Native Americans, LGBT+, immigrants and poor people crowded into inner cities and forgotten rural areas to name a few. Marginalized populations, regardless of color, creed, identity or handicap, have been living with prejudice, inequality, impoverishment and hopelessness for generations. It's no mystery that their life expectancies have been consistently lower than their White contemporaries. Hidden from media attention and lost in the generalizations of statistical analysis, their plight didn't register concern or funding for research by our enabled authorities and elected officials. It was easier to blame their acknowledged lower life expectancy on the prevailing and convenient supposition of genetics, addictions and other personal frailties.

Middle-aged White men are not immune from prejudice, poverty and hopelessness. According to the studies on premature death, what sets them apart from other ethnic or gender groups is that they, more than any other segment of our population, have lived with personal expectations of greater opportunity. Middle-aged White men grew up believing that the quality of their lives would be better than that of their parents and for decades, reasonable effort meant they could expect and would likely realize a higher standard of living than the generation before them. The fact that this White male segment of our population is now struggling and succumbing to deaths of despair at a greater proportion than the larger population is a blaring alarm that something has gone terribly wrong...and not just for middle-aged White men. Studies clearly demonstrate this devastating reality applies across all segments of our population. The truth is, economic hardship, socioeconomic inequality and the desperate impoverishment sustained by lack of jobs, lack of opportunity, inadequate educational resources and insecurity regarding basic needs (food, housing, healthcare) are *causing the kind of catastrophic stress that limits life itself.*

Beyond these alarming revelations comes our future. As the gap between the very wealthy and the very poor widens and the middle class shrinks away, premature death from chronic illnesses and deaths of despair continue to rise. This trend continues even now and it will be felt by all of us across race, ethnicity and gender identity.

Diseases of Despair

Deaths of despair are caused by diseases of despair. These diseases include but are not limited to all types of risky behavior, such as unprotected sex and driving while impaired, addictions of all types, depression, suicidal thoughts and ideations, and even chronic illnesses. A collaborative effort studying the health decline in rural areas of Pennsylvania (2009-2018) indicates that *diseases of despair are on the increase in both male and females across the entire adult age-span.* Notably, there were major increases in substance and alcohol abuse and a marked increase in alcohol related illnesses in adult women of all ages and in men over age 35. Those who live in neighborhoods disadvantaged by lower socio-economic status and those who relied on Medicaid were at even greater risk. Suicidal thoughts and behaviors were also up dramatically for men and women of all ages, but for those who were *younger than 35 years, the incidence tripled.*

The findings of this Pennsylvania study aren't an anomaly in the United States. The trending health concerns they describe are mirrored in other national and regional studies. Our quality of life, our opportunities to get ahead and the perception that we can have a better life than our parents had has been steadily eroding since the 1970's. This is affecting most of us in some way, and it's affecting our health and happiness even as we remain uninformed or unaware of the root causes and the larger effects.

Diseases and deaths of despair are not isolated to the U. S. Inequality, poverty and social injustices exist all over the world and have for some time. The fact that it's affecting the U. S. in the way it has in recent decades is a clear sign of a grave imbalance taking place at an accelerated rate and affecting larger portions of the population. What needs to be very troubling to all of us…all of us…is the fact that the causes of inequality, poverty and despair are not being identified at the root cause. Without finding and resolving the root cause of the problem, it will be impossible to improve the quality of life for a growing number of people in this country…and in the world.

Mass Shootings—Glaring Examples of Inadequate Resolve

In the last few years the number of murders by mass shooting have multiplied by factors that will be out of date before this book is finished. It seems no one is safe, and innocent children, people of color and those whose religious beliefs and gender identities are less familiar to us have borne much of the burden. With each occurrence there is fear, anger and confusion, maybe even a sense of hopelessness. In spite of the tremendous pain and suffering, we don't seem to be able to resolve this growing threat to innocent people and diverse communities.

Without guns, those who wish to make their point and express their rage, fear, blame and hatred will use anything at hand to attack the perceived cause of their pain. While we should have little use for guns, guns are not the problem. They are only a symbol for brokenness, fear and despair. As a nation of concerned individuals, we're not asking the most critical and essential question, *"How did these people come to believe that killing a group of innocent people was the only solution they could find for their problems?"* This is the question we *all* need to be asking. These horrific crimes, no matter where they occur, are the result of a belief in separation and impoverished thinking, years of neglect, abuse and emotional pain culminating in a violent explosion of rage looking for expression and relief.

Many of the perpetrators of these crimes also showed signs of self-harm, suicidal thoughts and other risky behaviors before their catastrophic finale. Regardless of other factors, there can be no debate…mass shootings are extreme acts of separation, distress and hopelessness at the core. The perpetrators' despair is caused by the same inequities as other deaths of despair. Until we look beyond the superficial explanation of a gun, disturbed perpetrator or maligned hate group and uncover the true causes of inequality, fear and hate, we have little hope of making substantive changes in the devastation we are observing as our collective experience.

CHAPTER 15

What Holds Such Desperation in Place?

"The eye sees all, but the mind shows us what we want to see."
– William Shakespeare

It's only denial that allows us to think we're not affected by the unfortunate events in our world, or that we are not somehow part of what's taking place. When we are confronted with information about tragedies, we feel the pain and desperation in our own bodies, and we attribute our feelings to outside circumstances. *The pain we feel is our innate wisdom sounding the alarm for change.* Our innate wisdom knows the truth…what happens to one of us happens to all of us.

We may not have lost a child to a school shooting or a husband, sister or friend to suicide, but it takes real effort on our part to shut down the pain we feel for those parents, friends and families who are suffering such a life-shattering loss. Their pain is our pain; their grief is our grief; their hopelessness is our hopelessness. Denial simply pushes the pain deeper, allowing it to fester and distort our perception of the world. It also increases our sense of separation, diminishes our sense of power and obscures our sense of responsibility to each other, and to ourselves. We can no longer afford the luxury of looking the other way and going on about our lives as if nothing has happened, hoping it will not happen again, or that it will not happen to us.

The Myth of Powerlessness— What Can I Do? I Am Only One

"I am only one" is the largest and most fundamental *lie* the human race has ever adopted into our belief system. It is synonymous with "separate from God" and perpetuates the next untruth—we are unworthy of the love, wisdom and power we were created with. In this misperception, we believe ourselves to be incapable of overcoming the negativity and pain in our world and undeserving of the peace and harmony arising from honest efforts to make positive changes. This lie is a mistake of the first order.

This erroneous belief keeps us immobilized and defeated before we even begin. It stops any reasonable action before we can consider the possible causes or contemplate a plan with our powerful minds. Once the beliefs of separation and unworthiness are planted, they are propagated and reinforced by the events we observe around us. Helplessness and hopelessness are societal diseases, and like all diseases, they started long before we had any conscious awareness of what was going on. We learned our helplessness and hopelessness as children. Some of us lived in situations where no matter what we did, we couldn't win or escape the painful situations that replayed continuously in our lives. We gave up and just followed along. Some of us may have learned that we needed our parents to intervene on our behalf. We didn't have much opportunity to fight our own battles and learn autonomy, responsibility, resilience and trust in our own abilities. We may have grown up believing that authorities and institutions ascribed as authority—government, religion, education, health, financial—were definitive sources of truth and could not be doubted or questioned. When the doctrines and dictates of these authorities conflict with our intuitions and the Still Small Voice Within, we doubt ourselves and discount our inner wisdom.

Some of our beliefs about powerlessness may have been handed down through our ancestors. We modeled our parents, and their parents before them, in the way we navigated our own life experiences. If they felt fearful and helpless, they modeled those attitudes and behaviors to us. If they felt angry and militant, we learned those ways of coping and behaving. If they felt resourceful, resilient and powerful, chances are good that we also grew up feeling and acting this way. Regardless of their world-view and perspective, their innate wisdom and modeling included the safety-in-the-numbers tribe mentality where being alone was inherently dangerous and they were drawn into well-defined and more isolated groups. As society becomes more complex, chaotic and apparently divisive, we all are withdrawing into smaller and more divided factions. Reducing our tribe to those who are like ourselves is actually exposing us to more harm than these group affiliations can protect us from. In our isolated groups we are adopting the negative beliefs (cause) of separation, fear and helplessness and ensuring the negative consequences (effect) of misunderstanding, abuse of power, inequality, struggle and failure.

In earlier and less complex times, our ancestors understood that safety in numbers applied to the whole group. They found courage in coming together and pooling their resources to put up a united front and conquer adversity. They allowed the fight-or-flight response to support their efforts to make effective change. They weren't influenced by side commentary inferring they were powerless and ineffectual or suggesting they had no right to information that could help solve the problems they faced. In earlier times, they just came together, agreed on a plan and worked in cooperation to do what had to be done.

As a part of the total human experience, our DNA also retains remnants of fear from our ancestral memory of the persecution that came to those who protested the sponsored and approved ideologies of the time. Without an awareness of where it comes from, some of us are leery of being too vocal or visible when we disagree with conventional thinking, authorities or even the majority of people in a room. We may also be aware that intolerance to opposing ideas and persecution of dissents are not problems of the past. Today's heretics—those who are thinking outside the boxes of financially supported ideologies and mass propaganda—put themselves at risk if the truth they speak becomes too loud and threatening to those who control the money and power.

Pressure on those who speak out against authority can manifest as threats to funding, jobs, professional credibility or licensing and in extreme cases, threats to their physical safety.

The real harm in the myth of powerlessness is thinking we can justify our lack of effective participation with logical reasoning. If we're powerless to change things, then we're absolved of any responsibility for what is happening around us. The myth of powerlessness is a spiraling negative force. Like a tornado, it holds us in the endless vacuum of ineffectual reasoning, confusion, hopelessness and chronic stress until it spits us out, broken and entangled in the chaos that surrounds us. When we believe we are separate from God, we dismiss the powerful and creative minds we were created with. We deny or discount the tools we have at our disposal—the very ones we need to heal the problems we are all experiencing. Instead, it's easier to blame someone else, blame the victims or ask the question, "Why does God allow such things to happen?" (As if God is to blame for what's going on.) The denial and misuse of the God-given powers within us are to blame for the suffering we observe.

When we look away in an attempt to shield ourselves from the pain of others or blame someone else for the ills we see, we are abdicating our responsibility. We are expecting someone else to step up and fix the problems without support or participation from us. We become even more disillusioned and distraught when the perceived leader doesn't get the job done, or the problem does not magically fix itself. The more this happens, the more we re-affirm our own powerlessness (repetitive learning; and cause), and the more desperate we become (effect).

The Balance of Power

In the beginning, we acknowledged the attributes of an Ever-present God as All-knowing, All-powerful and All-loving and in Their Image and Likeness our purpose is to grow into the completeness of that image. We must also recognize that peace, love and fulfillment can only be achieved when these attributes are in balance with one another, for each is a power in its own right. Health and happiness in our personal lives and in the collective consciousness come from this balance; imbalance results in distress and disease.

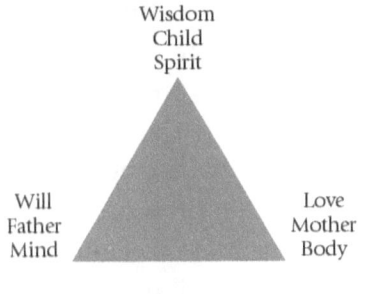

Each attribute possesses power and contributes equally to maintain balance of the trinity…at all levels of existence.

Misguided use of an attribute's power results in imbalance, instability and disease, personally and collectively.

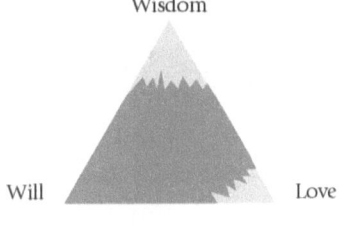

Abuse of will's power overrules wisdom's power and rejects love's power.

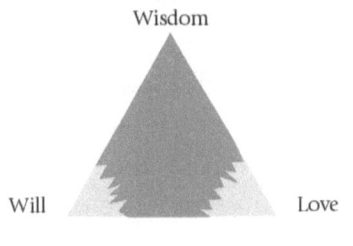

Manipulation and misuse of knowledge subverts will and love, undermining the foundation of balance.

Misuse of love's power in order to manipulate others creates a vacuum where little can survive.

The myth of powerlessness is promoted and reinforced through many of our institutions. When we see this happening, we must label it for what it is, an abuse of power, and take appropriate actions to resolve such abuses.

Governments, through legislation, regulatory policies, oversight, program funding and enforcement are instrumental in maintaining a just and equal society. This is the stated purpose. Failure to act fairly and responsibly from a holistic and just concern for the greater good is both a dereliction of duty and an abuse of the power granted by the people. Laws, regulations and policies that intentionally disadvantage and marginalize people and foster hopelessness need *to be identified by the governed* and dealt with by effective means to undo the damage and suffering such unjust regulations perpetrate.

Those religious authorities who stand as intermediaries between God and their congregations, extolling their truth while promoting separation based on religious dogma, ethnicity, race, gender or gender identity, are not teaching the fundamentals of the Golden Rule or the truth that every human being is a divine child, created in God's Image and Likeness. When religious leaders are not raising awareness for the inequities of marginalized people of all colors and proclivities and are not actively promoting effective action to remediate inequities wherever they are found, they are effectively promoting separation and the mistaken notion that some are more equal and more worthy than others. This is an abuse of power, aligned with separation and injustice.

For a variety of reasons, many institutions of learning have been disempowered or at least limited in their ability to teach independent and critical thinking as part of their curriculum. Many are handicapped with inadequate resources and maligned priorities, limiting their ability to offer what is needed to lift up children and adults who have been marginalized by inequality, corruption and the belief of separation. As a result educational institutions and society at large are producing young people who believe they are helpless and hopeless due to institutionalized indoctrination lacking in creativity and critical thinking skills. They have learned that the only way to succeed is to go with the flow and not make too much noise. *We are sculpting widgets.* We must ask ourselves why so many of our young people are losing hope…and dying? While some institutions are part of the problem, many of them are hobbled by the dictates of their governing bodies…all the way to the top. This is an abuse of power and an abuse of wisdom and knowledge as we knowingly handicap greater portions of our population with inadequate means to pull themselves up.

A more subtle and damaging form of abuse is the abuse of will, love and wisdom's powers. Individuals, institutions and corporations who use technology and the scientific insights regarding the functioning of our subconscious minds in order to manipulate information and exploit people's basic needs is nothing short of evil. These entities build their presentations and marketing strategies around our innate survival imperative for safety, belonging and love and fortify it with pretty images, emotional appeal and repetition. Their intention is to make us *believe* that their product, service or value system is the missing component necessary for achieving our deepest desires. Offering love or security in return for conformity and compliance is another form of such abuse.

As individuals, we must use mindfulness, discernment and our emotionalized intention to be *all that we are* in order to reclaim the balance of power and take responsibility for what is going on. Our institutions were established with the highest intentions and have brought much that is good to our society but we must not be lulled to sleep by past successes even as our institutions are being hijacked by those who abuse power to their own benefit and maligned intent.

The Ever-present, All-powerful God within you is your source of hope. Just as your Spark of Divinity keeps drawing you back to your birthright as the image and likeness of God, so too does it keep nudging you, through your pained awareness. It incites you to be an active participant in correcting the imbalances harming us all. Loving yourself whole means remembering you are one with God and all of humanity. Loving your neighbor as yourself is the path to reclaiming your power and participating with your unique gifts and talents in truly responsible and life-changing ways.

The Myth of Scarcity—Us Versus Them

The next myth holding our collective pain and desperation in place is the myth of scarcity. It spawns from the belief we are separate from each other and from our failure to love our neighbor as ourselves. It is based on the belief that there isn't enough for every one to have what they need to be happy, healthy and fulfilled. Scarcity is real to us because there is never enough when we continually feel unfulfilled by our misdirected attempts to find happiness and feel loved. We haven't discovered the root cause of our unhappiness.

Scarcity is the product of "false gods." In losing touch with our intimate connections to God and to one another and forgetting the full intent of the Golden Rule, we've lost sight of the truth that we are all equal in the Mind of God. We've replaced our innate imperatives for love, the common good and the wellbeing of our human tribe with man-made priorities of wealth, power, prestige and possessions based on the illusions of separation and scarcity. We have adopted an acquisitive mentality that is blinding us to the truth that balance, love and joy are found by being in harmony with our true nature and living life as an expression of God's Love. In our pursuit to "keep up with the Joneses" and have bigger bank accounts, houses, cars, phones and TVs, we have become slaves to jobs, possessions, marketing, media and influencers. As we give more attention to our false gods, we become entrained in belief systems that are intentionally engineered to manipulate our minds and keep us clamoring for bigger, better and more. We are so busy trying to get ahead, as defined by others, that we don't see what is really going on and how it's affecting us individually and collectively. We become an increasingly overworked, overwrought and desperate society lacking the time and energy for introspection, awareness and the ability to rethink our lives or the processes that are making them a living hell. More important, we are distancing ourselves from the skills of mindfulness and discernment that would open our hearts and minds to inspired wisdom and loving thoughts, words and actions and a more balanced, healthy way of life.

As life becomes more complex, frenzied and confusing, we consciously or unconsciously withdraw into more isolated states of self-insulation, self-protection and separation. To varying degrees, we believe ourselves to be on our own…helpless, powerless and struggling to get by…and so we perceive (observe) our lives as a constant scramble to hold onto our piece of the finite resources we now believe we must have. We have learned to equate material possessions with happiness and survival. When we live in separation and fear and believe life is a struggle to maintain stability and security, we turn away from the suffering of those whose lives have been washed away in conditions caused by corruption, inequality and injustice. We distance ourselves from those who struggle to get by in the most basic of ways.

But we must remember, these people are "the least of my brethren." Reflecting back on the disturbing trends in chronic diseases and deaths of despair, it's apparent that those suffering the most are those who are too marginalized and oppressed to speak out and effectively defend themselves from the societal changes and inequalities that brought most of them to such desperation. Somewhere deep inside, our inner wisdom knows we are connected and that their struggle is our struggle. The restlessness or discomfort we feel as we go about our lives is the alarm calling for the changes necessary to bring us all back into balance and peace. Our innate wisdom is guiding us to participate in these changes, each in our own unique way. Being an active participant for society's healing is part of your own journey. You are the outward expression of God's Love. You only need to follow the guidance of your heart.

CHAPTER 16

The Road Home—
The Gifts of Love, Wisdom and Power

"Love will find a way through paths where wolves fear to prey."
– Lord Byron

In our Universe, nothing has ever happened that was not already known in the Mind of God/Field of Possibility. Our highest aspirations and our greatest fears are there, along with all the events that have ever taken place…good and bad. This is the meaning of Infinite, Eternal and All-knowing. At this point in our evolution, we're not so enlightened as to be able to understand all the causes, effects and synchronicities that create the web of reality we are experiencing. We can't know the Mind of God and so we are best served to live with the knowing—or faith—that God as our Higher Power holds all things in love until we join Them on that highest plane of correspondence. As a Spark in the Mind of God, we are each working toward a greater understanding of our divine inheritance and we still have work to do before we attain full mastery of our gifts. Our greatest advances toward mastery will come with a better understanding of how, through the Law of Cause and Effect, we are creating our reality and with that, we are responsible for what we are experiencing. On a quantum level, this has already been proven; our bias-based thoughts and observations are the creative energy collapsing waves into the particles reflected back to us as our reality here and now.

The social unrest, imbalance of power, prejudice, inequality and hopelessness have been part of humanity's collective journey for eons. They are not new; they are only more visible now. As with our individual struggles, society's problems are caused by our collective belief in separation. Misuse of our God-given gifts of willpower, wisdom and love is the effect caused by separation. The abuse of our gifts became the cause of what has been playing out for eons; the effects we are still dealing with today. What we are experiencing is the work of our human mental creations. The Law of Cause and Effect, working through each of us is how we collectively contribute to the mayhem and despair we are living. The pain and suffering of humanity can only be redeemed by this same Law and by modifying our personal contributions to *cause* a different reality.

There is no mistake that you are here now. You are part of the great transformation that is taking place. Your participation comes in two very important parts. Your first and most important contribution is through your dedication and efforts to love yourself on every level as you step into your Divinity and discover full use of your gifts. This you accomplish through all the tools discussed in Parts Two and Three. The more you use those tools, the higher your vibration becomes and the more you contribute to the higher vibration of the collective. Loving yourself as God loves you is your greatest contribution. As the Masters taught, "the Kingdom of Heaven is within."

The second way you contribute is by listening to the wisdom of your heart and participating in the changes that need to take place. This you must do according to your own unique gifts and purpose. Just know, *everything you do matters!* With every effort to love your neighbor as yourself, every act of compassion toward others, and every thought and word of gratitude, forgiveness, humility, courage and hope you express in your life, you are interacting with and positively influencing the energy of the collective held in the Mind of God/Field of Possibility. This is you lifting up all of us! Beyond being a higher vibration in Mind/Field, we are all driven by our survival instinct (physical), pained awareness (mental) and the knowledge of good and evil (spiritual) to do more to love our neighbors as ourselves. If every man, woman and child is "a member of [our] family" as Jesus advised, then we must do much more than we are doing if we are to love them as we want to be loved. Rather than being distressed and disempowered by the magnitude of the problems we see around us, we each must find ways to *participate in lasting change.*

It may be difficult to imagine yourself as a healer, advocate, activist, way-shower or even savior. But in reality, that's exactly who you are. You are an essential participant in the changes shaping humanity's evolution. Please do not underestimate your power and ability to make a difference. The truth is, you are just the person the world has been waiting for. Someone with your exact skill set to participate as the unique expression of God's Love that you are.

You have the ancestral inheritance of the great teachers and the molecular building blocks of your ancestors. This amazing heritage is just waiting for you to love yourself, acknowledge your gifts, stand up and let your light shine in the world. You may not be called to be an elected official, teacher or famous crusader for justice and equality. Your most important contribution is the one that answers the call of your heart. When you look out into the world and see the struggles of your brothers and sisters, follow the guidance of that Still Small Voice Within and you will know just what to do.

Don't be overwhelmed in thinking you must do something right this minute, just be open for the guidance that will come. You are not alone. There are others you do not yet know who think like you and are waiting for you to join them. There are those who will see your shining light and come running to join you. Your innate wisdom will connect you with those you need to find. Your ancestral heritage and the teachings and examples of enlightened Masters still illuminate the path opening before you. Most importantly, the Mind of God where you live and move and have your being is always present, supporting you with Love, Wisdom and Divine Will whenever you ask for guidance and assistance. You are unstoppable when you love yourself as God loves you and when you love your neighbor as yourself.

How Will I Know What To Do?
What Would Jesus Do?
(Or Any of the Great Teachers?)

Leaders the likes of Jesus, Buddha, Muhammad, Gandhi and Martin Luther King, Jr. did not sit at the dinner table wringing their hands or act paralyzed, blaming a system too big, too entrenched or too evil to be changed. They prayed, they meditated and they loved God, themselves and their brothers and sisters. They believed in truth and the great potential that lives within the divine spirit of every person. They dedicated their lives to the neglected, downtrodden and outcasts of their societies. They channeled their passion into resolve and action. They did not teach hate and retribution, endorse separatism, or rally the multitudes to anger and violence, instead they taught resistance and modeled civil disobedience. They rallied in defiance to negative forces they believed perpetuated the social injustice undermining the balance and justice in their respective societies. They thought and acted outside the box of acceptability, personal safety and convention, standing as beacons of light in the darkness. Their power was in their love and their intention to make the world a better place. Their messages spoke out for equality and love of neighbor. They taught peace and their actions offered living examples for a different paradigm. They showed us that the higher vibrations of oneness, love and compassion would overcome the negative forces of separation, hate and fear. From the Ancient Wisdom proclaimed by Buddha, Jesus and Muhammad through to the Civil Rights Movement of today, our greatest teachers and leaders received the wisdom and truths of a Higher Authority through visions, dreams and intuitive knowing. They accepted their insights and followed their hearts, speaking out to raise awareness and lead the way for meaningful change.

Historical accounts of these great activists and leaders make it seem as if their significant works were the efforts of a single person but their stories are more nuanced if we look deeper. They acknowledged their strength came from their faith in God or the knowing of their oneness with God. Their faith and knowing allowed them to stand up as testaments to God's Love, Power and Wisdom (God's Image), unshakable in their knowledge of the Truth and dedicated to teaching a more enlightened way. Like the North Star, others found truth and solace in their teachings and followed their guidance as disciples, converts and believers. Together, these followers formed the unconquerable forces still inspiring hope and action today. Like a single candle lighting other candles, these teachers, through their followers, brought light to a dark world. As they taught justice, harmony and love, they inspired the same in others, and the Earth's inhabitants were forever changed. Their lives and the impact each had on society are validation of the healing power available when we open our hearts and minds to the wisdom and guidance of God. Through their examples and their teachings, they have passed the torch to us so that we too may express the Love, Wisdom and Power of God's Image in our world.

So now it's time to follow the examples of the Masters. If you have come this far, you will recognize the tools you've been given to be the change you wish to see. Reviewing them in this context magnifies their importance and practical application.

LOVE YOURSELF — In every way possible, love yourself as God loves you. God is right there with you, loving you unconditionally no matter how often you stumble. The more you love yourself, the stronger and more resolute you will be at standing in your truth, unshaken by the thoughts, words and actions of others and the events unfolding around you. Use the tools of mindfulness, curiosity, love, compassion, gratitude, humility, courage, vulnerability, faith, hope, honesty and equanimity to be and radiate love. You are an expression of God's Love.

LOVE YOUR NEIGHBOR AS YOURSELF — The Golden Rule is all you need to know. Hold all others in love and *compassion with no judgment*. You can never know another person's journey or the purpose they came to fulfill. You *can* know with certainty that you want to be safe, loved, lifted up when you're down and assisted when you struggle to participate as an equal. When you love your neighbor as yourself, you want for them what you want for yourself. You are innately drawn to participate in ways to make this happen…just as you would want others to do for you.

NON-JUDGMENT — "Hate the sin; love the sinner."—Mahatma Gandhi.

There is a difference between non-judgment and no consequences. The Law of Cause and Effect applies universally and impartially to all things. As an absolute truth, this means there is an order and a reason for the way things happen, even if we can't see it clearly. If we have faith in Divine Wisdom, of which the Law of Cause and Effect is but one part, then we can let go of judgment and the distress that comes from it. At this point in our evolution, there are so many things we cannot fully comprehend. There are people whose lives are beyond our capacity to understand. We can't imagine how they're contributing to our collective evolution. But with God in all things, we can have faith that *God is working through every single person*. When we suspend judgment and open our hearts, we may find unexpected insights, forgiveness, compassion and understanding.

When we look beyond our own experiences, we can see other people struggling with unfortunate conditions. As with our personal struggles, their situations offer them the potential for growth and healing. Like us, their struggles and triumphs are not only about their personal healing because as they heal themselves, they are contributing positive energy to the collective. Consider the example of courage demonstrated by a woman or man who discovers the self-awareness, fortitude and self-love to walk away from an abusive relationship and move forward into a more self-affirming life. This new place of self-love is the result of a hard fought campaign to overcome negative beliefs and messages that were planted very early. Such a difficult life is one avenue through which self-love can be learned. On the other side, such a learning experience requires an antagonist to stir up the inner conflict. While it's difficult to appreciate or feel compassion for someone who abuses or demeans others, they are also serving humanity by opening space for reflection and opportunities for change, growth and a better way of being. As a human collective, we still have many faulty beliefs calling out for healing and so we need those who will set the stage for learning the lessons of worthiness, love, peace and oneness. As we individually and collectively shift to higher levels of consciousness and make the necessary changes, we will no longer need such lessons or the misguided behaviors that bring these lessons to us.

We may judge victims of abuse as weak or enabling their own victimization. Such judgments or characterizations *are not valid* and do nothing to relieve suffering. As our brothers and sisters work through their life lessons, they also provide us with opportunities for learning and growth; opportunities to grow in compassion and non-judgment; opportunities to participate as advocates and social change activists; even opportunities to see the anger and fear we ourselves may have pushed from our awareness. The struggles you see around you offer many opportunities for insight, change and growth. You have been given the gift of inner wisdom, insight and the ability to see and feel the pain of others. You have also been given the power to shift those struggles to a higher vibration of peace and love.

DO NOT TURN AWAY — Just as you find ways to help others after natural disasters, so too will your heart tell you what is needed in conditions affecting the "least of our brethren." Be steadfast in your efforts to bring relief to the conditions that call out for your unique gifts. The Masters brought attention to the plight of people without a voice—the sick, downtrodden and outcasts—those without the power to help themselves. They remained dedicated to their purpose even in the face of personal oppression and threats to their wellbeing. Turning our awareness away from the suffering of others simply continues the pain and stress for each and every one of us.

BE A BEACON IN THE WORLD AND JOIN A TRIBE — Be visible as a participant and as a voice for change. The wisdom and teachings of the Masters had a profound impact on their followers. The followers became the tribe whose unwavering efforts contributed to the shifting of humanity's consciousness to the higher vibrations of Love and Oneness. We are still being lifted up by their contributions. Now *you* are the torch-bearer and you are the light needed to bring justice, balance and peace to our world. Join together with others who are aligned with the Truth of Love and loving our neighbors as ourselves. Where two or more are gathered, God is multiplying the power of love beyond our capacity to know.

PARTICIPATE according to the call of your heart and your unique gifts and talents. Life is filled with opportunities to participate in making the world a more safe and just home for us all. How do you know which situations call out for your involvement? Your divinely inspired intuitions and emotions are always there to guide you in the best use of self. The more you pay attention to that Still Small Voice Within, the more confident, supported and resolute you become.

~~~

Emotions and intuitions are the messengers. When negative emotions such as sadness, anger, violation, hopelessness and fear are triggered, you are sensing a situation in need of change. The stronger you feel these emotions and the longer they stick with you (if you are otherwise balanced and peaceful), the more you are being guided to participate in correcting that very situation. You are *innately compelled to alleviate the suffering* of your brothers and sisters, no matter where such suffering originates. Just as with your own struggles, you can't stop your innate stress response by simply turning way or letting time distance you from troubling events. Strong emotions are a call for change, but that doesn't mean you must jump on every bandwagon passing by. Take time for introspection and feel into the wisdom of your heart as you choose how you will participate. You may find unexpected insights and guidance. Accurate information and discernment also offer important guidance.

One revelation that might be hard to acknowledge is that some of the anger we feel in man-made disasters is, in part, anger with ourselves. We are angry because we know things must change to eliminate the problems we see repeated time and again, but we sense nothing is being done to address the problems. If we honestly contemplate how we're feeling, it's likely that we are angry with ourselves because deep inside we know we have put on the mantle of helplessness and fearfulness as the natural outgrowth of "What can one person do?" We have given our power over to those who claim to know what's best and that they alone have what it takes to "fix it." If we were honest, we would acknowledge that at some point, we knew better than to believe the "quick fix" stories we are being told. Our anger or helplessness tells us that we know it's not getting fixed and the world is no safer, peaceful or loving. Our innate wisdom knows better than the rhetoric of confusion and fear mongering that has become the "explanations" given for the problems we see. Our anger is coming from inside; we have not honored our gifts and inner knowing and we have assumed a position of powerlessness. We do not love ourselves or our neighbors when we don't stand up and act intelligently, compassionately and responsibly with our God-given powers. Once we come to terms with how we have undermined our own powers of will, wisdom and love, we can choose to participate differently—becoming active as leaders, crusaders, advocates and healers.

We are each called to use our gifts in service to the greater good and the evolution of humanity. We must actively participate to correct social injustice and inequality in all its derangements. We must take care of the Earth that sustains us. We must care for the sick, the poor and the oppressed, loving our neighbor as ourselves. We must understand that because we are all inseparable as one human experience, our neighbor may be a world away, but they are still our neighbor. We must be vigilant, continuing our best efforts until every man, woman and child has an equal opportunity to pursue their hopes and dreams with the expectation that their best efforts will bring them to the same securities, peace and prosperity we expect for ourselves.

There are many issues confronting civilization at this time, too many to list. All of them have a beginning, though the beginning often dates back so many generations that it has become an accepted standard in our society. Once a practice, policy, standard or way of thinking gained a foothold, it was able to slowly mutate into a more divisive and destructive norm so that now we simply accept it as just the way it is. The root causes of these problems are not unknowable; they are hidden in fear-provoking images and statements of the obvious to disempower analytical thinking where the question why could be contemplated and effective solutions could be created. Your active and meaningful participation requires discernment, following the guidance of your inner wisdom and digging to find the root cause of the struggles and pain you are witnessing in this world.

The events and situations you feel the most passionate about are the ones calling for your unique skills and talents. Your inner wisdom is connected to the Mind of God where your gifts, potential and purpose are all known, though you may not be fully aware of them just yet. Your passion, sometimes masquerading as anger, is your call to action. It's up to you to choose how you will respond and how you will participate in the changes needed if we are to find our way. All you will ever need to know to serve your purpose is this: You are One with an All-knowing, All-powerful, Ever-present God. Love yourself and honor your growing awareness that you are on the perfect path for you. Use the powers of prayer and meditation to seek wisdom, guidance and support in your best efforts to make a difference. Be part of groups that work together to deal with the distress and injustices you are called to help heal. Remember that darkness is transformed by light. Love is the light and the energy that transforms the negative creations of human mistakes, misperception, abuses and imbalance.

You are one of over seven billion people living this three-dimensional reality on Earth. Each person's contribution to the collective consciousness has equal weight as we go about our day, thinking, speaking, feeling and acting according to our unique personalities and belief systems. Consciously or unconsciously, we are putting our energy into the Mind/Field and must own the reflected reality we are experiencing. It's safe to say, most of us agree we need to see changes, whether for ourselves, the environment or the state of distress and turmoil in the world. What most of us want with all our hearts is a just and equal world where all beings are safe, loved, happy and satisfied. Getting to that place depends on all of us. We must work together for peace and harmony. The good news is that we don't all have to be of the same mind and we don't all need to act in the same way. Our diversity makes us stronger and opens the door for greater possibilities because each of us is an aspect of the One, like the facets in a diamond. That said, reaching a place where peace and harmony are the glue holding society in balance requires that more of us love ourselves enough to stand up and use our voices for necessary change. It requires more of us loving our neighbors as ourselves as we honor each other's uniqueness. It demands that we listen with respect, reaching across the superficial divides that separate us so we can negotiate answers based on equality and justice for all. We have a ways to go, but we are on the path.

Everything you think, say and do matters…to all of us. Magnify the power of your thoughts, words and actions with loving intention.

PART FIVE

Being Love's Expression

"We know that we have passed from death to life because we love one another."
– 1 John 3:14

CHAPTER 17

The Art of Mental Transmutation

"You never change things by fighting the existing reality. To change something, build a new model that makes the existing model obsolete."
– Buckminster Fuller

You live in a world filled with pain, struggle and conflict. You also live in a world filled with beauty, compassion, hope and love. In every moment, you choose which world you will give your attention and intention to and which reality you are co-creating. Loving yourself whole means actively participating in bringing all life back into balance and peace. "Seek ye first the Kingdom of God" and "Love your neighbor as yourself" are the teachings of the Masters.

Master Jesus also spoke of the reward and the difficulties we would find as we travel the high road to happiness. "Rejoice and be glad, for your reward is great in heaven, for in the same way they persecuted the prophets who were before you." (Matthew 5:12) If you are familiar with this passage, you may have learned as I did, that Heaven was a distant place you could get to if you lived a "good" life. As we have discussed, Heaven, the Kingdom of God and the Kingdom of Heaven are all the same place. They are the space where the Peace that passes all understanding is found...inside of you...when you tap into the Love of

God that *is* you. Your reward is living in the peace, love and happiness you have been searching for. You create heaven with your beliefs and the ways you choose to live as a result. But what of the persecution you will experience (as did the prophets before you), as you walk this path? If you were raised like me, your mind flashes on crucifixion, stoning, burning and being torn apart by lions, though none of those things are likely to be part of our experience now. In our time, persecution means to oppress, harass, bully, torture and mistreat. We can definitely see that the Masters, Mystics and everyday people who believed and practiced a less conventional and more intimate belief in a Higher Power did indeed suffer one or more forms of persecution. (Even today, some fanatic religious sects espouse prejudice, ridicule, hatred and violence against those who think differently.) Some spiritual seekers may live in a world where it's safer to express spiritual beliefs, but even when teachers aren't persecuted to the extent the word might imply, thinking outside the box may provoke cynicism, criticism and alienation. To this concern, I can only assure you: the peace you find as you love yourself and align with the Highest Powers of Love and Wisdom are a much greater reward than living in denial of your true essence. As you move into coherence with God's Will for you, you are entering into the Kingdom of Heaven within and you are becoming the very love you seek. You are also becoming unshakable in a chaotic world, and influential in ways you can't yet fully know and appreciate.

The more you use your gifts, tools and talents according to the call of your heart and the Still Small Voice Within, the higher your vibration becomes and the more solid you feel in every aspect of your life. Even in your most difficult challenges, you will hear Love, Wisdom and Power speak your name as They guide you along higher ground. As you grow into the magnificent and expanded version of yourself, you begin to witness yourself as a part of the human condition and you will be drawn to participate in ways you might not have considered before. Even without fully acknowledging all you are contributing, the more you love yourself, the more you have to give to others, and the greater the gifts of love that return to you.

In reality, you are standing at the Gate of Heaven and with every thought, word, feeling and action you choose if you are worthy to step back into Paradise.

Our unseen and unrecognized contributions are explained by ancient Hermetic Wisdom, which informs us that those who understand the Law of Mentalism gain mastery in the Art of Mental Transmutation. Even without understanding what this means, we are constantly involved in mental transmutation. Mental transmutation is the process of shifting energy to create our personal reality and contributing as equal members to our collective experience of reality. The *Art* of it reveals the greater power and potential of our minds when we truly understand ourselves as part of the Higher Consciousness. The Art of Transmutation means being consciously involved in the process of creating beauty, harmony and love. With this Law, we can change our own thoughts and we can *change the thoughts and realities of others*. This is the long lost art of alchemy taught in the Mystery Schools.

Since the Hermetic Laws are Universal Truths, they are impartial and apply to all things equally…good and bad, light and dark. We saw how the Law of Mentalism worked in Hitler's takeover of Germany twisting its populace with evil intent and emotionalized language. We saw it in action in 2020 with the polarization, civil unrest and public dis-ease caused by rhetoric, innuendo, lies and selective information broadcast to the American people. Influencing the mental processes of others can happen easily through mental manipulation, herd mentality and fear mongering. These are blatant examples of the Law of Mentalism working on the side of darkness, as it has for eons. Since there is balance in all things, it's easier to influence the minds of those who have given their power away or are simply unaware of their own power. When people feel helpless, fearful and powerless, they are more likely to adopt the ideologies of others as explanations for their own struggles and pain. This is one reason why diligence, discernment and seeking the higher planes of Love and Wisdom are vital to us all. It's why loving ourselves, embracing our God-given powers and projecting them into the Mind/Field is critical.

The true power behind the Art of Mental Transmutation is the power of love. The more you love yourself and your neighbor as yourself, the more you are aligned with Higher Consciousness. This is the Law of Polarity shifting the balance higher up the scale of love and light. In this place, your thoughts are backed by loving intention, aligned with the Love of God and have the power to influence the most recalcitrant minds, even without their participation. This is the true Art of Transmutation and it is your greatest contribution to the ascension of humanity. This is how you walk in the footsteps of the Masters and this *is the experience* of bliss and harmony as you feel your Spark of Divinity rejoicing in your heart.

You don't need to be fully actualized to practice the Art of Transmutation. You don't even need to understand the Hermetic Laws to use them. These Laws are actually working through you to create reality and influence the arc of human evolution. Through your choices, you decide how you contribute and Universal Laws obey your thoughts, intentions and the power of your mind.

I would like to conclude with what I regard as practices for being *in* the world, not *of* the world. These are activities of love you can do no matter where you find yourself. I also make this promise: if you practice expressing love in the world, you will know greater peace and happiness than you have ever known, and you will come ever closer to the Kingdom of Heaven and Heaven on Earth. You'll know it because you'll feel it in your body. You will be perfecting the Art of Mental Transmutation.

Ecstasy—The Sweet Release of Surrender

In more delicate times, to "know" a man or woman meant to have carnal knowledge, that one had been physically intimate with another. Physical intimacy, which can be accompanied by emotional, mental and even spiritual intimacy, is the only way some of us appreciate the experience of ecstasy. While the pursuit of this amazing experience and the momentary feeling of connectedness may be a primary motivator to seek out sexual orgasm, the expansive feeling of ecstasy is available to us through many other avenues.

To truly know God is also an intimate experience that is accompanied by feelings of ecstasy. Throughout history, the major religions of the world addressed the ultimate goal of knowing and experiencing God in their own terms; Nirvana, Bliss, Ecstasy, Joy and Enlightenment. They offered techniques, which would allow devout practitioners to reach such levels of knowing. These techniques include prayer, meditation, repentance, asceticism and agony, among others. The goal was union with God and the experience of Divine Love. We may have heard stories about the experiences of St. Theresa of Avila, St. Francis of Assisi, St. Padre Pio and St. Hildegard of Birgen or perhaps seen videos showing the Sufi Whirling Dervishes, all of whom had regular practices that opened them an intimate connection with God and the experience of ecstasy. It is also thought that some of the great philosophers, artists, musicians and scientists entered into such states to receive their brilliant contributions to humanity.

The experience of ecstasy comes to us as we let go of our human identification (ego) and merge into Higher Consciousness, the Mind of God. We become part of something greater than ourselves. It's an altered state of consciousness where the limitations of ego identification dissolve and we *know* we are one with God. We may not be able to identify with Saints, Mystics, Sufi Dervishes or renowned thinkers and artisans, but we all have the ability to achieve this wondrous state. It only requires devotion, practice and a willingness to surrender to the Kingdom Within.

> In my promise that this state is possible for all of us, I would like to tell you about some of the times this has happened to me.
>
> The first time, I was on a spiritual retreat. After dinner, we all sat together in a group meditation and at some point during this meditation, I became aware that I could not feel my body. It was not a numbness, but a feeling of immense calm. I could not feel the edges of myself. There was no place where I ended and everything else began…I was one with something I did not know. I could hear people talking and knew the meditation had ended and people were leaving the room. As the room changed from quiet chatter to silence, I was aware that there

was no change in how I was feeling. Even thinking about how different I felt and trying to understand what I was feeling didn't bring me out of this very expansive, balanced state I could not otherwise describe...except that it was heavenly, a Peace that passed all my understanding.

The second time, I was working an 8-hour shift as a Hospice nurse. I was sent to provide respite for a family overwhelmed with the 24/7 duties of caring for an admittedly difficult man, now dying of cancer. Sitting in his armchair, this man didn't move the entire time I was there. He didn't speak, lift his arm or blink an eye. It was a very quiet day. At one point during this shift, I knelt down beside his chair and put my hand on his arm. My only thought was that he must be lonely. And then for just a few moments, I felt what I could only liken to an orgasmic sensation flooding my body, as the man remained seemingly unaware of my presence in the room. After a few minutes, I stood up and moved away from him, wondering, "What just happened?" When I recounted the experience to others, I told them I could only describe it as a "soul merge" though I wasn't really certain if such a thing was possible at the time.

Many years later, I was talking with a woman as she drew my blood. We were commiserating and sharing our personal stories. As she was talking, a feeling of empathy came to me; it was so expansive that again, I couldn't feel the edges of myself. I felt warm and light as she stayed engaged with her duties. As with earlier experiences, I could only describe it as a soul merge.

As I learned, such experiences of bliss or ecstasy are truly possible if we surrender to the power of love flowing through us as we stay present to the moment.

I would like to give you (and myself) a precise formula for reaching this state of peace, expansion and ecstasy, but I have not yet fully mastered my ego self. In retrospect, each of these experiences took place as I was mindfully engaged in an encounter. Whether I defined it as meditation, soul merge, empathy or loving intention, it involved giving myself over to the moment. Without being aware of a process, these were moments of letting go, of surrendering myself and becoming one with something greater than myself...a stream of Loving Consciousness flowing in, around and through me. I will tell you that the more I try to re-create this feeling, the more elusive it becomes. In my experience, ecstasy is more available as we refine our gifts and merge with the Love that holds all things together. The practice of meditation, being lovingly present in each moment and having the faith to surrender to the Will of God are the tools that will bring us to the divine experience of ecstasy and the mastery of alchemy and transmutation.

Visualizations And The Art Of Transmutation

Visualization is a technique that harnesses the power of your mind and intentions as you project a vision into the Mind/Field. You are imagining or *imaging in* a specific scene or situation with your mind. With visualizations, you are actually observing a reality that can be different than the one you have been or are experiencing. The more loving your intention and the more aligned your image is with the Will of God, the greater the impact your image will have, though it may take some time to appreciate the outcome you are visualizing. In the collective of humanity, other people may be projecting similar visions, so your thoughts are magnified through the power of group agreement and cohesion.

Whether through prayer, spoken affirmations or mental visualization, much has been written about the power of our minds to create what we most desire. The more detailed our mental pictures and the more we embrace them with positive energy, the more power they have. Say for example, we pray for peace on Earth; we use our mind to create a picture that represents peace to us, like people of all colors and ethnicities holding hands around a bounty-filled table, or solders laying down their guns to help rebuild broken homes. Next we add feelings of love as emotionalized intent and gratitude for the outcome realized; we are literally breathing love and life into our creation of peace. The more often you practice this form of mental alchemy, the more you shift the energy in the collective field of humanity. Have faith and trust that you are making an impact. Visualizations can be used for your personal needs, but please, consider the needs of our world whenever you sit in meditation and prayer.

Sometimes we witness things happening around us and we feel concerned, uneasy, angry or fearful. It could be a couple fighting in a restaurant or a person who appears obviously distressed. We want to do something to help the situation, but often, there is little we can do overtly. To be judgmental or to simply feel bad is to contribute negative energy to the Mind/Field. But if we keep a few positive visualizations available as quickly accessible remedies for any difficult situation we can, at the very least, offer a counterbalance to the negative energy of distressing situations. I encourage you to create a few quick images that make you happy and then broadcast them into our collective mind whenever you see a need.

Start building your repertoire with these few examples:

When you become aware of a tense or troubling situation or you are personally involved in a stressful situation, imagine those people—situations or institutions—surrounded in a luminescent white light of transformation and purity or an emerald green mist of healing energy or a violet flame of perfection or a pink blanket of divine love. Think in color and with intention.

My favorite visualization includes using body movement. I use this technique in situations such as being cut off in heavy traffic, seeing a panhandler at an intersection, encountering a person with a negative perspective or a child being harshly reprimanded. With a physical gesture similar to throwing a ball, I imagine I'm throwing pink and purple fairy dust (or glitter) and watch it sprinkle over the person, situation or institution. Each part of this visualization has significance. Pink represents unconditional love. Purple is the color of divine perfection and transmutation. Fairies are magical. Whether throwing fairy dust or glitter, it is sparkly, light, innocent and messy fun (ask any child). As I throw love, healing and happiness onto a troubling situation, I'm invoking love, healing and happiness for those who are struggling. I offer this visualization to you because every time I have used it, I immediately feel relief and joy and more importantly, I'm released from my own negative feelings. I feel certain that if you use this visualization, you will feel better instantly, regardless of what happens with the situation you shower with that blessing.

No matter what you're trying to accomplish in your life and no matter what major shift you wish for our world, visualizations propelled with love, compassion and gratitude are powerful tools to promote change. These simple visualizations may seem silly or insignificant, but they're not. They are the Law of Cause and Effect in action. When you practice them, you are proving to yourself that your thoughts *do* make a difference. As you project your loving intentions and visualizations (cause) into the Mind/Field, they are received in ways that you may not see (effect) and the Mind/Field returns your loving intention (cause) to you as the good feelings (effect) you experience as a result of your effort. You are the giver and the receiver of your love. Be open to your creative instincts and abilities and you will discover even more ways to be a beacon of love and hope in our world.

Transmutation Through The Child Mind
Be As The Little Children

When we are "in the world" we have ample opportunity and reason to be vigilant, analytical, discerning and responsible; it's part of our upbringing. Sadly, too many of us have come to accept these adult attributes as the price we pay for growing up. This way of thinking has caused us to forget we are not "of the world." When we are of the world, we trap ourselves in high pressure, low satisfaction lifestyles with false gods promoted by some entity we have given our power to. Children don't do this. They let us know when they are tired, hungry and uncomfortable. They live in the moment and pull us into the moment with them when they demand our attention for their needs, wants and expanding experiences. They don't understand the urgency of a newspaper, TV programs or text messages when they want our attention. They are *in* our world but they definitely are not *of* our world. We dismiss this, saying children don't understand the pressures of the adult world, but it's likely they are exhibiting more wisdom than we give them credit for. They live in the moment, unburdened by the past or the future.

When you embrace the child-like qualities of openness, curiosity and playfulness, and find joy in your willingness to express vulnerability and trust, you're more free to explore and experience the world without preconceived notions and the burdens of past experience that can diminish your happiness and health. What if each day was an adventure and each person a new friend to explore it with? What if your work and interactions were delightful revelations as you learned more about yourself and the world around you? What if you had the self-awareness to just say "no" when something really didn't suit your interest? What if you could reach out for support and guidance with no fear that you might be judged as weak or taken advantage of? What if you were open to letting the gifts and strengths of others lift you to new levels of understanding and then expressed your gratitude and excitement with smiles, laughter and hugs?

The child-mind is a relative state of peace and abandon that comes with innocence, engaged curiosity and a desire to know what matters most in the moment. Walking in the world with a child-like attitude is a balanced circle of giving and receiving. It's the Law of Cause and Effect. You become a loving, trusting, giving and joy-filled example as you shine in the world. You are the new shiny face of love and peace. And in this space, you are open to receive the gifts of others who encourage, support and lift you up as you share the journey with them. As you willingly receive the good will and love of others, you know you are worthy, safe and loved in this circle of free flowing energy where all is in harmony.

Radiating God's Love Into The World

Moving through life with a child-like approach may seem somewhat naïve or ill-advised in some situations, but that doesn't mean you can't be a bright face radiating peace, gratitude, compassion and love into the world around you. The more you love yourself, the more grounded and centered you feel. From this point of balance you are more aware of others and you may sense the energetic forces connecting you to them.

You may feel tenderness as you witness people moving through their lives and you inherently wish the same love and peace for them as you desire for yourself. This is the expansive energy of love filling you and radiating into the world and it reinforces the subtle awareness that you are one with your brothers and sisters.

In Part Four, we discussed following our heart and passions to be involved in the changes necessary to bring justice, equality and peace to all people. Beyond these resource-intensive efforts are small, day-to-day efforts that cost little or nothing but can make a significant impact. Gifts of self will, in time, affect the receiver but they affect the giver almost instantly. Such gifts include giving food, money or a cup of coffee to a person who's homeless, supporting local food banks, leaving a larger tip for wait staff at a diner, picking up items that were accidently dropped, or helping a person struggling with packages get through a closed door. There are many ways to bring a smile to another. Their smile or thank you is proof that you have affected their day and their energy. After all, how would you feel if someone did the same for you? You can feel the difference such actions make. And there are other equally profound ways you can transmute the energy as you radiate love and receive that reflection back to yourself.

PRESENCE is the gift of yourself. As you go through your day, look people you meet directly in their eyes and smile. Smile genuinely from that bright shining place inside and say hello from your heart. Do that same brilliant eye contact and smile with "thank you" and "you're welcome." Use these phrases more times than you ever have before, with the grocery store clerk, the coffee barista, the waitress who delivers your food and fills your coffee cup, the stranger who holds the door open for you, your child who carries their plate to the sink, your significant other who takes out the trash or folds the laundry or gives the kids a bath so you can take a break. Not just thank you, but eye contact and a smile with heart-felt appreciation. Maybe even with a gentle touch.

Almost everything you do can be done with a smile and the sparkling eyes of kindness that convey, "I see you." Such a personal connection may not seem like much, but it really makes a difference. If the person acknowledges your efforts with a smile or responds by relaxing their face or shoulder muscles, you have made an impact in that moment. In this exchange, you can *feel* the connection and you'll be aware that you feel even better than when you first reached out beyond yourself. You may even feel your heart smile as the Universe responds, beaming love back to you.

All human beings want and need acknowledgement and connection and in these moments, you have met two basic needs. If the person acknowledges your effort with a bright smile and eye contact, they are returning the gift of "I see you" and "thank you" as you receive back the gift you gave. If the person doesn't acknowledge you or responds in a neutral or negative way, this is another opportunity to shine your light with compassion and non-judgment. This is a person who is struggling with a burden you can't see, but your love and compassion will help lighten the load they carry as your love transmutes energy in the field. You may never know how your gift of compassion and love affected them, but as you extend love and compassion in even difficult interactions, you are loving your neighbor as yourself. You are also maintaining your own balanced and peace-filled state. In this moment, you are increasing the vibration of our collective conscious. As one is lifted up, we are all lifted up because, of course, we are all one.

HUMAN TOUCH is one of the most basic and essential forms of communication. We have long known that babies who aren't touched and held regularly fair much worse than babies who are. The same is true of the elderly. In fact, there is a name for the condition that occurs when touch is absent or insufficient—failure to thrive. If touch is important to infants and the elderly, it's quite likely that it's equally important throughout our own lives.

You are the hands of God expressing love in this three-dimensional reality. For many of us, our hands are our instruments. They are the way we do our work and minister to the world. They are also conduits for the loving energy you project from your heart. Some among us have mastered the skill of projecting healing energy through our hands. Those of us who experience such practitioners can feel their warmth and energy when they touch us. We are all capable of this. With intention, we can do it all the time. Your mindfulness and the simple intention to be open to the flow of love as it moves through you to another is all that's needed. Visualize and *feel* God's loving energy flowing into you and then flowing through your heart, down your arms and out of your hands as you:

~ Shake someone's hand.
~ Place a stethoscope on a chest or a blood pressure cuff on an arm.
~ Wash or cut someone's hair.
~ Massage someone's hands and paint their nails.
~ Hold the hand of a child.
~ Put your hand on someone's arm to connect or console.
~ Every time you touch someone.

You can amplify this gift of love by looking them in the eyes with kindness, and smiling as you reach out.

Many of us work in fields that don't require or allow us to touch others. In such occupations and professions, your presence, purpose, talents and heart energy are just as essential as those who do touch people as part of their work. How you project love and compassion into the world is very similar to those who can touch people. Simply be mindful that you are the expression of God's Love and visualize your loving energy radiating out from your heart in all directions. Remember the power of eye contact with loving intention and your beautiful genuine smile. You don't need to push or force love to extend it, just be balanced and grounded in happy and loving thoughts as you do your work, *knowing* your love is radiating out from you, like a light bulb warms and illuminates the space around it. The energy of loving intention is the critical element. You are a healer and your contribution is so very important.

As you practice radiating your loving intentions in your work or leisure activities, you can use the light bulb imagery. Imagine yourself as a light bulb receiving power from the Source, just as a light bulb receives electricity into its elements, which then illuminates the space around it. See this loving energy flowing into your heart. Experience yourself as warm, illuminating and purposeful, simply because of the energy flowing through you. Since the Source of your love and light is

All-powerful and Ever-present, your ability to be loving is limitless; no effort needed. Starting your day with this visualization and the intention of being a loving presence sets you up to be at peace, and to be a positive influence as you fill your environment with high vibration energy. The more you practice this, the more automatic it becomes as you grow a whole new operating system in your subconscious mind. A simple deep breath with the intention to be the expression of love and light is all it takes to bring you into this powerful space. It can also keep you calm and balanced when difficult situations arise.

When you radiate the gift of love, you receive it back in greater measure. People around you may or may not be aware of the energetic gift of your loving presence, but the Ever-present God in them and in the Mind/Field is reflecting your gift back to you as the circle of love is complete. The more consciously you extend love to others, the more aware you will be when it comes back to you. In these moments, you are practicing the Art of Transmutation and contributing to the higher vibration of humanity.

HUGS are close and personal encounters; they are intimate and powerful. Hugs convey many things. Along with purity of loving intention, hugs have the power to change lives, relieve pain and remind us that we are worthy and not alone. They can express gratitude, compassion, love, protection and presence. When you hug someone, you are stepping through personal space and boundaries. Such a sharing of personal space implies a level of recognition, openness, safety and trust and it requires honor and respect for both yourself and the other person. When accompanied by loving intention, a hug creates a bond and a heart to heart connection that becomes an energetic circuit where the giver is also receiving and the receiver is also giving. When you are open to giving and receiving in this way, you are blessed with loving and healing energy that flows from the Divine Source and unites you with another. In this holy moment, the love of both people is amplified by the power of two or more gathered in Oneness.

There is no way to overstate the peace and joy available when you shift your perspective to a higher consciousness and reprogram you mind with loving and empowering beliefs about yourself and the world. The more you practice techniques that bring you into stillness and balance and the more you practice radiating your love as a natural extension of who you are, the more joy-filled, loved and fulfilled you become. It's a process and, like all processes, each step and each effort builds on the one that came before. As you move forward, you will feel the difference your practice is making in your life.

CHAPTER 18

You Are The Expression Of God's Love

*"Let us make humankind in our image,
according to our likeness..."*
– Genesis 1:26

No matter what we do in life, *we are all in service* to humanity. No matter how we define ourselves, *we are all healers*. And together as one, we are healing the misperceptions we have projected into our collective consciousness. We are healing the collective mind as we heal ourselves and become more aligned with Love's vibration. We can only be in alignment with this higher vibration by embracing the truth that each and every one of us is here now as an essential part in this collective effort to heal and move beyond this reality we are experiencing. Part of our own growth is to embrace the truth that we *are all equal* and inextricably connected and that *each person is necessary and unique*, bringing their own talents, gifts and understanding as they serve their purpose.

---
*In the Mind of God/Field of Possibility,
we each are an essential part of the Divine Matrix.*

Some of our life stress comes from having lost sight of the truth of our equality and oneness. We became lost in the illusion of hierarchy where some are determined to be more important than others. This illusion is an unfortunate corollary of the myth of separation and it is reinforced by the complexities of modern living. When we're confused by the illusion of hierarchy and besieged with the stress of contemporary living and the external demands we have adopted as our own, we discount our divine gifts and become estranged from each other and our Source. We are making our journey more complicated than it needs to be.

As we lose our ability to stay balanced and aligned with Love's vibration, we start to feel unappreciated, burned-out and distressed in even our most meaningful work. Feeling burned-out and unappreciated can happen to any of us regardless of the service we perform but it seems especially true for people in the healing and helping professions. Burn-out can put us at greater risk of harming ourselves through the lower vibrations of judgment, indifference and cynicism, the detrimental side effects of separation, hierarchy and the misperception we have regarding our role in the lives of others. When we define ourselves as an expert or authority, it's possible our own sense of unworthiness and inadequacy is buried beneath an attitude of superiority and entitlement as we distance from our own pain and from the plight of those seeking our help. Between our indoctrination to quickly label problems so an action plan can be applied and our coping mechanism of distancing through the illusion of hierarchy, there's little time or inclination to connect with those we serve and consider their situation from a holistic and human perspective that might produce a better plan of action. We can become frustrated when our clients don't follow the recommended course or respond in ways we had hoped they would. We may discount them as lazy, ignorant or weak. This discounting and the separation such labels afford us may feel protective as we attempt to insulate ourselves from frustration or blame someone else for how we feel. But this is an illusion obscuring the real struggle. On some level, we are judging our own effectiveness, adequacy and worthiness based on actions and conditions of someone else. The more we feel this way about ourselves and our work, the more likely it is that we will become cynical, indifferent, depressed and even hopeless. When such feelings settle in and cloud our attitudes, they're not limited to our interactions with just a few clients. These feelings contaminate other encounters and our perceptions about humanity in general and as they do, they create more separation. While outside factors can hijack our passion and our deep desire to help others, nothing will destroy our ability to be of true service as quickly as losing touch with the gifts of love and compassion that originally brought us to our calling. This becomes a vicious cycle and as a result, we feel more isolated, unappreciated and unworthy. We may look for ways to numb these feelings and not infrequently, we develop counterproductive and unhealthy ways to express our personal distress.

This same cycle of hierarchical distancing, indifference and distress is common in far too many lives today. In addition to the helping professions, those who work in management and other positions of power and decision-making as well as those who labor on the front lines of any industry are also at high risk when company policies prioritize profit over the wellbeing of employees, customers and society. Those who make work space and personnel decisions creating unreasonable or unsafe conditions for employees or product decisions that compromise the wellbeing of customers, society or the environment must step out of alignment with their God-self to make such decisions. Front-line workers who must work in conditions that are unsafe to them or compromise the safety of others in order to survive are at the same risk. Regardless of what we do and the stories we tell ourselves to justify our decisions, if we are out of alignment with the God-given gift of wisdom that guides us back to harmony, peace and satisfaction, then we will be distant, isolated and depressed. Some of us will bury our distress beneath cynicism, judgment or addictions, but our dis-ease remains chronic and our energy is hurting us and the human condition we came to serve.

Our distress and the problems we see in our world today are the blessings of growth opportunities. The sole purpose of distress is to mobilize us to change and adapt to what is happening around us. The old paradigm has been to go with the flow and follow the illusion of success and our misunderstanding of love and willpower…our intention. You are here to transform this old way into the new paradigm of love-based inspiration and life-altering change. You are gifted beyond your imagination; you have all you need to reach the higher planes of correspondence where Love, Wisdom and Willpower wait for you to reclaim your birthright and shift to the Higher Consciousness breathed into you in the beginning.

"The God In Me Greets The God In You."

What would your demeanor be if you stood face to face with God? Would you feel humbled? Would you bring your full attention, listen with focused intent and embrace this opportunity completely? Would you be open to being changed by the interaction?

Take a moment to contemplate this possibility because this is the belief and the attitude that will take you to Heaven. When you approach every situation as an opportunity to come closer to the ultimate happiness you are innately drawn to find and treat every person with the reverence you would give to God, you will know the Kingdom of Heaven. Loving yourself as God loves you and loving your neighbor as yourself is the only path. As you walk this path, treat each person you meet as your equal. Look them in the eyes, and radiate this thought with love, "The God in me greets the God in you." This perception of reality is filled with the power of intent, love and wisdom…it becomes *the word* that creates a new paradigm. It strengthens connections and opens space for the flow of many blessings we have available to make our path lighter and brighter. They will be familiar to you:

HUMILITY — When the God in me greets the God in you, there is no hierarchy because you are equal. You are acknowledging the worthiness and magnificence inherently present. You are honoring their life journey and acknowledge they are doing the best they can in this moment…just as you are. A posture of humility also relieves the burden of feeling you must fix their problem. It conveys your faith and trust in them because you *know* the God in them provides all the resources they need to solve their situation when they are ready to do so.

PRESENCE — When the God in me greets the God in you, you are present in that space with them, paying attention, listening without prejudice, judgment or impatience. As you do this, there is the possibility you will find something deeper and more expansive than you have ever experienced before. Being fully present, looking them in the eyes, listening to their story with patience, openness and acceptance, says, "I see you." It also conveys, "You are important and worthy." Such recognition and validation have the power to transform lives without any other assistance. Would you sit with God and offer any less of yourself?

ACCEPTANCE AND RESPECT — When the God in me greets the God in you, there is no judgment. You wouldn't try to change God's thoughts and ideas. You wouldn't push your convictions onto Them as the only possibilities. God doesn't try to change you. An All-knowing God accepts you as you are and intervenes only when you are open to receive assistance. This attitude of acceptance and respect says, "You are perfect just as you are." It requires nothing more than simply being who you are in the moment.

BALANCE AND HARMONY — In an attitude of humility, acceptance and respect, there is equality and balance. While you may be the expert with knowledge and information others seek, how you interact and how you deliver the information speaks volumes about how you value and respect that person...and yourself. When you are accepting and respectful, you honor that they are in control of themselves and free to make decisions and choices based on the many unknown factors affecting their lives. This creates a calm space where a person can consider what you offer and then make his/her own decisions without guilt, shame or animosity. Such a calm and positive attitude creates a healing space and this may be all someone needs to finally appreciate his/her own worthiness and powerful ability to make necessary changes. Such an open and balanced attitude also relieves you of the pressure to fix something you have no control over. It spares you from the feelings of frustration, isolation or distress when they look at their life differently than you do. Your presence and acceptance makes a powerful difference; you just don't always get to see how it manifests.

LOVE AND COMPASSION — God is Unconditional Love…compassionately present with each of us in our pain and struggles. When the God in me greets the God in you, you radiate God's love to the other person. With your intention, you are reflecting the love within them back to them. It's there, in all of us. Even though they may not have found that part of themselves yet, it's still there. Being in your loving presence makes a difference in ways you may never know. It's also a two-way street. When you look at them with humility, love, compassion and acceptance, it's all reflected back to you as a confirmation of your true God-self manifesting in the world. There truly is no greater reward than this experience. Be mindful to embrace and appreciate that feeling each time you experience it!

"The God in me, greets the God in you."

You Are The Savior The World Is Waiting For

You are a healer…a powerful healer! As a Spark in the Mind of God, your most important work is healing yourself with awareness, understanding, forgiveness, compassion and love. As you do this, you expand, intensify and radiate your Spark into the fullest expression of who you truly are…a unique expression of the image and likeness of God; you are the eternally loving, wise, creative power of God. Becoming this fullest expression of your magnificence is the process of healing all the misperceptions and pain of humanity and it's the purpose of your life. As you accomplish this holy work, your example becomes the light and your love becomes the powerful energy elevating humanity to ever-higher levels of Peace and Harmony. You are the beacon drawing others onto the path of Truth and Love. You are the vibration shifting our collective conscious to its highest expression of Love and Light. In your triumphs and in your challenges, honor yourself for your great service to The All. You are following your Divine Plan and you are doing exactly what you came to do…be your fullest expression of God's Love in this world.

You are this magnificent!

**Loving Yourself Whole
Be In The World
With Purpose and In Service
A Living Expression
Of
The Love of God**

ADDITIONAL RESOURCES

Bruce H Lipton, PhD.
Biologist, author and presenter on consciousness evolution, the power of the mind and epigenetics.
www.brucelipton.com

The Foundations of Wellbeing
Rick Hanson, PhD.
Psychologist, professor, bestselling author, presenter and facilitator for practical programs leading to inner peace, empowerment and, of course, wellbeing.
www.thefoundationsofwellbeing.com

Patricia Cota-Robles
Retired marriage and family counselor, world renown teacher, visionary and author and presenter for World Conference on Illumination and weekly vlogs for evolutionary ascension.
www.eraofpeace.org

Patricia Thompson, MSN, RN, CHt
Retired registered nurse, adult nurse practitioner, medical support hypnotherapist, author, presenter and facilitator for seminars on spirit-mind-body connection, healing the self and response-ability in achieving health and happiness.
www.healthbyhappiness.com

Thomas Campbell, PhD.
Physicist, consciousness researcher, author, international lecturer and facilitator for consciousness seminars and retreats.
www.my-big-toe.com

Gaia, Inc
Gaia, Inc.is an international alternative media video streaming service and online community offering yoga and alternative thoughts on consciousness, health and what science is telling us.
www.gaia.com

ACKNOWLEDGMENTS

Loving Yourself Whole has been a work in progress for more than 20 years. What I thought was important enough to share then is only a fraction of what is offered here. And so it is with the deepest gratitude I acknowledge the Presence of God in all the opportunities and challenges that allow me to present this information. I recognize the support and encouragement of the higher planes of correspondence flowing through with patience and persistence, especially Jesus, the Christ and Teacher, and Kuan Yin, Bodhisattva of compassion, mercy and kindness as they supported me with love, wisdom and understanding.

Also in gratitude and humility, I acknowledge my parents, Frank and Mary for their many forms of support and encouragement. Even while I know that there were many times they couldn't figure out what the heck I was doing, they offered kind words of encouragement. This was increasingly true in recent years, even as I appeared to be deviating from all I was taught. To you both, I am grateful for the fertile soil and opportunities that shaped me into who I have become. And, as family, I am deeply grateful for my brothers, Quentin and Mark and my sisters Janice, Barbara and Carolyn. You are my heart. You made life meaningful, funny and do-able even when it seemed a difficult road. Each in your own way, you have been a great encouragement to me in pursuing this dream. A special thank you to Mark for your technical knowledge and wizardry, along with your generous availability and assistance. You made the successes of the last 10 years possible.

For my children, Kaylee and Frank, I have the deepest gratitude. You are woven through these pages in ways you will never know. You are the love, wisdom, humility and understanding that come from a thousand lifetimes of connection, support and encouragement. Even in your moments of doubt, it was always your love and faith that inspired me. You are beating of my heart.

I will ever be grateful for my friend, Marilyn Stemp, who has been one of my greatest supporters in all aspects of my life. She has offered assistance and encouragement toward this effort for over 20 years. As the editor of *Loving Yourself Whole*, she encouraged me to speak my voice even when it was necessary to refine that voice, and she has made these pages infinitely more readable. She also put me in contact with Cindy Segrest, the graphic design artist who oversaw and completed the graphics in this book and crafted the layout for the printed edition. Cindy was also the fire bringing *Loving Yourself Whole* to completion. Thank you both!

I would also like to acknowledge my friend Martha Boose and her friends Ellen Kuyper and Laura Fairbanks for agreeing to read through the early draft. Their insightful critiques helped pave the way for the manuscript Marilyn eventually received. Thank you for your love and support and helping me refine my thoughts.

Lastly, I have had amazing friends who have also been my teachers at various points in my life. You have walked with me, influenced my life, lifted me up when I was down and carried me when I felt broken. There are not sufficient words for my gratitude, but please know that I carry you with me always. You are the seeds of beauty I hope to be sowing into our collective consciousness.

I know I will miss calling out the names of some important people in my life, but I want to acknowledge as many as is possible. With much love and gratitude for all the ways you have been present in my life, thank you to Alice Fernando-Ahmie, Annette Wilson, Darryl Schoon, Debbie Mitchell, Frances Smith, Holly Byerly, Jack Zingg, Jeanne Carleton-Lee, Jennifer Cloney, Joe Thomas, Julie Evans, Liz Anderson, Martha Boose, Martha Schoon, Marilyn Stemp, Mary Ann Flood, Mary Birdsong, Marsha Drozdoff, Nav Daheley, Nikki Miller, Peter Scott, Walter Evans and Vincent Stemp.

ENDNOTES

Loving Yourself Whole is a compilation of my formal education, books I have read, seminars I have attended and my life experiences, including my personal searching and so many meaningful relationships. It is not possible to reference all the information offered here because it has become my understanding through years of seeking and then knowing in my heart that it is truth. Over the years, many authors and teachers have offered similar information and universal truths and now, to the best of my ability, I give credit for their gifts of knowledge, and suggest other sources that have contributed to my wellbeing. I hope these references will be of assistance to you as well.

Chapter 1: You Are Much Greater Than You Know
1. Berg, Y. (2004). *The Power of Kabbalah: Technology for the Soul* (4th ed.). Kabbalah Center International.
2. The Dalai Lama, Desmond Tutu with Douglas Abrams. (2016) *The Book of Joy; Lasting Happiness in a Changing World*. Avery

Chapter 2: Does Believing In An Ever-present God Really Matter?
1. Three Initiates. (2012). *The Kybalion: A Study of The Hermetic Philosophy of Ancient Egypt and Greece* (p. 37). Rough Draft Printing.
2. Ibid., 7-8.
3. Ibid., 27-31.
4. *The New Oxford Annotated Bible with the Apocrypha*. New Revised Standard Version. (1977). Oxford University Press.
5. Three Initiates. (2012). *The Kybalion: A Study of The Hermetic Philosophy of Ancient Egypt and Greece* (p. 21) Rough Draft Printing.
6. Ibid., 55-63.

Chapter 3: Reclaiming Your Personal Power
1. Lipton, B. H.; & Bhaerman, S. (2009). *Spontaneous Evolution: Our Positive Future (And A Way To Get There From Here)*. Hay House, Inc. This is one of my favorite books for summarizing the discoveries of science and the tumultuous relationship between the realms of science and religion. Their researched timelines, accountings and interpretations presented in this entertaining and informative book is well worth the read if you are inclined to know more about how we became so disconnected from ourselves.

Chapter 4: Understanding the Key Concepts
1. Three Initiates. (2012). *The Kybalion: A Study of The Hermetic Philosophy of Ancient Egypt and Greece.* (p.17). Rough Draft Printing.
2. Francis, M. R. (2016, May 2). *What is a Particle?* Symmetry. https://

www.symmetrymagazine.org/article/what-is-a-particle. Retrieved September 11, 2020.

3. LondonCityGirl. (2015, May 14). *Quantum Mechanics for Dummies*. [Video]. YouTube. https://www.youtube.com/watch?v=JP9KP-fwFhk. Retrieved September 11, 2020.

4. Lipton, B. H.; & Bhaerman, S. (2009). *Spontaneous Evolution: Our Positive Future (And A Way To Get There From Here)*. (pp. 97-99). Hay House, Inc.

5. World Peace Group. (n.d.). *Washington meditation project reverses violent crime trend by 23.3%.*http://www.worldpeacegroup.org/washington_crime_prevention_full_article.html. Retrieved November 22, 2019.

6. Ball, P. (2019, June5). *Quantum Leaps, Long Assumed to Be Instantaneous, Take Time*. Quanta. https://www.quantamagazine.org/quantum-leaps-long-assumed-to-be-instantaneous-take-time-20190605/. Retrieved December 12, 2020.

7. Three Initiates. (2012). *The Kybalion: A Study of The Hermetic Philosophy of Ancient Egypt and Greece* (p. 81). Rough Draft Printing.

8. Lipton, B. H.; & Bhaerman, S. (2009). *Spontaneous Evolution: Our Positive Future (And A Way To Get There From Here)* (pp. 270-275). Hay House, Inc.

9. LondonCityGirl. (2015, May 14). *Quantum Mechanics for Dummies*. [Video]. YouTube. https://www.youtube.com/watch?v=JP9KP-fwFhk. Retrieved September 11, 2020.

10. Williams, M. (2011, January 18). *What Is The Double Slit Experiment?* Universe Today. https://www.universitytoday.com/83380/double-slit-experiment. Retrieved November 22, 2019.

11. IDG Books Worldwide, Inc. (2001). Belief. In *Webster's New World College Dictionary.* (4th ed., 132). IDG Books Worldwide, Inc.

12. Brainworks. (n.d.). *What Are Brainwaves?* Brainworksneurotherapy. http://www.brainworksneurotherapy.com/what-are-brainwaves. Retrieved December 6, 2020.

13. Neuroscience. (1997, December 22). *What is the function of the various brainwaves?* [online]. Scientific America. https://www.scientificamerican.com/article/what-is-the-function-of-t-1997-12-22/ Retrieved December 6, 2020.

14. Lipton, B. H.; & Bhaerman, S. (2009). *Spontaneous Evolution: Our Positive Future (And A Way To Get There From Here)* (pp. 36-39). Hay House, Inc.

15. Gephardt, S. (2004). *Why love matters: How affection shapes a baby's brain*. Brunner-Routledge.

16. Simmerman Sierra, T., & Simmerman Sierra, A. (1995). *HYPNOTHERAPY TRAINING MANUAL: Module 1*. Hypnotherapy Academy of America.

17. Basic Knowledge 101. (2020). *Human Brain-Neuroscience-Cognitive*. https://www.basicknowledge101.com/subjects/brain.html. Retrieved September 14, 2020.

18. Center on the Developing Child. (n.d.). Brain Architecture. *Harvard University.* https://developingchild.harvard.edu/science/key-concepts/brain-architecture/. Retrieved November 11, 2019.

19. Smith, S. C. (2014, November 23). The Gifted Mind: Learning to Think. *SEEN, Southeast Education Network*. https://www.seenmagazine.us/Articles/Article-Detail/articleid/4390/the-gifted-mind-1. Retrieved September 14, 2020.

20. Queensland Brain Institute. (2017, November 17). Can you grow new

brain cells?. *The University of Queensland.* https://qbi.uq.edu.au/blog/2017/11/can-you-grow-new-brain-cells. Accessed September 19, 2020.

21. Argentieri, M. A., Nagarajan, S., Seddighzadeh, B., Baccarelli, A. A., & Shields, A. E. (2017). Epigenetic Pathways in Human Disease: The Impact of DNA Methylation on Stress-Related Pathogenesis and Current Challenges in Biomarker Development. *EBioMedicine,* 18, 327–350. https://doi.org/10.1016/j.ebiom.2017.03.044

22. Lipton, B. H. (2013). *The Honeymoon Effect: The science of creating heaven on earth.* (pp. 77-80). Hay House.

23. Zukav, G. (1989). *THE SEAT OF THE SOUL.* Simon & Schuster, Inc.

24. Your Kidneys and How They Work. (2018, June). *National Institute of Diabetes and Digestive and Kidney Diseases.* https://www.niddk.nih.gov/health-information/kidney-disease/kidneys-how-they-work. Accessed September 17, 2020.

25. Soosalu, G.,Henwood, S. & Deo, A. (2019, March 18). Head, Heart, and Gut in Decision Making: Development of a Multiple Brain Preference Questionnaire. *Sage Open.* https://doi.org/10.1177/2158244019837439.

26. Young, E. (2012, December 18). Gut instincts: The secrets of your second brain. *Neurosciencestuff.tumblr.com.* https://neurosciencestuff.tumblr.com/post/38271759345/gut-instincts-the-secrets-of-your-second-brain. Accessed September 17, 2020.

27. Breit,, S.,Kupferbert, A., Rogler, G., & Hasler, G. (2018). Vagus Nerve as Modulator of the Brain–Gut Axis in Psychiatric and Inflammatory Disorders. *Front. Psychiatry,* 9(44). https://doi.org/10.3389/fpsyt.2018.00044

28. *Science of the Heart: Exploring the Role of the Heart in Human Performance; Chapter 1: Heart-Brain Connection.* (n.d.) HeartMath Institute [Online publication]. https://www.heartmath.org/research/science-of-the-heart/ Accessed September 18, 2020.

29. NIH Human Microbiome Project defines normal bacterial makeup of the body. (2012, June 13). *National Institutes of Health* [News Releases].

30. Doyle, L. M., & Wang, M. Z. (2019). Overview of Extracellular Vesicles, Their Origin, Composition, Purpose, and Methods for Exosome Isolation and Analysis. *Cells.* 8(7) 727. http://doi.org/10.3390/cells8070727.

31. Opfer, C. (2014, June 6). Does your body really replace itself every seven years?. *HowStuffWorks.com.* <https://science.howstuffworks.com/life/cellular-microscopic/does-body-really-replace-seven-years.htm> Accessed September 19 2020.

32. Queensland Brain Institute. (2017, November 17). Can you grow new brain cells?. *The University of Queensland.* https://qbi.uq.edu.au/blog/2017/11/can-you-grow-new-brain-cells. Accessed September 19, 2020.

Chapter 6: The Root Cause of Illness

1. Bailey, A. A. (1935). *Esoteric Healing* (p. 5). Lucis Publishing Company.

2. Wright, A. (n.d.). Chapter 6: Limbic System: Amygdala. Neuroscience Online; *University of Texas Health.* https://nba.uth.tmc.edu/neuroscience/m/s4/chapter06.html. Accessed September 20, 2020.

3. Rotenberg, S., & McGrath, J. J. (2016). Inter-relation between autonomic and HPA axis activity in children and adolescents. *Biological Psychology,* 117, 16–25.

https://doi.org/10.1016/j.biopsycho.2016.01.015

4. Swenson, R. (Ed.). (2006). Review of Clinical and Functional Neuroscience-Swenson: Chapter 9—Limbic System. *Dartmouth Medical School.* https://www.dartmouth.edu/~rswenson/NeuroSci/chapter_9.html.Accessed September 20, 2020.

4. Queensland Brain Institute. (2017, November 17). Can you grow new brain cells?. *The University of Queensland.* https://qbi.uq.edu.au/blog/2017/11/can-you-grow-new-brain-cells. Accessed September 19,2020.

5. Kumar, A., Rinwa, P., Kaur, G., & Machawal, L. (2013). Stress: Neurobiology, consequences and management. *Journal of Pharmacy & Bioallied Sciences, 5*(2), 91–97. https://doi.org/10.4103/0975-7406.111818

6. Patient and Caregiver Education. (n.d.). Brain Basics: The Life and Death of a Neuron. *National Institute of Neurological Disorders and Stroke.* https://www.ninds.nih.gov/Disorders/Patient-Caregiver-Education/Life-and-Death-Neuron. Accessed September 27, 2020.

7. _____. You're your Brain: Hypothalamus. (2014, May 11). *Neuroscientifically Challenged.* https://www.neuroscientificallychallenged.com/blog/2014/5/10/hypothalamus-know-your-brain Accessed January 9, 2020.

8. _____. Pituitary Gland /Hormone Health Network. (2019, January). *Hormone.org Endocrine Society.* https://www.hormone.org/your-health-and-hormones/glands-and-hormones-a-to-z/glands/pituitary-gland Accessed January 9, 2020

9. Torrico, T. J., & Munakomi, S. (2020, July 31). Neuroanatomy, Thalamus. In *StatPearls* [Internet] StatPearls Publishing. https://www.ncbi.nlm.nih.gov/books/NBK542184/ Accessed September 20,2020

10. Hannibal, K. E., & Bishop, M. D. (2014). Chronic Stress, Cortisol Dysfunction, and Pain: A Psychoneuroendocrine Rationale for Stress Management in Pain Rehabilitation. *Physical Therapy, 94*(12), 1816–1825. https://doi.org/10.2522/ptj.20130597.

11. Rotenberg, S., & McGrath, J. J. (2016). Inter-relation between autonomic and HPA axis activity in children and adolescents. *Biological psychology, 117,* 16–25. https://doi.org/10.1016/j.biopsycho.2016.01.015

12. McCorry, L. K. (2007, August 15) Physiology of the Autonomic Nervous System. *American Journal of Pharmaceutical Education;* 71(4): 78. https://doi.org/10.5688/aj710478.

13. Young, E. (2012, December 18). Gut instincts: The secrets of your second brain. *Neurosciencestuff.tumblr.com.* https://neurosciencestuff.tumblr.com/post/38271759345/gut-instincts-the-secrets-of-your-second-brain. Accessed September 17, 2020.

14. Breit,, S.,Kupferbert, A., Rogler, G., & Hasler, G. (2018). Vagus Nerve as Modulator of the Brain–Gut Axis in Psychiatric and Inflammatory Disorders. *Front. Psychiatry,* 9(44). https://doi.org/10.3389/fpsyt.2018.00044

Chapter 7: It's All About Stress

1. Kim, E. J., Pellman, B., & Kim, J. J. (2015). *Stress effects on the hippocampus: a critical review.* Learning & memory (Cold Spring Harbor, N.Y.), 22(9), 411–416. https://doi.org/10.1101/lm.037291.114

2. Lipton, B. H. (2008). *The Biology of Belief: Unleashing the Power of Consciousness, Matter and Miracles* (pp. 29-34). Hay House, Inc.
3. Hannibal, K. E., & Bishop, M. D. (2014). Chronic Stress, Cortisol Dysfunction, and Pain: A Psychoneuroendocrine Rationale for Stress Management in Pain Rehabilitation. *Physical Therapy, 94*(12), 1816–1825. https://doi.org/10.2522/ptj.20130597.
4. Morey, J. N., Boggero, I. A., Scott, A. B., & Segerstrom, S. C. (2015). Current Directions in Stress and Human Immune Function. *Current opinion in psychology, 5*, 13–17. https://doi.org/10.1016/j.copsyc.2015.03.007
5. Cafasso, J. (2018, November 1). Adrenaline Rush: Everything You Should Know. *Healthline.* https://www.healthline.com/health/adrenaline-rush#symptoms. Accessed January 15, 2020.
6. Mittal, R., Debs, L. H., Patel, A. P., Nguyen, D., Patel, K., O'Connor, G., Grati, M., Mittal, J., Yan, D., Eshraghi, A. A., Deo, S. K., Daunert, S., & Liu, X. Z. (2017). Neurotransmitters: The Critical Modulators Regulating Gut-Brain Axis. *Journal of Cellular Physiology, 232*(9), 2359–2372. https://doi.org/10.1002/jcp.25518.
7. Aronson, D. (2009) Cortisol—Its Role in Stress, Inflammation, and Indications for Diet Therapy. *Today's Dieitian, 11*(11). 38.
8. _____. *Understanding the Stress Response.* (2020, July 6). Harvard Medical School. Harvard Health Publishing. https://www.health.harvard.edu/staying-healthy/understanding-the-stress-response. Retrieved September 21, 2020.
9. Dartmouth. (2011, February 3). The Physiology of Stress: Cortisol and the Hypothalamus-Pituitary-Adrenal Axis. *Dartmouth Undergraduate Journal of Science.* https://sites.dartmouth.edu/dujs/2011/02/03/the-physiology-of-stress-cortisol-and-the-hypothalamic-pituitary-adrenal-axis/ Accessed September 20, 2020.
10. Hannibal, K. E., & Bishop, M. D. (2014). Chronic Stress, Cortisol Dysfunction, and Pain: A Psychoneuroendocrine Rationale for Stress Management in Pain Rehabilitation. *Physical Therapy, 94*(12), 1816–1825. https://doi.org/10.2522/ptj.20130597.
11. McEwen B. S. (2008). Central effects of stress hormones in health and disease: Understanding the protective and damaging effects of stress and stress mediators. *European journal of pharmacology, 583*(2-3), 174–185. https://doi.org/10.1016/j.ejphar.2007.11.071.
12. Kumar, A., Rinwa, P., Kaur, G., & Machawal, L. (2013). Stress: Neurobiology, Consequences and Management. *Journal of Pharmacy & Bioallied Sciences, 5*(2), 91–97. https://doi.org/10.4103/0975-7406.111818
13. Lipton, B. H. (2008). *The Biology of Beliefs: Unleashing the Power of Consciousness, Matter and Miracles* (pp. 29-37). Hay House, Inc.
14. Zhang, X., & Ho, S. M. (2011). Epigenetics Meets Endocrinology. *Journal of Molecular Endocrinology, 46*(1), R11–R32. https://doi.org/10.1677/jme-10-0053
15. Argentieri, M. A., Nagarajan, S., Seddighzadeh, B., Baccarelli, A. A., & Shields, A. E. (2017). Epigenetic Pathways in Human Disease: The Impact of DNA Methylation on Stress-Related Pathogenesis and Current Challenges in Biomarker Development. *EBioMedicine, 18*, 327–350. https://doi.org/10.1016/j.ebiom.2017.03.044
16. Hay, L., & Schulz, M.L. (2013). *All Is Well, Heal Your Body with Medicine, Affirmations, and Intuition* (p. 202). Hay House.

17. *Ibid.*, 202.
18. *Ibid.*, 192.
19. *Ibid.*, 194.
20. Qinghui, M., Kirby, J., Reilly, C. M., &Lue, X. M. (2017, May 23). Leaky Gut As a Danger Signal for Autoimmune Diseases. *Frontiers in Immunology.* https://doi.org/10.3389/fimmu.2017.00598
21. Campos, M. (2019, October 22). Leaky gut: What is it, and what does it mean to you?. *Harvard Health.* https://www.health.harvard.edu/blog/leaky-gut-what-is-it-and-what-does-it-mean-for-you-2017092212451. Accessed October 3, 2020.
22. Zoltan, P. R. (2013, April 10). Altered Immunity and Leaky Gut Syndrome. *AFPF Wellness.* https://www.afpafitness.com/research-articles/altered-immunity-leaky-gut-syndrome. Accessed October 3, 2020.
23. Hay, L., & Schultz, M.L. (2013). *All Is Well, Heal Your Body with Medicine, Affirmations, and Intuition (p. 217).* Hay House.
24. *Ibid.*, 194.
25. *Ibid.*, 209.
26. *Ibid.*, 208.
27. *Ibid.*, 202.
28. National Institute of Mental Health. (2020). *Post-Traumatic Stress Disorder.* National Institutes of Health. https://www.nimh.nih.gov/health/publications/post-traumatic-stress-disorder-ptsd/index.shtml. Accessed October 3, 2020.
29. *National Suicide Prevention Lifeline* toll-free at 1-800-273-TALK (8255) or the toll-free TTY number at 1-800-799-4TTY (4889). Or text the Crisis Text Line (HELLO to 741741). From National Institute of Mental Health. Accessed October 3, 2020.
30. World Health Organization. (2020, January 30). Depression: Fact Sheet. https://www.who.int/news-room/fact-sheets/detail/depression. Accessed January 31, 2020.

Chapter 11: Loving Yourself Whole
1. Campbell, T. (2007). *My Big Toe: Awakening, Discovery, Inner Workings: A Trilogy Unifying Philosophy, Physics, and Metaphysics.* Lightning Strike Books.
2. Campbell, T. https://www.my-big-toe.com. Thomas Campbell is an author, physicist and consciousness researcher. He facilitates seminars and retreats offering a much expanded view of the our possibilities and our connection to a higher consciousness. His gentle and comprehensive understandings and guidance offer practical instruction for grasping the nature of a larger universe and for becoming love, which Tom tells us is the purpose of life.
3. Li, J., Lee, D. H., Ju, J., Tabung, F. K., Li, Y., Bhupathiraju, S. N., Rimm, E. B., Rexrode, K. M., Manson, J. E., Willett, W. C., Giovannucci, E. L., & Hu, F. B. (2020). Dietary Inflammatory Potential and Risk of Cardiovascular Disease Among Men and Women in the U.S. *Journal of the American Collage of Cardiology,* 76(19). Elsevier. https://doi.org/10.1016/j.jacc.2020.09.535
4. Mayo Clinic Staff. (2020, October 14). Water: How much should you drink every day?. *Healthy Lifestyle Nutrition and Healthy Eating.* Mayo Clinic. https://www.mayoclinic.org/healthy-lifestyle/nutrition-and-healthy-eating/

in-depth/water/art 20044256#:~:text=So%20how%20much%20fluid%20does, fluids%20a%20day%20for%20women. Accessed October 24, 2020.

Chapter 13: We Are Social Beings—Inextricably Connected to One Another
1. *The New Oxford Annotated Bible with the Apocrypha*. New Revised Standard Version. (1977). Oxford University Press.

Chapter 14: Distress Is The Call For Change
1. Shanahan, L., Hill, S. N., Gaydosh, L. M., Steinhoff, A., Costello, E. J., Dodge, K. A., Harris, K. M., & Copeland, W. E. (2019). Does Despair Really Kill? A Roadmap for an Evidence-Based Answer. *American Journal of Public Health*, 109(6), 854–858. https://doi.org/10.2105/AJPH.2019.305016
2. *Addressing Diseases of Despair in a Rural Community*. (2019, November 13). National Institutes of Health. U. S. Department of Health and Human Services. https://ncats.nih.gov/ctsa/projects/ruralhealth/CTSI-PSU. Accessed February 24, 2020.

Chapter 15: What Holds Such Desperation in Place?
1. Stiglitz, J. E. (2012). *THE PRICE OF INEQUALITY: How Today's Divided Society Endangers OurFuture*. W. W. Norton & Company. A clear, articulate and in-depth accounting of changes in legislation, policy makers and stakeholders involved in the numerous financial disasters and social inequalities that are affecting a growing number of Americans. You will not find this information on your nightly news or social media alerts. But this is the information you need to be aware of as you look for the answers to the question, "Why?" J. E. Stiglitz, winner of the Nobel Prize in Economics, also offers us answers to the dilemmas we now find ourselves enmeshed in.
2. Taibbi, M. (2011). *GRIFTOPIA: A Story of Bankers, Politicians, and the Most Audacious Power Grab in American History*. Spiegal and Grau. This is a deep dive into the politics, policy makers and maligned intentions of those who bent and disregarded all rules to take advantage of everyone they could, stealing from the citizenry of the United States. Matt Taibbi's book is frank, factual, satirical and well researched. We should all be as alarmed and demanding of change as he is. This book names the culprits, methods and consequences as it reveals causes of the problems affecting us all.
3. Taibbi, M. (2014). *The Divide: American Injustice in the Age of the Wealth Gap*. Spiegal and Grau. This is what investigative journalism is capable of when individuals are committed to truth and exposing the actual causes of the problems we see in our society. Matt Taibbi exposes the growing income disparity, criminalization of poverty and the inequality and injustice that is being played out with impunity against a growing number of U. S. citizens, but most notably people of color.

Chapter 17: The Art of Mental Transmutation
1. Three Initiates. (2012). *The Kybalion: A Study of The Hermetic Philosophy of Ancient Egypt and Greece* (pp. 23-31). Rough Draft Printing.
2. Tonizzo, J. (2001). Religions and Ecstasy: God, Man and the Ecstasy. *La*

Mechanique Universelle [Online Publication]. https://mecaniqueuniverselle.net/happiness/religion-ecstasy.php. Accessed November 10, 2020.

3. Goldhill, O. (2016, September 10). The Many Overlooked Benefits of Ecstasy. *Quartz* [Online Publication]. https://qz.com/773596/the-many-overlooked-benefits-of-ecstatic-experiences/. Accessed Novemeber 7, 2020.

4. Glucklich, A. (2015, May). Pain and Ecstatic Religious Experience. *Oxford Handbooks* [Online Publication]. https://doi.org/10.1093/oxfordhb/9780199935420.013.38.

ABOUT THE AUTHOR

Patricia Thompson is a visionary, teacher and advocate for holistic health through self-empowerment. Her personal, academic and professional efforts have provided her with a wide range of experiences, inspiring her to search for answers through both traditional and unconventional forums. She received her Bachelor of Nursing Science from Mount Saint Mary's University in Los Angeles, California and her Masters of Nursing Science from Vanderbilt University in Nashville, Tennessee. She is a life-long student of Ancient Wisdom, Esoteric Healing and complementary and alternative healing modalities. In her professional capacity, Patricia has served as a Registered Nurse, Board Certified Adult-Geriatric Nurse Practitioner, nurse educator, massage therapist, esoteric healer and medical support clinical hypnotherapist. Now retired from clinical practice, she is dedicated to sharing her knowledge with others so they may embrace their inherent gifts and feel empowered to choose a happier and healthier life for themselves.

Her diverse background bridges understanding between the benefits of conventional medical science, lifestyle choices and esoteric healing practices. Her visionary interpretation of the commonalities linking these seemingly divergent fields informs her belief that each person was born with the innate ability and desire to be happy, healthy and whole. Patricia offers a detailed explanation of psychological and biological concepts, current science and Ancient Wisdom teachings and then weaves them together to establish the spiritual and quantum nature of life, its struggles and the brilliant potential inherent in every soul. Her passion is helping others find the key of understanding that will open the door and reveal the magic, magnificence and power that resides in every human heart. Today her efforts focus on enabling others to connect with their innate wisdom and reclaim their birthrights of health and happiness. Patricia is the author of *Loving Yourself Whole*. Visit her at www.healthbyhappiness.com

www.ingramcontent.com/pod-product-compliance
Lightning Source LLC
Chambersburg PA
CBHW020901080526
44589CB00011B/388